BRITISH M

RUNNING LEC

1980s

www.gabriellecollison.com

BRITISH MARATHON RUNNING LEGENDS OF THE 1980s

Gabrielle Collison

Proofread by Robert Wilson

Cover photograph by Ray O'Donoghue

Jacket design by Paul Collicutt

Acknowledgements

I'd like to thank the interviewees for their time and enthusiasm – it is little wonder that you were all so successful.

I'd also like to thank the following people for their help and support with this project: Geoff Hill, Ian Hodge, Alan Storey, Paul Collicutt, Ray O'Donoghue, Robert Wilson and Caroline Rodgers (2.44.17).

Lastly, I'd like to extend my gratitude to Sir Eddie Kulukundis for sponsoring my original MSc thesis work in 1999.

Contents

Introduction

In 1999, as part fulfilment of my MSc Sports Science degree course at University College Chichester, I researched the factors surrounding the success of British marathon runners in the 1980s.

Throughout the 1990s, British marathon running standards not only stagnated but also declined. This was despite the continued advancements in scientific backup, training methods, equipment, full-time professionalism and sponsorship. This trend has since continued (with one of two exceptions) into the 21st century.

In the 1980s, the UK rankings show that there were eight men who ran under two hours ten minutes and six women who ran under two hours thirty minutes. These were times considered benchmarks for a world-class performance and times under which most major marathons were won.

During the 1990s, there were only two and three respectively and by the end of 2009, two and five.

The 1980s saw forty-five British men in the world top 100 and thirty-four women. This compared with only eighteen and thirteen respectively in the 1990s and three and five by the end of 2009.

Moreover, if those runners who made their marathon debuts in the 1980s are removed from the 1990s rankings, then we are left with the even more worrying figures of eleven men and nine women. Similarly, if we take the first decade of the 21st century in comparison to the '90s, it reduces still further to two men and five women debutants.

According to UK Athletic statistician, Ian Hodge, in 1980 the 100th best UK male clocked 2.26.28 and this improved to 2.19.52 in 1983. However, by 1989 it had slipped back to 2.26.05 and by 1999 had regressed still further to 2.32.15. In 2009, the 100th best time was 2.33.59. As for the women, in 1989 the 100th fastest time was 3.06.05. This fell to 3.09.02 for 80th in 1999 (100 women not listed). It improved slightly to 3.03.11 for 100th in 2009.

Since Charlie Spedding's bronze medal at the 1984 Los Angeles Olympics, only Paula Radcliffe has achieved a medal on the world stage by winning gold at the 2005 World Championships in Helsinki.

There have been no successes at European Championships although there have been a number of bronze medallists at the Commonwealth Games in each decade as follows:

1982 Brisbane - Mike Gratton - 2.12.06

1990 Auckland - Angela Pain (Hulley) - 2.36.35

1994 Victoria - Mark Hudspith - 2.15.11

1994 Victoria - Yvonne Danson - 2.32.24

2006 Melbourne - Dan Robinson - 2.14.50

2006 Melbourne - Elizabeth Yelling - 2.32.19

Many "Big City" marathon wins were achieved by British runners in the 1980s, for example, Steve Jones (Chicago, New York & London), Charlie Spedding (London), Mike Gratton (London), Paul Davies-Hale (Chicago), Geoff Smith (Boston), Hugh Jones (London), Priscilla Welch (New York), Veronique Marot (London) and Joyce Smith (London). Steve Jones also held the world best for five months (2.08.05 - Chicago, 1984) and later went on to set the British record of 2.07.13 (Chicago, 1985), which still stands today.

In the 1990s, Allister Hutton (London), Eamonn Martin (Chicago & London), Paul Evans (Chicago), Marian Sutton (Chicago) and Liz McColgan (Boston & London) all won "Big City" marathons. However, in the 21st century only Paula Radcliffe (New York & London) has done so to date.

It is clear that the number of countries in the world marathon rankings has increased over the years, notably

3

with a flooding of the market by high-altitude born African runners in particular. There have also been suspicions of a number of countries providing drugs programmes to assist their athletes. However, there are still only very few British runners running the times that those of the 1980s ran, and there does appear to be a definite overall decline in road running standards.

Until Paul Evans' winning 2.08.52 Chicago Marathon performance in October 1996 (followed by 2.09.18 at London in 1997), no Briton had bettered two hours ten minutes for seven years; Tony Milovsorov's 2.09.54 run in the London Marathon of 1989 being the last. Since then, there have only been three other men to break the two-hour ten barrier: Richard Nerurkar (2.08.36 - London), Jon Brown (2.09.31 & 2.09.44 - London), and Mark Steinle (2.09.17 - London).

In 1993, Trevor Frecknall, in an Athletics Weekly article entitled "Signs of Hope," wrote that while:

> '...Nerurkar has earned a fine reputation as a championships marathon runner...Britain's endurance runners have slipped further behind on the world stage and have been overtaken by Spain and Portugal in particular at European level.'

In 1996, the Flora London Marathon recognised this worrying decline in standards and joined forces with the then British Athletics Federation (BAF) and the

Foundation for Sports & Arts to launch a scheme with the aim of trying to help improve standards. The scheme involved a mixed squad of 20 elite British runners and 10 coaches jointly funded by the three bodies to the tune of £60,000. It was known as the "British Athletics Endurance Initiative" and offered services, such as warm-weather training, altitude training, competition support and medical screening.

While this help was welcomed, and probably much needed at the time, it was perhaps just as important to listen to and seek out the advice of the previous generation of marathon runners, who had performed with such great distinction. Charlie Spedding, for one, was surprised that no one other than Tony Milovsorov bothered to ask him how he achieved his success. Speaking to Athletics Weekly in 1996, he said:

> 'I was always surprised that no one asked me how I prepared for LA and how I coped with the heat...but I am just one example of that.'

Alan Storey, the National Event Coach for the Marathon in 1999 and a previous General Manager of the London Marathon, also pointed out that many great marathon runners of the past felt that their advice had been somewhat neglected and their knowledge and experience wasted.

This was therefore the background to my research conducted in 1999, and I aimed to seek out the thoughts and opinions of those who I interviewed in order to find out if there were any common factors surrounding their success.

This book will not repeat my entire study and findings but merely wishes to share the interviews with those who have an interest in what those of the 1980s had to say. I've also included the pilot study interviews with three men from a previous era.

The conclusion to my study was that the following factors were common to the interviewees and their success: childhood social factors, a well-rounded athletic background, peer group influence, a general long-distance running subculture, the running boom, training and competing to their bodily limits, and a dedicated and committed approach.

While I have endeavoured to make the interviews read more coherently from their original transcription, I have tried not to alter the flow of conversation and the personal communication style of the interviewee or to make the interviews seem too rigid and structured.

Answers to questions were not always given immediately and quite often arrived at by a rather roundabout route. However, I think this gives a flavour of the person and interview. Naturally, some people are more direct and straightforward whereas others tend to be less so.

A mere list of someone's training, while of interest, does not help you to get to know the person and to find out what made them tick. Therefore, I hope that the occasional divergences in answering questions tells you as much as the answers themselves and does not detract from the interviews' readability.

Gabrielle Collison

www.gabriellecollison.com

INTRODUCTION

The Interviews

John Boyes

PB: 2.13.20 – Maassluis 1985

Highest World Ranking in the 1980s: 86th

Marathon Achievements:

Winner - Maassluis Marathon 1985

How did you become involved in athletics?

I did a track race when I was about 12 years old at school. It was an 800m on a grass track, and I won it. I even beat the school champion, so I was really pleased. I then did school cross-country. We used to train by running around a big field. We just turned up and did it. It was quite good. I then went on to join the army and was there for five years. I was in the army junior cross-country team from 16 to 18 years of age, and later, when I joined the army fully, I went to Germany where we became the Army Cross-Country Champions. I never actually represented the army at cross-country, but I was in the team that won those championships and the Rhine Championships. Because we won the championships, they took us off-duty. We were training three times a day, as we couldn't be seen not to be doing

9

anything, and we ended up getting to a fairly good standard. I ran 15.27 for 5000m. I left the army at 21 and had around five months off. After that, I started running again because I missed it so much. I got hold of Ron Hill's books and read them. They were very inspiring and led me to go down to Bournemouth Athletic Club where I met a couple of guys of international standard called Roger Brown and Harold Chadwick. We started training, and I did my first marathon in 1981.

So, you didn't have any successes at English Schools' or anything like that?

No, nothing like that at all. It was after I joined the army that I had all my successes. The army gave me the background.

Did you do any more track over 5000m and 10,000m or cross-country before doing this first marathon?

Not 10,000m really and I struggled to make the Bournemouth team over 5000m, so I had to do the steeplechase. I did that twice in the Southern League and was unbeaten, but I didn't want to do that any more because it was too painful. Eventually, I concentrated on the 1500m and 5000m.

Were you quick?

Yes, reasonably but not compared to the really quick guys. I got under four minutes for 1500m, which I was really pleased with. I used to do a lot of track like 1500m, 5000m and that. I actually hold the track record at Withdean Stadium [Brighton's track] for 10,000m. I ran 29.18.02. I broke it in about 1986; it had stood since 1958.

Had you done many road races before the first marathon?

Very little. We used to do the Salisbury 10 Miles road race. I ran quite fast there; I ran 48.59. We also did the Woking 10. We had that sort of background. I did 23.45 for five miles, so I was quite quick, but I never broke 30 minutes for 10,000m until I got really fast on the roads. It sort of went road first and then track over 10,000m.

So, why did you decide to do a marathon?

It was 1981 and the first London Marathon, and we all thought we would go for it, but I was actually rejected. However, we also had a team going for one on the Isle of Wight, which was in May, and as someone dropped out, they asked me to do it at the last moment. I hadn't trained for it, but I did it and ran my slowest ever time of 2.39.45. I then ran 2.24 in 1982 and another 2.24 in Rotherham, which was the Post Office Championships. After that, I did a couple more and went back to 2.28 and 2.30. So, I decided to really train for it. I ran 100 miles a week and made a breakthrough in London in 1984. I ran 2.17 and was picked to run for England in the

11

Glasgow Marathon in September. England won the team race, and I ran 2.14. I then ran in Holland in 1985 and did my PB of 2.13.20.

Was that your eighth marathon?

Yes.

How long before marathons did you decide to do them?

I used a 12-week build-up, and it was a definite build-up.

Can you outline a typical training week in a build-up to a marathon?

We always used to go for London in March/April, so I would have two weeks really easy at Christmas and then build up very slowly through January. I'd do 60, 70, 80, 90 and finally 10 weeks of 100 miles a week. I would also build up the long run to about 22 miles and then try to go down again the following weeks. I was doing 17, 16 or even 14 sometimes. I tried not to do two long runs in a row. I did various sorts of speedwork, and when I ran the 2.13.20, I also did a lot of hills. I'd do eight two-minute efforts up a hill on a Tuesday. I was combining this with being a postman. I would do the hills on my own in the afternoon with a six-mile warm-up and a six-mile warm-down, which totalled about 17 miles by the end. I used to do two 10-mile runs on a Wednesday: a 10 at lunchtime and then quite a hard 10 in the evening. The group of us who went out used to do a measured mile in the evening as well. The best I ever did for that was about 4.18, and it is an accurate mile. So, we were training very hard without really knowing it. We'd then go and do speedwork again on the Thursday.

How did you combine this with being a postman?

I was getting up at 4.15 A.M. and doing a hard physical day until 12 P.M.; I was either cycling or walking. I'd then get back, go straight out for a run and get a couple of hours sleep. Later, I did another run. Basically, it was sheer bloody hard work. You can only do it for a certain number of years though. The trap is when you get successful at the marathon and get asked to do a lot of them. You are tempted, but you can only do so many. You might get a call asking if you want to go to Melbourne in five weeks, and then what do you say? That is the downfall. You try to do too many. It's as simple as that. I tried to get in specific races like a half-marathon five weeks before, or we used to do the full distance. We might find a marathon and run it a minute a mile slower. Alternatively, we used to go down to the Worthing 20 and do a lap of the course first plus an extra mile to make it up to the full distance. We'd run that at about six-minute mile pace. So, I always tried to do the full distance about five weeks before.

Did you do any 10km or 5-mile races as well?

Yes, we used to race quite a lot. I used to take them as they came and didn't ease down for all of them. In fact, about 10 days before a couple of my best marathons, I actually did a 3000m on the track, and I was running PBs for both 1500m and 3000m at this time. While I was in a build-up to a marathon, I was so strong. I did the New Forest Marathon in 1988 as a training run before Berlin, and I won it in 2.32. Five weeks later, I ran 2.14.5 in Berlin.

So, you did the full distance a few times in training?

Yes, but only five weeks before and I would try to run a minute a mile outside my racing pace. The only time I have run further than the distance was when I got my wife to drop me off at Dorchester, which is 30 miles away, and I ran back. However, I got injured, so I never did that again. I tended to think 26 miles is far enough anyway, so why would you want to go any further?

Were your interval sessions mostly on the track?

I tried them on the track, but they were always better on the road. From about 1987 onwards, I was coached by Dave Cannon, and he got us going out and doing a 10 to 12-mile run on the road with 6 x 5 minutes in it. I always made the second one along the measured mile, and when I was in 2.13 sort of shape I was going through in about 4.35 pace. That was when I knew I was flying. It was usually during about the third week of doing them. We used to do them religiously every Tuesday. This was in 1989. On Thursday, we used to go out and do sharper stuff like 8 x 400m. It was usually on the road or along the promenade. I tried doing 6 x 1 mile on the track once, but I found it better doing them on the road. You are simulating what you are doing in the race.

Did you do any tempo runs or fartlek?

Not really, although we would do a five-mile time trial two weeks before, and we'd run quite fast on that just to give us an idea of what we were doing. If there were a five-mile road race around at that time, we'd go do that instead. We'd just try to run a controlled five miles. A whole group of us did that in 1989, and we all set PBs. We were all doing the same schedule.

So, you averaged 100 miles a week?

Between 100 and 120. I never went below 100 for those 10 weeks. It was a really good build-up. Two weeks before, I would come down to 80, and it would feel like having a week off.

So, you started your taper two weeks before?

Yes. My last long run was three weeks before. I'd probably do a 12-mile run on the Sunday the week before and 17 miles the week prior to that, or it may have even been 14 actually. I didn't want to be running too far if I was going to be doing 26 miles in two weeks' time.

How about the sessions during the taper?

We used to sharpen them up a bit. On the Tuesday 10 days before, we'd go out and do 14 x 400m. I ended up doing them in about 62 seconds. We'd then go out on the Thursday and do 6 x 800m. After the 12-mile run on the Sunday, I'd do the carbohydrate depletion diet until the Wednesday night, and I wouldn't do any more speed; we'd do a run on the Wednesday and that would be it. I would then start eating carbohydrate again and not run a step until race day.

Do you think that the diet helped?

Yes, I would say it definitely worked the first few times. The only problem with the diet is that when you are at that stage of fitness, you are susceptible to getting a cold. In 1996, I was really fit; I did the diet and promptly got a cold. But if you have done the diet and it has worked, and then you don't on another occasion, it is on your mind. It's psychological; so much of it is in the mind.

Were you also a top 10km runner at this time?

No, because the standard was so good then. I was regularly running 29.30, and I was nowhere with that. I was just another 10km runner.

Did you use any form of mental techniques before or during the race?

I used to sing in my head while I was going round. I would sing that Whitney Houston one called "One Moment in Time." It got me round some good ones. I was just singing and getting hyped up. You can get through a mile singing "Bohemian Rhapsody" or something. It really does help, but it is just sheer utter concentration in the end. In Berlin in 1988, I just kept telling myself to hang on. I kept thinking that the longer I could hang on, the better I was going to do, and the less time I was going to be by myself. Before the race, I was always confident of my fitness; I knew if I was going well. However, you are always so nervous about doing a marathon because so much can go wrong during it. You have to have done the training and the preparation. It's as simple as that. After that, it is just a matter of concentrating for the amount of time.

Did you do any other forms of training, such as weights?

Sometimes, I would swim afterwards to recover. I also used to have a couple of weeks off running and just go swimming. I always cycled up every hill as a postman. It was a matter of honour. I would never get off the bike and walk. I was on my feet for four hours a day walking as well.

Did you work full-time throughout your running career?

Yes, as a postman, and as I said earlier, it was a demanding day. There is no doubt that we are too lazy these days.

Were you coached throughout your career?

On and off. I don't think I am very easy to coach, as I like doing my own thing. Even with Dave [Cannon], I tended to like to race too much. As I previously mentioned, I was starting to get in the position where people were inviting me to Holland and France etc. It was hard to say no, especially when you are just a postman. But yes, I did get some very good advice from Dave. Jim Bailey also used to help me at first, and he probably laid a lot of the background. He started me off when I got out of the army. It was more advice than coaching though. Dave lived up in Cumbria, and we used to speak every now and again, but there wasn't any guy standing at the side of the track with a whistle and stopwatch. It was more a case of someone to knock ideas off with really. If I agreed with them, I would do them, and if I didn't, I wouldn't.

Did you mostly train with a group or on your own?

Mostly with groups. It pushes you and gets you out when you don't want to go. There were good guys to train with like Pete Russell, who was a very good cross-country runner. He ran 2.15, and we would always be watching each other. We'd train together and race the guts out of each other on the road.

Were most of your runs done quite fast?

Not my steady runs. I made a rule that easy runs were easy. I would definitely go slowly on some of the runs, especially the Sunday run. I used to go out with 2.35 guys, and I couldn't keep up with them. I didn't want to though because I wanted to do my hard session on the Tuesday. Sometimes, we ran fairly hard on a Sunday; sometimes we got a bit stupid. However, I worked so hard during the week that I mostly used to just want to get the time under my belt and enjoy it. The only one I did fast was the one five weeks before. Easy runs are easy!

Did you have any forms of sponsorship or financial assistance?

I was sponsored by Brooks for a while and then Asics sponsored me just before the Westland Marathon. I did a 20km race and came third in 59.59. I was sponsored from then until McColgan got all the money. They dropped us all then. There was no cash. It was just shoes – purely gear.

So, there was never a time when you thought you could give up your job?

Never! The most I ever got was in the Mersey in the Commonwealth Games Trials in 1989. I came fourth and received about £1500. I should have won that; Carl Thackery won it. I pulled a calf muscle at 13 miles because the pace was too slow. I was away from Geoff Wightman at that point. So I just plodded along in 2.20, and Geoff came through and got the Commonwealth Games spot, which annoyed me at the time because I think I should have been there, but that's history. I was the fastest in the field, and I was really fit for it. They gave it a lot of sponsorship, and it was big money for Britain at that time. I think Carl got about £5000. However, it was a one-off. I got $500 in London in 1989 although I think Chris Brasher did actually double that to $1000, as I hadn't got any appearance money. That was for running 2.13.45. The following year, I got $1000 to do London.

Did you have a special diet or take any supplements?

I just used to eat loads and drink loads, including beer. I never took any supplements except vitamin C for cold prevention.

What about any electrolyte drinks?

No, I never trusted them on my stomach. The problem with the marathon was that I felt sick at the end. In fact, I usually was sick. During the race, I would just drink plain water although I mostly tipped it over my head and didn't actually drink much of it. I would also take sponges. However, I would drink a lot before. I won the Miami Marathon in 1987 in 78°F and didn't drink. I also had two bottles of Heineken the night before my PB. It is just what you are used to.

What is your height, and what was your racing weight?

I am six-foot, and I think at my best I weighed 10 stone 7 to 10 stone 10.

What factors do you think made you and the others in the 1980s so good?

It was just so competitive in our day. We all did the Southern and National Cross-Country Championships, and it was very tough. I think you will find that most of us really good marathon runners came from a cross-country background. We'd then go on the roads and hammer each other there. You'd go to a road race and have to run 48 minutes for 10 miles to win it. We would look at the times run and think we could also do them because we had beaten the guys before in another race. We weren't afraid to try. I used to go through halfway in 64.50, and my best for that distance was only 64.30. I didn't worry about the pace as long as it felt right. I wouldn't think anything scientific or that I had to do negative splits. I just used to run how I felt and stuff it. I found I could always hang on over the last six miles. I trained very hard, and I think a lot harder than people do now. There is a lot of science going into it and people saying you don't have to do so many miles etc., but I think you will find that most of us did a lot of mileage and only the most talented could get away with not doing that. I know Dave Cannon did 2.11 on only 80 miles a week, but it was 80 miles on the fells and at 5.45 pace all the way. It was therefore a very hard 80 miles. So we were training very hard, and there were a lot of us doing that. There were a lot of us averaging 17/18 miles a day. We'd even go out and do our Sunday run of 22 miles and then meet up again at 5 P.M. in our racing shoes to jog another six. We'd do silly things like that. A lot of the group guys were going out and running 2.22, 2.25, 2.26, and you wouldn't think they were very good runners; you wouldn't even consider these guys. They were going out and running 2.25 because we were all training together. We had a bloody good group, who would push each other. You'd know that at 6 P.M. on a Tuesday night there would be a dozen of you, and you'd have to turn up and push each other. I also don't think there are that many youngsters coming through now. You go to races and all you are getting are veterans winning.

Steve Brace

PB: 2.10.35 - Houston 1996

[1980s: 2.11.50 - Chicago 1988]

Highest World Ranking in the 1980s: 49th

Marathon Achievements:

Winner - Paris Marathon 1989

Winner - Paris Marathon 1990

Winner - Berlin Marathon 1991

27th - Barcelona Olympic Games 1992

52nd - Helsinki European Championships 1994

60th - Atlanta Olympic Games 1996

How did you become involved in athletics?

I dabbled with it in school, but I was from a rugby dominant area, so I played rugby for a number of years. I was 21 when I started running for fitness, and I entered the 1981 People's Marathon in Birmingham. I ran three hours twenty-three. That was my first introduction back into athletics. Once I had run one, I wanted to run a bit faster, and so it really stemmed from there. You say you are never going to run another one, but when the legs are better, you do a bit more training. For the next few years, I did about six or seven marathons a year in a fun run capacity.

Did you have any success in athletics at school?

Yes, I used to make the school cross-country team and the county championships. I remember going to represent the county in North Wales but that was by virtue of the fact that no one turned up for the county steeplechase. I was usually third or fourth scorer for the school cross-country team.

So, there were no successes at Welsh Schools' or anything?

Oh no! No, I never got through to Welsh Schools' level. I only ever did county level really. Rugby was always my first sport, and I actually played soccer for a while.

Basically, we only ever did running when the fields were flooded, and we couldn't play rugby.

How many marathons did you do before you ran your PB?

When I did 2.10.35 at Houston in 1996, it was my 49th. I had run a 2.10 back in 1991, which was only slightly slower, and that was when I won Berlin. In the early 1990s, I ran an awful lot of them in 2.10s, 2.11s and 2.12s.

In the 1980s, your fastest marathon was 2.11.50 in Chicago though, right?

That's right. I ran 2.11.50 in 1988. I also ran 2.12 in London in 1988. It was the trial, and I finished just behind Charlie Spedding.

How long before running marathons did you decide to do them?

Well, I had a high level of fitness all the time anyway. Basically, I used to average 80/90 miles a week for 52 weeks of the year, year after year. It was just fine tuning really. I became a full-time athlete in 1989, and so I had to run two marathons a year in order to make a living, as I didn't make much money out of the sport at other distances. I also liked to try to run for Great Britain if it were feasible. I always did a spring and an autumn marathon. So I'd start putting in the long runs after

Christmas for the spring marathon and then the same again later on in the year for the autumn one. The rest of the stuff was fairly bread and butter training throughout the year. I was specifically a marathon runner. I wasn't very good at 10km or anything else. I just did a lot of mileage.

Can you outline a typical training week in a build-up to a marathon?

I used to run 110 to 120 miles a week leading up to a marathon, and I always had an easy Saturday. Basically, I would pack the mileage into the first three days. I did 10 miles every morning on Monday, Tuesday and Wednesday and then the evenings would be as follows: an effort session on the track or road on Monday, where I would do anything from 10 to 15 miles in total, 10 to 15 miles again on a Tuesday and another 10 miles on a Wednesday. On Thursday, I would ease up slightly; I'd do a 5 to 10-mile run in the morning and then an effort session during a run in the evening. It would usually be longer efforts than on Monday. I would generally pack in between 80 to 90 miles in that four day period, and then I would have an easy Friday and Saturday, which would be just enough to regenerate my body. On Sunday, I would usually do a race. I raced most weekends throughout my career. In the late 1980s and early 1990s, I was doing anything from 50 to 70 races a year.

Would you say that your steady runs were fast?

Everything was very club orientated because we had so many good runners at Bridgend. We had seven British marathon internationals. So it was very much a case of tying in with them. Greg Newhams, in particular, lived fairly close. It was always steady-paced running based on how you felt. I would run to the club, do a few miles there and then a few miles back home afterwards. I would say it was usually six-minute miling. There would be competitive sessions, but these would mainly be left to the Thursday night efforts. They would be anything from a kilometre or three-minute efforts through to a mile, 2000m or 10-minute efforts with everything short recovery.

What about hill training?

We used to alternate track - we have a grass track - hills and road circuits. There was a little bit of variety. However, it is hilly around here anyway. You could do a flattish eight-mile run but anything over that had hills. We had one 10-mile run that had eight hills. Ian Hamer and I used to do it, and we'd hit each one hard. We'd then regroup and jog on to the next. Everything was very informal. Sometimes we'd do a 20 to 30-minute tempo run. It wasn't always planned. It was casual in the way the Kenyans often train. When they head out the door, they don't know what they are going to do to some degree. Some things are planned and other things are set by something else like the weather conditions. It doesn't have to be that specific as long as you are working fairly hard and doing a lot of it. It is not that hard to get right. Other than when you are fine-tuning, a lot of it is bread and butter stuff, week in, week out. I would suggest that for 40 weeks of the year it is not a difficult sport to plan. Some people make it very complex, but it is really rather simplistic. If you are doing too much, then your body tells you. If you are coping and progressing, then you know. There are no shortcuts. It is all about hard work. I have not got the perfect runner's shape but with hard work your body becomes far more efficient at running. It is just a long-term investment of effort.

Did you do any other forms of training like weights?

When I was nearing the end of my career, I did more, but this was mainly due to injury. I used to get off the road and run on grass though as much as I could. I have a lot of grass areas straight outside my door, such as school fields, a floodlit grass circuit around an industrial estate, golf courses and the common around Ogmore. I am also very close to Merthyr Mawr. I used to wear a lot of clothing as well just to work hard without punishing the body. Obviously, everything has caught up with me to some degree. Towards the end, I would use a step machine, which I still do now. I also do a bit of cycling and use a skiing machine. I only did 28 miles this week, but I usually supplement that with a couple of sessions in the gym where I am working hard as well.

But when you were running at your best, you didn't do this?

I did just about all running because there wasn't much time for anything else. You maximise your running. At the end of the day, you are running 26 miles, so there isn't too much upper body conditioning required. It is just time on your feet and those are the energy systems you have to encourage.

Did you mostly train on your own or in a group?

I am very much a social runner. I came into the sport as a fun runner, and with my rugby instincts I am also very much a club man. I have only ever been with one club. We had a great group of runners, and we mixed ideas. I think a club is a place to do all your learning. I was self-coached throughout my career.

So, you never had a coach?

Early on in my career, in 1984, I went to college in Caerleon, Newport. Steve Jones was there at that time, as well as a group of good athletes, and I used to stay up in the week and do a bit of training with them. So until about 1987, I would sort of link up with Mike Rowlands, who was Steve's marathon coach. It was not in a coaching capacity but more for suggestions and advice. I'd just chat to people. I'll give advice to anyone because at the end of the day you still have to get out of the door and do it. As I said earlier, the formula for training is fairly easy. It is all about hard work and not getting injured, as well as being focused, knowing where you are going and having a long-term commitment. So throughout my career, I was a very practical type person. I would glean all this information from different places and adapt it to suit my situation. It was a sort of design process like when I was a carpenter at college. You have to take the best ideas, work out what is right for you and adapt them. I have always been quite adaptable and can assess things quite well both in the short-term and long-term. However, while you get the glory of any achievements, you also get the aggravation if things go wrong; when everybody decides you should have done it this way and not that way. But I tended to only take notice of people that had run under 2.15. Anyone can tell you things, but if they hadn't been there and done it, then it would usually go in one ear and out the other.

Were you also a top 10km runner at this time?

No, I didn't break 29 minutes. I think I ran 29.04 or 29.05 on the Swansea Bay course a couple of times, and for my standard of marathon running that is relatively modest. I was not world class over 10km. I did some physiological tests, and it was found that I just have the capacity to run close to my threshold for a long time. This has enabled me to run good marathons. However, I never had an adequate VO2 max to be able to cope with anything at a higher level or shorter distances.

How did you taper for marathons? Did you do the carbohydrate depletion/loading diet?

I've done everything; it varied enormously. Towards the end of the 1980s, I was doing the full bleed out, which was really good and had a great effect if I was fit. However, because I was doing so many marathons, I was having the odd bad run. Basically, I fathomed out that when there was high humidity, it was causing immense problems with the carbohydrate loading phase. There was a time in the mid 1980s when all the carbohydrate drinks from Scandinavia were becoming more of a force, and I was doing a lot of learning at this point with all these things. I am convinced that a full bleed out is the X factor that puts you half to one per cent up on where you should be. However, you have to be in great shape, the marathon course reasonable and there must be good conditions. The diet also leaves you quite beaten up in terms of running your body down and then regenerating it after. For this reason, I tended just to carbohydrate load in the last three days. There were also some hotter marathons where the carbohydrate loading didn't have a great effect in the heat and humidity. New York could even be warm, and all the championships were usually in warm climates.

But, in general, you think it helped?

Yes, definitely. However, it also depends on your mental state. By Wednesday, you are physically and mentally shattered, and then you realise that you have to run 26 miles. It takes some doing to believe that your body can do it. I was teaching too at that time, and it can be hard if you have kids all day. Your blood sugar is low, so you can't concentrate, and it can wear you out more.

So, how did you taper?

It varied enormously. I nearly always did a 15 miler or an hour-and-a-half run the Sunday before, and obviously, if I was doing the diet, I had to run reasonably until the Wednesday. I did a bit of an effort session on the Tuesday at race pace. It was usually 8 x 3 minutes with three minutes recovery just to get pace judgement. The last three days were pretty much always the same. I'd do 30 minutes, then 25 minutes and then 20 minutes of very easy running. Sometimes I did a race. In Houston, I did a 10km the week before my fastest marathon, but other times I didn't race after two weeks before. I am someone who very much enjoys racing, and I don't find it too stressful. I can accept losing, and at the end of the day, I could focus on the marathon.

Did you pick specific races in your build-up to a marathon?

No, I never did. I did three or four half-marathons on the trot at one point. I just enjoyed competition.

Did you ever do any track or cross-country in your build-up?

Yes, it was no problem really, but I was relatively not that good at either of them. I was primarily a marathon runner. I would do races for the club but not in their own right or for performances as such.

Did you use any form of mental techniques before and during a marathon?

I think that having experience and having been there before, as well as simulating it in training as much as possible, are the main things. Even when I went to a race, I would do a 20-minute run in the morning and then maybe three, four or five miles before the race itself. This trained the mind and the body to be tired and depleted. I used a lot of carbohydrate drinks and flavoured them with sugared squash. This was not only to replace the glycogen but also for mental concentration. It's fine having a recharged battery, but if you can't apply it with concentration, then it is not of much use. It is very much a mental thing. If you can stay focused on what you are doing, then it is an advantage and gives you confidence. I won four of my marathons in sprint finishes. I knew if I was there at the end, I had the confidence factor, and I'd hang in there until grim death. I would rarely be beaten in the closing stages. It was concentration, confidence, stubborn determination and having done it before, as well as the training having gone well. The main thing is getting the training right, but in the marathon it seems as important to get all the little things right and to get all the aspects coming together. This is the difference between it happening on the day and a performance working out, and it not. It might be things, such as using Vaseline, not getting blisters, getting your drinks right and having faith in your shoes. All these things give you confidence. You don't get it right every time, but it has been one of my biggest attributes in my career: the ability to get all these aspects right immediately leading up to a marathon and on the day of the race. I am also very competitive in whatever I do. Whether it is playing tiddlywinks or running a marathon, I want to win. Even in training, I still want to lead that last effort.

Did you ever use altitude or warm-weather training?

Rarely. I went to altitude at Steve Jones' place in Boulder. It was OK, but the thing is you tended to fit in with what the runners there were doing, and I'd run too much and too hard. I didn't go there in great shape, and I'd come away in worse. I didn't go warm-weather training often. I used to find I got better results at home. I am someone who very much likes a routine, to know where I am going and to know what I am doing. I operated throughout my career with runners in the area. I was lucky, as I had many good runners of suitable ability to train with, and the local conditions were great. I also had a young family, so there was that aspect to consider as well. In recent years, I have been to Florida quite a bit, and I have more or less used that. However, this has only been in the 1990s, not in the 1980s at all.

So, were you a full-time athlete for most of your career?

I went to college from 1984 to 1988, and then I taught locally until 1989 to get my probationary year out of the way. After that, I became a full-time athlete until more or less last year [which was 1998].

Did you have any forms of financial assistance or sponsorship?

I had Adidas for my clothing, bonuses and some retainers for a few years. However, that sort of dried up as the sportswear industry found it tougher and tougher. I had "Elite Cymru" during the last two years but that has gone now because I am no longer of the calibre to retain it. I also had my medical bills sorted out by some people along the way, but other than that it was just little bits and pieces. Basically, I lived off what I won. When I first became a full-time athlete in 1989, I was very much going from race to race picking up £50, £60, £80, £100 or whatever. However, after the Commonwealth Games marathon at the end of January 1990, I won the Paris Marathon in April, so that tied me over for a short while. I went from one race to another for a number of years and that is what made me consistent. I knew I had to get a payday every time I stood on the start line. Maybe it would have been nice to have gambled a lot more, but I knew appearance money was for if you finished. Therefore, it was better to get a par performance under the belt than to gamble too much and go out too hard.

Did you follow a special diet or take supplements?

I took mineral supplements, multi-vitamins, vitamin C and that sort of thing. When you are training hard at that level, you need minerals and salts because you are sweating so much. Plus, I used to wear a lot of kit for resistance, so I was sweating even more. I still do wear a lot of kit. Other than that, your body craves what it needs, which is mainly 80% carbohydrate and water. I have no doubt that the majority of distance runners are dehydrated to some degree most of the time and dehydration to any degree means a drop in performance. It is something that I have been a stickler for. I have a glass of water on the draining board at all times and keep sipping from it. It becomes second nature after a while. Everyone invests all this money in training and going away, but a drop of tap water now and again would boost performance by 50% because many people are dehydrated.

Did you drink electrolyte drinks as well?

Yes, I did from time to time, but they weren't so readily available. Usually, it would be some carbohydrate with electrolytes like Isostar, especially after long runs.

Did you ever get anaemic?

No, I never suffered seriously like that from a nutritional point of view.

What did you drink during marathons?

It varied, but usually it was a carbohydrate drink like Leppin. In the 1990s, I put squash in my drinks more, as I came to understand why I was having problems in some races. It was mainly due to the concentration. The 6 to 8% they tell you is nowhere near acceptable in a lot of conditions. You need 2 to 4%. In New York, I was in great shape, but by 16 miles I was dehydrated because there was too much carbohydrate in my gut, and this was not allowing the water out to the muscles. It is crucial to know the conditions from that point of view. Carbohydrate drinks are the way forward for the majority of marathon runners, not just in marathons but also as part of the daily diet. The only time I just drank water was when I was at a level where I couldn't put my own drinks out, but from the mid 1980s that wasn't a problem.

What is your height, and what was your racing weight?

I am 1.74 m, which I think is five-foot nine-and-a-half, and I weighed 10 stone 2 to 10 stone 4.

Can you tell me any factors as to why you and the other marathon runners of the 1980s were so good?

The obvious one is 10,000m running. In general, marathon performances only reflect the state of 10,000m running, as a proportion of 10,000m runners move up to the marathon. I don't think we have the 10,000m athletes now, and you haven't got the whole track ethos around within clubs these days. I know I didn't come through that door, but if you look at Steve Jones' sort of era, they generally had a track background. They persevered with the track and had basic speed, and then they moved up to 10,000m. It all comes down to basic speed at the end of the day. You can have the odd quirk like myself, that is, someone who can't quite do it over 10km and who can run 2.10, but then 2.10 is really quite modest by today's standards. You've got to be able to run 27 minutes for 10km to be able to live with the pace of today's marathon runners. Despite not coming from a track background, I served a long apprenticeship, and it was of use. I didn't just suddenly arrive on the scene. I knew why I had got there. There was a large base to the pyramid in the running boom of the 1980s. You need a wide base. The larger the base, the higher the level of performers involved. I think the world of sport is far bigger now as well. There are a considerable number of sports available these days, and there are not many people encouraging athletics. Schools don't do a good job at selling the sport, and it is very much based on the strength of the teacher. Teachers will do what they are good at, and there aren't many of them with much of a background in athletics. This is at the very grass roots and then, of course, if you don't get people joining clubs, they don't move onto county level and so on. I don't think the road scene has helped either. There is so much available on the roads, and people don't have the focus of one race. If they have a bad race one week, then there is always another one the following week. In the early 1980s, there weren't so many races, and later on it changed to more emphasis on 5km and 10km road races. Another thing is that you can go and run abroad just as cheaply nowadays. They only used to pick teams off of the London Marathon results but now people are jumping straight into marathons around the world. Lastly, I think people are a bit afraid of the marathon for one reason or another. You'd think with the slower times to get vests and into championships it would encourage more people to try, but it doesn't seem to be the case.

Dave Cannon

PB: 2.11.22 – Montreal 1980

Highest World Ranking in the 1980s: 21st

Marathon Achievements:

Winner - Montreal Marathon 1980

2nd - Auckland Marathon 1980

Winner - Auckland Marathon 1981

Joint Winner - Paris Marathon 1981

12th - Athens European Championships 1982

How did you become involved in athletics?

I started when I was around 11 years old at grammar school. We had a games period where we had cross-country races. I was winning them, and so the games master told me about a county championship trial to be held one Saturday. I was one of those people who didn't like school and so to be told to come back on a Saturday was not the greatest thing for me. However, he managed to persuade me, and I won it. The following week was the actual county championships, and I also won that. From there, I went on to the English Schools', and while I was away for the weekend Kendal Athletic Club asked me if I would join them. So that is how it all started really, and I basically went through the age groups running cross-country and a few road races.

Did you do any track?

No, I didn't do any track. We only had a grass track.

So, it seems that you were quite successful straight away?

Yes, more or less straight away. I used to win all the school things. When I went to my first English Schools', I finished 24th and that was a failure to me, but in later years I realised it was very good. It took a long time before anybody from my county bettered that.

How far were the road races that you were doing then?

About three miles.

How old were you when you joined Kendal AC?

I joined when I was 12 years old.

So, how did you progress to become a marathon runner?

Well, it seemed the further the distances went, the better I was. I progressed through the age groups, building from the three miles to as far as I could run, which was probably six miles. Occasionally, I would do a 10 miler and found that I was very good. There were no other 17

41

year olds running the sort of times I was running. Where I live in Cumbria, we are surrounded by hills, and so I moved on to fell running and competed in the junior races. When I got to 16, I had to decide whether to stay as an amateur or run for two bob and become a professional. I decided to stay as an amateur and carried on with the fell running right the way through until I was 26. I was British Champion four times. When I was 21, I tried to do a marathon, but I dropped out. I just went and did it off of my fell running and was probably far too ambitious. I wanted to win, and I was leading until I ran out of steam. So I gave marathons a miss for a couple of years, and then at 23 I went back to the exact same marathon and won it in 2.21. This time, I had trained for it and set off much more conservatively. The write-ups in the magazines started saying I could be the next Olympic champion from Great Britain, but I ran another two marathons later that year and early the next, and they were both 2.21. I was finishing them absolutely spent. I was trying to intermingle the marathons with my fell running. My coach and my brother both said that I should leave the fell running alone and concentrate on the road. The problem was if I went on the roads, I was just another runner, but if I went on the fells, I was a winner and that was what I was in it for. I was only in athletics to win. In May 1976 at Rotherham, it was the trial for the Olympic Games. I decided that I would set off conservatively and just run within myself until 15 miles and then see what I could do. It worked a treat, as I was able to stand up and talk to people rather than crawl the last couple of miles. The time was still 2.21, but I found out how I could run marathons. By the end of 1976, I went to do the Harlow Marathon, a race in which I had run 2.21 before. I won it in 2.19 using the same tactics. I was not thinking that I could win or desperately wanting to win, but I was able to dictate the pace for most of the race and so that really gave me confidence. I think you have to serve your time at the marathon a little bit, and I had by then. The next year, I got a trip. I had never run for Great Britain, and so I was dead chuffed. I ran a half-marathon in Holland in 63 minutes and was really pleased. That was probably one of my fastest back then and from doing that, I got invited to do the Amsterdam Marathon. Unfortunately, it was within three weeks of the AAA's Championships, and there was a rule, which said that you couldn't run three weeks either side of the national championships. They wouldn't give me permission to go, which really annoyed me at the time, as it was going to be my first international marathon. So I had to go and run at Rugby, but as it turned out, it was probably the best thing that could have happened because I won the race in 2.15.02, which was another 4-minute improvement.

How many marathons did you run before you set your PB?

I probably ran about eight or nine. The 2.15 got me a chance to run in the unofficial World Championships in Fukuoka in 1977, but as it was only May, and the race wasn't until December, I decided to run in the Enschede Marathon. I did 2.17 there in fairly hot conditions. Later, I ran 2.16 to finish seventh in Japan. After that, being as I was the AAA's Champion, I decided to try for the positions available in the Commonwealth and European teams the following year. I desperately wanted to go to at least one. The trial race was in Sandbach, and I lined up thinking that everyone was expecting me to win. However, as I just wanted to make the teams, I ran to make sure that I did and finished very strongly, making another improvement to 2.13.29. Tony Simmons won it in 2.12. As a result, I went to Prague for the 1978 European Championships where I finished ninth in 2.14. It was a solid performance, but I had stomach problems during the race and had to stop twice, so I lost touch with the leaders. Anyway, by this time, I knew if I got things right, I could win a medal. Naturally, my thoughts then moved on to 1980 because 1979 wasn't a championship year. By the end of 1978, I finished second to Ian Thompson in Auckland in 2.16 and then in 1979 I won the Toronto Marathon very easily by three-and-a-half minutes, once again in 2.16. Around this time, the promoter of the Auckland Marathon rang me to ask if I would go back to the race, which was going to be held in the January or February of 1980. I declined the invitation because I was hell bent on getting in the Olympic team, and the trials would be in March. However, he persuaded me by offering to put me up for six weeks and for my wife to come along as well. I asked the selectors what the policy would be, and they said if I came up with a fast time, they would consider it, but if not, I'd have to run the trials like everyone else. So I decided to take the risk, and I went out there. I was also thinking that even if I didn't come up with a really belting run, training in Auckland was going to be a lot nicer than Cumbria at that time of year. It was very hot, and the race started at six o'clock in the evening, so the further we went, the cooler it got. I took off sensibly and was always in the second group. I actually took the lead with six miles to go, but Quax came with me and eventually disappeared. His superior leg speed did me over the last mile or so, but I still ran 2.13 and therefore within seconds of my personal best. I thought it would be good enough to be selected. However, the selectors thought otherwise and said that I'd have to run the trial. So, I come back five weeks before the race at Milton Keynes and ran in the Hartlepool 10, which is a race I had always run. I held the course record of 48 minutes-something, and I ran low 47. I was absolutely delighted and thought that I must be in really good shape. However, unfortunately that was when I should have run the trial. By the time the race came along, it was too late; I had gone over the top. I ran 2.16, but Ian Thompson won it in 2.14. The selectors didn't take into account my other performances, and I wasn't selected. I was devastated. It was probably the worst moment of my athletic career, and sadly the three guys they selected failed to finish. Anyway, a lot of good came out of it because it made me more determined to show them that they hadn't picked the right guy. I got a chance to run in the Montreal Marathon, which was in the September following the Olympics, and it went like a dream. A lot of countries had boycotted Moscow, and they came to do that race instead; all the Americans were there. I went thinking that if I finished in the top 10, I would have done okay, as even with my 2.13.29 I was only 11th fastest in the field. However, I won it in 2.11.22. I was absolutely over the moon. That sort of time would have won me a medal in Moscow. I knew I was in good shape as I had beaten Ian Thompson by two minutes over a 12 miler before the Games, and I had won about five races - shorter ones - on the trot. I was very determined at that time.

Did you plan a meticulous build-up to these marathons, bearing in mind the closeness of some of them?

Basically, I had a fair career at running shorter distances, but I didn't actually make any British teams. I found the event I was best at and became British Champion at it. From then on, in order to be successful, there was nowhere left to go but to run marathons. Naturally, I sat down at the beginning of the year to decide on the marathons I would run. This would usually be the trial and then a championship, which meant I never did New York or Boston because they didn't fit in. I'd run the first marathon and then take two or three weeks "off" just jogging. After that, I would build up again and quietly work for another 12 or perhaps 16 weeks, that is, I'd work from 12 to 16 weeks away from the marathon. So, I'd do a few short road races and a half-marathon or something like that and then start my build-up when the time was right. I was quite meticulous in my preparation. If I didn't feel right, I wouldn't do it. I think I ran 21 in total, and my average was 2.16.

What would be a typical training week in a build-up to a marathon?

Compared to a lot of marathon runners, I was a relatively low mileage trainer. This was basically for a few reasons, one of which was that I had a manual job

47

digging holes and things like that. It was strenuous; I was climbing up electricity poles. I'd start work at eight o'clock and finish at five o'clock, so I had to do my morning runs, which were five miles, very easy and then my main session at night after work. If I was in a marathon build-up, I'd do 20 miles or thereabouts every other Sunday.

Did you ever go any further?

Yes. When I got to seven weeks away from the actual marathon, I would increase the run to 23 miles. However, at six weeks to go, I'd drop it back down to 12 or 14 miles although I'd probably try to race that week as well. The following week, which would be five weeks to go, it would be a 26-mile run. I would then go back once again to 12 or 14 miles the next week and possibly do a 10km or something on the Saturday because we had a lot of Saturday races then. Later on, Saturday races disappeared, and they were all on Sundays. If it did happen that a race was on a Sunday, then the long Sunday run would go. I would probably do 12 miles on a Wednesday, and then my last long run would be a 22 miler three weeks before. In between, Monday would be an easy five and eight miles.

How easy was your easy?

The easy morning run would be at six-and-a-half-minute mile pace, but as I said earlier, being a relatively low mileage trainer, I used to run most of my runs at under six-minute mile pace. The evening runs were generally at five-and-a-half-minute mile pace or thereabouts, including the 12 miler, and I have even run the 26 miler at that pace. On Tuesday, there was a five-mile run, and then I would do some sort of session in the evening. It would probably be an eight-mile run with something like 5 x 1 mile efforts included. I'd warm-up for a mile, do a mile hard, then a half-mile jog, another mile hard and so on. There was no pressure on it. I didn't time them, but they would be hard and quite fast. I'd do something similar on Thursdays; I'd do three-minute efforts on the road or something like that. It was nothing really structured. Instead of say doing 1000m reps, I'd do four-minute efforts. I kept everything quite basic, and it was mostly miles and half-miles. On Wednesdays, I'd do the 12 miler. Where I live is hilly, so it was tough. If I had a race on a Saturday, I did nothing on Friday. Some people didn't believe me but that is what I did. It was like a holiday not to have to get up and go running, and not to have to come home and go running. I really looked forward to the Saturday races for the day off on Friday. If there weren't a race on the Saturday, I'd go on the country. I made a point of going on the country to get off the road because early mornings and nights in the winter meant it was all on the road. It was always an easy run. It was a place where there are lots of open and ploughed fields. Being a local lad, the farmers didn't mind me running through the fields. I used to go down and maybe do a little bit of fartlek, but it was mostly just an hour of easy running.

Being that you lived in such a hilly area, did you bother with specific hill sessions?

Once I became a marathon runner, I didn't bother with hills as such, but when I was a fell runner I actually did very specific sessions. I would run to this valley and then up a hill that was probably no more than 50 metres. I used to use my arms and legs as though I was running up a sand hill and give it everything. I would then walk back down and do it again. I'd probably do a set of 10 to 15. I'd then go off for 10 minutes of easy running on the fields, and come back and repeat it. After the second 10 minutes of easy running, I'd do some strides. The muscles you build up for fell running are different from those you use on the roads, so when it came to marathon running the hill sessions were replaced by a 400m or 800m stretch on the road that was as flat as possible. However, I could never really find a very flat stretch, and so I used to run up and down the same bit of road. I'd do an 800m with one little hill at the end and just jog at that end for a couple of minutes and come back the other way.

Did you do any other forms of training like weights?

When I was a kid, I had really weak arms, so I used to run with bits of metal and dumbbells. However, once I became a manual worker that was sufficient really; it was bodybuilding in itself.

Were you also a top 10km runner?

There weren't really many 10km races. The road races were 10 miles, and if I didn't run under 50 minutes, I'd be disappointed, regardless as to whether I had just run a marathon or not. I was rarely beaten, certainly in the North East and Cumbria. I'd only get beaten if someone like an Ian Thompson turned up. I ran around 29 minutes for 10km. In fact, I think my best was 28.59. My best 10 miles was a race from Bradford to Leeds, but it has a lot of downhill, so that should maybe be discounted. I ran 46-and-a-half minutes there. I ran 47 minutes on about four occasions on four different courses and that was when I was at my peak in the marathon as well. Marathons do knock you back, which is why I only did two a year. If you do more, you become slower at the other events and that wasn't helpful to the marathon anyway.

What races did you like to do in your build-up?

Everything was planned, and the races I planned were those that fitted in. If it fitted in, then that is where I would run even if it meant travelling a long way to do it. I would usually run in the Northern and National 12-Stage Relays for Gateshead, and I would use them as speed sessions. I would always have the Friday off, but I wouldn't taper down for those races. If it was a 10 miler, then I would always ease off from the Wednesday, and I wouldn't do a session on the Thursday. If the race didn't go well, I might do another sharpener the following week, but I played it by ear. The blueprint was there; the way it would be in a perfect world. However, it hardly ever is a perfect world, so I'd chop and change when necessary. As long as you have the whole plan in your mind, that is the main thing, and I think I was very good at that, I really do. I got 100% out of myself. As time went on, I also got more sensible and did less silly things. Experience tells you that if you've got a cold, you don't go out.

What was your average mileage?

In my best years at the marathon, that is 1979 to 1983, I was averaging 69 miles a week. If I had told the lads that at the time, they wouldn't have believed me. They would've thought I was trying to pull the wool over their eyes.

Were you coached at any time?

I was coached by Gordon Surtees from when I was 15 years old, but he had no more experience than me at marathons. In fact, I probably helped him as much as he helped me because we were learning together. I see a coach as someone to talk to and plan things with, not necessarily someone who stands next to you on a track shouting and bawling at you or saying that you are doing 60 seconds a quarter or whatever. We spoke, and we learned. I think we both had a lot of successes in those years together. He also had Steve Kenyon coming through, and we placed first and second in the AAA's Championship in 1982: Steve was first, and I was second. Naturally, being in a club like Gateshead Harriers, I would listen to Joe Soap, and if I thought it would help me, I would try it out. We had people there of the calibre of Brendan Foster, who I was friendly with and admired. I would also read what Ron Hill had done because he was an idol of mine, and there were people around like Bill Adcocks who I would talk to. I tried things; I would never discard anything. If I thought it would help me, I used it.

Did you mostly train on your own or with a group?

I mostly trained on my own. In fact, I'd say 99% of it was on my own because of work and where I lived. In the early days, I would probably have had to look 50 miles away to find another runner, let alone someone to train with. It made me hard and determined. I remember Brendan Foster saying to me that I was not the best runner in the world, but if I had a snifter of winning, I'd take it because I had to win. I don't think that is bad. In fact, I am quite proud of it.

How did you taper for the marathon?

Three weeks to go was the last long run, which would be a 22 miler on the Sunday. I'd then just do easy running until the Wednesday, that is, over six-minute miling and then a hard effort session on the Thursday. If I had a 5/6 miles or 10km race though the following weekend, then I'd go through the whole week easy and use that as my session. If I didn't have a race, then Saturday would be easy and I'd do another hard effort session on Sunday. Monday and Tuesday were back to easy and then on the Wednesday I'd probably do a session of 6 x 800m with a lap jog. That was a key session and used to tell me how I was going. Gordon would actually stand by the track for that one, and I'd get nervous for it. I used to average around 2.10/2.11. My best ever was 2.08. I wasn't quick; my fastest mile was 4.20. The lap jog was done in two minutes though, so the recovery was done quite quickly. I used to know coming off of that session that providing nothing went wrong I would be OK on race day. Mentally, it could have worked the other way, of course, but apart from 1980 I never really had a disaster. That time I knew I wasn't right before the session. In fact, I dropped out of it. I still ran 2.16 in the trial, but I knew I wasn't fresh. So, after that session I'd go and do another one on the

Friday. It would be 12 x 400m reps with the same lap jog recovery. I'd just stride them out in 63/64 seconds but still working hard; they were still fast as far as I was concerned. On the Saturday, I just jogged and then on the Sunday I'd do a 12 mile-run. After that it would be eight miles on Monday, six on Tuesday and just a jog on Wednesday. On Thursday and Friday, I'd do nothing. People couldn't believe that, especially when I went away with teams. They'd say, "Aren't you running today?" and I'd reply, "No, all the work is done." I would also do the diet.

Did you do the full depletion phase as well?

Yes.

Do you think that it worked?

Yes, it definitely worked without a shadow of a doubt. Basically, after the 12-mile run on the Sunday, I would start the depletion part of the diet and would not eat sweets or starches right up until the Wednesday or Thursday, depending if the race was on a Saturday or Sunday. It was hellish really, but I was determined to do things 100%. I used to end up only eating meat, fish, eggs and cheese, and drinking tea with no sugar. There was no sugar or cake. By Wednesday, when I was tapering down to the last run, it was an effort just to do it, and I used to wonder how the heck I was going to run on the Saturday. Once you've done it though, and it

55

works, you are confident that it is normal and all will be OK. The first time I did it, I thought I was ill. After the run on Wednesday, I would eat everything. I'd eat sweets and sticky stuff; I'd eat the lot. In fact, as soon as I'd got back from the run, and before I'd even had a shower, I was eating. I'd do that from Wednesday night up until Friday lunchtime. I'd then reduce it a bit and have smaller amounts, so that I didn't have stomach problems. It definitely worked for me although it was a thing you couldn't necessarily do every time because it wrecks your body. At first, I did it every marathon, but later I only used it for championships and tried to get away with not doing it for the trials. I actually modified it by the end and did two days on, two days off. I felt it still worked.

Did you use any form of mental techniques before or during a marathon?

Yes, especially with training on my own. When you are on your own, you have a lot of time to think. I was very focused on planning, and as it got nearer, I would be running the race many times in training and thinking of all the possible things that could happen. As the race approached, I would also be keeping an eye on what my competitors were doing and who was going well. I'd then mentally prepare for them to be there. I'd say to myself that they had to beat me too and that I just had to be there with them. I used to do a lot of that in training. When I did the diet, I would also use that as a psychological thing leading up to the race.

What about during the race?

I used to find that if I had a bad race, it happened early on, and I'd be on for a bad one for a very long time. It would then just be a case of surviving. When I ran well, I was in control. The problem was when I came out of control mode. I remember running London in 1983, and they set off at a very fast pace. It was the year Mike Gratton won. I was with Mike at 10 miles, and we went through in around 48.40. I was absolutely hanging on. The leaders had gone through in about 48.10, and I was thinking that they couldn't keep that up. Basically, I had lost a lot of training before the race, and I wasn't confident enough. I started to doubt whether I could keep it going, and I sort of let Mike go. Well, Mike buggered off and left me, and I hadn't got the confidence to go with him. After 20 miles, I was passing people. I hadn't thought it through. Something happened that I hadn't expected to happen, and the thing in my mind was that I had missed a lot of the last sessions because of illness. I mentally boobed a bit that day; I lost my chance to do a 2.10. I also used to talk to people in races. I remember talking to Brendan Foster in his only marathon in New Zealand. Dick Quax was looking at me as if I was mad. It was psychological, and the further the race went, the more confident and cocky

I got. It wasn't meant in a nasty way. It was just that everything was happening the way I had planned, and if I got that snifter of winning, then I was really up. So yes, I worked on the mental aspect a lot in my own way.

Did you ever use altitude or warm-weather training?

No. Being as I was in full-time work, I never had the time.

So, you were never a full-time athlete?

No, I could never afford it. I was married with a couple of kids, and the mortgage had to be paid. Plus, we weren't making any money in those days.

Did you have any forms of financial assistance or sponsorship?

Not financial. I had a contract with Asics from 1977 but that was just shoes until 1980, at which point I got full kit. I didn't have a salary. However, once I'd run my 2.11s, they gave me a retainer and bonuses if I ran well. It was certainly a help, but it was never enough to be able to pack in work and keep my wife and kids or pay the mortgage or anything.

Did you win much prize money?

I think I got £200 when I won the Toronto Marathon, and I thought I had won the world. A couple of years later, Kevin Forster did the same race and won $2000. I am not bitter. I look at it this way, Ron Hill was a much better athlete than I ever was, and he got nothing in those early days. I don't begrudge what people are getting in the London Marathon or wherever now. I just wish I were 20 years younger. Any money I won just made life a little bit easier.

What was your diet like? Did you take any supplements?

When I was training and doing a manual job, I ate anything; I was like a dustbin. I would even finish my kids' leftovers. During the day, while I was going round in my van for work, I'd stop to get bars of chocolate. I reckon as long as you are getting lots of good food, you can also eat plenty of rubbish. I used to take a vitamin tablet every day in the winter and that was it really.

Did you drink a lot as well?

I just drank when I was thirsty. Nowadays, you see 99% of the athletes walking around the hotel a few days before the London Marathon with a bottle of water permanently in their hand. I never had a bottle of water in my hand.

What about during the race?

It was drummed into me right from the early days that even if it was a cold day, you always took a drink and that it was no good waiting until you were thirsty. You took it before and at every opportunity, even if it was just to swill around your mouth and spit out. It was just water unless it was a championship event where you could put a bottle out. You never knew what the weather was going to be like, and sometimes you missed them, but I used to have Accolade put out. It was like Gatorade - body replacement fluids and salts. I used to take one other thing before a marathon (which Charlie [Spedding] would know about because he was a pharmacist, and I used to get them from him) and that was slow-release sodium tablets. I found I got cramps in a couple of marathons, so I would have a couple of tablets two hours before the race, and they'd slowly dissolve in my system as the race went on.

What is your height, and what was your racing weight?

I am just a fraction over six feet, and my racing weight was between 10 stone 7 and 10 stone 10. I think 10 stone 7 was the lightest I ever got down to and that was in 1980 after doing a lot of training. I'd say that 10 stone 10 was my best weight; it was when I got my best results. I was no different from anyone else in thinking if I was a bit lighter, I could go faster, but it just doesn't work like that.

What factors do you think made you and the others in the 1980s so good?

Basically, I think the lads and lasses of that time wanted to win more than now. The determination seems to be missing these days; they don't have to win. We had to win to make a stand for ourselves. I think in the 1960s and 1970s, and through to the 1980s, people generally weren't as well off as they are now. The youth of today have so many other things they can do. Where I lived in Cumbria, we couldn't even afford a football, so we used to kick a tin can around. There would be 20 of us kicking that tin around. Now the kids have everything. They have computers, and they don't need to find fun. It is the parents' fault, and I am just as much a problem because my kids get what they want. I think the parents are the biggest offenders, but the kids don't seem to have the will to want to be noticed or to be seen to be the best. Then there are the daft things like non-competitive sport in schools. I think the other thing, as far as I am concerned, is that you have to be a bit mad, which I probably am, and you have to want to take risks. I won the Ben Nevis race in Scotland five times. To run up and down there, you have to take risks. You've got to be determined, and I think I got that determination and strength from fell running. There were other people who left fell running and achieved success at the marathon like Jeff Norman, and a lad that

61

I coached called Kenny Stuart. Basically, I got a lot of strength, both mental and physical, from fell running. It was absolutely marvellous. We all went and raced, and then we all went and sat in the same tub. It is a little bit different from road running. I think I got 110% out of myself. One regret I have is not going to an Olympic Games. I went to two World Championships and two European Championships, which could have been Commonwealths, but it just so happened that they were within three weeks of each other. Marathon runners couldn't do both. Well, I couldn't have anyway. There are probably odd people that could have. But yes, not making the Olympics was my biggest regret. The other one was not running 2.10. After running three 2.11s and three 2.12s on different courses in different countries, I feel sure that I should have done a 2.10 somewhere and that would have been very nice.

Sheila Catford (Boyde)

PB: 2.33.04 - London 1989

Highest World Ranking in the 1980s: 41st

Marathon Achievements:

2nd - Berlin Marathon 1988

What was your background in athletics?

I always competed at school, and I really enjoyed it. I did cross-country and track, and all the other sports. When I left school, I carried on doing a lot of swimming, and I used to go out running a few times a week. A friend, who was quite a bit older than me, had entered a road race and when someone asked me why I was training but not competing, I decided to enter the race as well. Although I had been very competitive at school, I didn't have a coach, and I was not involved in a club or anything, so I had no idea about road races

How old were you at this time?

It was just before my 21st birthday. I think I came second on very little training, and a local club asked me to join. I joined the club, and a woman there, who was a good track athlete, said that Frank Horwill [a coach] would be very interested in me. So I contacted Frank, and he took me on board. He decided that I had the ability to make the Olympic Games. However, I didn't stay with Frank that long because I joined Leeds Athletic Club, which was closer to me, and I started training with Angie Hulley - or Pain as she was then - and Veronique Marot. I entered more races and started doing really well. I was more inclined towards the longer distances though, as I wasn't particularly electric over the shorter ones, and initially I was way behind the other two on track

63

sessions. I just didn't have the speedwork background they had at that stage, and I had to work very hard at it. I was training hard before I went to Leeds, but when I went there, it just became awesome. We were racing each other in all our sessions. However, it did become detrimental to our training at times, and looking back with hindsight I think we trained a little too hard. We got very good results from it, but there is a limit, and I don't think we had enough rest periods. Our sessions probably should have been monitored a lot more, and we shouldn't have been racing in almost every one. In fact, my immune system suffered badly because of the intensity of the training we were doing. You can get away with a lot when you are in your early 20s, but it eventually catches up with you. I have to say though that I think even when I wasn't in a group situation, I pushed myself just as hard. Later on, when I was coached by Alan Storey, I was doing his sessions faster than he set, and his sessions were tough. The intensity of training meant I ran well, but I broke down from it. It wasn't just the running though as there were other personal factors involved, which were putting an awful lot of stress on me.

When did you do your first marathon?

I was in my early 20s, and I ran in Birmingham. I did it just for fun, and before I became involved with anyone or any club. I think I did about 2.52. I had only been running competitively for about eight months, and I had no idea what I was supposed to do.

So when you joined Leeds, you took it all a lot more seriously?

I had actually been involved with Thirsk Athletic Club for a couple of years before I joined Leeds, but I devised most of my own training. On going to Leeds, I got a much more structured training schedule.

So, when did Frank coach you?

I think I was with Frank for less than a year or maybe a year.

Did you have a coach in Leeds?

Yes, Brian Scobie. He was very good but then again there were three girls there who all wanted to be the best. Every time we went out for a run, it was competitive. All three of us were very good at training hard, and we would do whatever we were set but that is not clever. In fact, it is not productive and can even be detrimental. You need to incorporate easy weeks and, in my view, you definitely need a day's rest occasionally. I never had them, and you need them.

So, when did you start running marathons seriously?

I would say it was when I packed in my job. When I was 25, Frank Horwill said to me that I could make the Olympic Games, and so I decided to really go for it.

How old were you when you set your PB?

My best times were when I was with Alan Storey. Alan made a huge difference to my career although unfortunately I didn't reach my potential with him. I should have done, as I was at my peak, but I got ill and had a number of personal problems. In fact, it was the personal problems that made me ill. Alan got me in shape to run sub 2.30. My PB of 2.33.04 was set in London in 1989, but I was also ill that day. I had systemic candida and after the Commonwealth Games in Auckland, I went down with it really badly. I shouldn't have entered it. I was sleeping 18 hours a day and was completely out of it, but I had trained so hard and was so fit. On the morning of the race, I had white thrush in my mouth. It was dreadful. This, and big personal problems and stress, did not help one iota. So after the Commonwealth Games, I came back home.

What did you run at the Commonwealth Games?

I ran 2.41. God knows how! I wanted to drop out after a mile. I thought it was ridiculous, but I was so stubborn. It is really amazing what you can push yourself to do.

After that, I went to see various specialists about getting it cured, but it is really difficult to get rid of if you've got it systemically. I then had a little flurry back. I went to try to run the qualifying time for the Olympic Games two years later, but I was on the verge of my divorce and more major stress. I was only 30 seconds off of the qualifying time, but following that I was wiped out again.

How many marathons did you run before you set your PB?

It was in Berlin that I first ran under 2.34. I think I might have done three or four by then. Berlin and London were the two where I ran 2.33 and were within six months of each other. I was 28 to 30 years old at this time and putting in big mileage and very hard sessions - seriously hard sessions.

What would you say was your biggest achievement?

The Berlin Marathon when I came second. I'd won marathons, but the field was very good there, and I ran 2.33. I felt really strong in that one and, in hindsight, I wish I'd gone off earlier because of how well I finished. Then again, you never know, do you? Getting to the Commonwealth Games was also an absolute elation, and the experience of being there was fantastic. It was my first major championships because I was constantly ill for the other ones. It was never injuries with me, just illness. I would like to have gone to an Olympic Games, and I am sure I would have done had the circumstances been right, but there you go.

How long before marathons did you decide to do them?

I would say probably about a four-month build-up towards them.

Could you outline the typical training you were doing in your build-up to a marathon?

It is very hard to remember. I ran around 75 to 90 miles a week. When I was training for the Commonwealth's, I did touch 100 one week but that definitely didn't suit me. You are completely knackered, and you are not doing anything other than eating, sleeping and running. Anyway, I'd say I ran 80 miles a week on average in a build-up. I would usually run twice a day on four days a week, and I did a long run on a Sunday - about 22 miles was the longest. I have done more than that, but the best marathon I did I don't think I even ran 22 miles; I think 20 miles was my longest. I can remember that for the Berlin Marathon, and the first time I ran 2.33, my longest midweek run was only 12 miles. It was done at a good lick though. I have done longer midweek runs; I have done a 15 miler.

So, were most of your runs done at a good pace?

Yes. My morning runs were appalling though. They were absolutely terrible; they were really slow. They weren't slow because I deliberately ran them slow; they were slow because I couldn't run any faster.

What would be the pace of some of your runs, such as your midweek run?

I would set off easy and then probably get down to low 6-minute miling although a part of it would be at below 6-minute miling - maybe even 5.50 pace. It did vary.

What about your long run?

It was supposed to be an easy run, but invariably it would be at a reasonable lick.

Were you running with other people?

No, I was running on my own.

What about other sessions in the week, such as fast work?

When I was in Leeds, I was certainly doing a couple of sessions a week on Tuesdays and Thursdays. I was doing track sessions for a while, but I found them too stressful.

Were both these sessions usually on the track?

Normally, I was on the track once a week, but occasionally it might have been twice. Sometimes it was a fartlek session on the road. When I ran my best times, I was actually doing my sessions within a run - say one minute, two-minute, three-minute efforts in an eight-mile run. I'd run them just as hard. I would still go to the track occasionally, but I didn't like it.

Was that with a group?

No, I'd stopped training with the group by then. I enjoyed it in one respect, but it became too stressful as everyone was trying to outdo each other all the time. It became negative.

So when you were running at your best, you were actually training on your own most of the time?

Yes. I ran good times when I was with the group, but I ran better when I was on my own. I did go across and do some training with the group on occasions, and my then husband also came across and did some sessions with me, but I found being on my own suited me.

What type of sessions were you doing on the track?

They would vary so much. Brian Scobie's and Alan Storey's were different. I can't remember exactly. If I could get my training diaries, I could tell you what they were. If I look at the Commonwealth Games period, there was a real mix of sessions. I'd do 5 x 1000m efforts with very little recovery, and then as soon as I'd finished running them, I'd go off and run 3km at some unbearable pace. Occasionally, I would do some mile reps at 5.20/5.25 pace. I would also do 12 x 400m. Some people do mega ones at some slow pace like 75 seconds whereas mine were run fast with Scobie; they were around 70 seconds. However, I don't think that was productive for a marathon runner. I ran them at 75 seconds when I went to Alan and ran faster at the marathon.

What recovery were you having?

I'd have about 30 seconds. However, if I were in a build-up, I'd start at a minute recovery and get down to that. I wish I had my diaries with me. The sessions were awesome. On Saturday, I might do a fast, continuous run: a tempo run. It was supposedly meant to be at 5.50 pace, but I would end up running it at about 5.45.

Did you race a lot?

One year, I did about 17. However, I remember when I did those two fast times, I didn't do anywhere near the same amount of races. There was more training going on then.

Did you do set races in your build-up to a marathon?

Absolutely! I'd do a half-marathon about five or six weeks before. A 10km was the shortest distance I raced.

Did you do any track or cross-country at this time too?

I did some cross-country, and I was in the Yorkshire team a few times, but I hated it. I only did it because they said it was good for you. I am not happy running cross-country, and I don't run well on it. I look dreadful. Angie Hulley is brilliant; she just flows. I do not!

What about track?

No, I hated track. I didn't like it one iota. Again, Angie did the track, but I just found it boring, and I wasn't happy. If I did the same distance on the road, I was fine. I loved the road. There was just something about going on the track and running round in circles that I didn't like, and I just didn't feel like I could run as fast.

So, you were purely a road runner?

Yes, absolutely! I am a road runner 100%.

Was your training therefore similar all year round?

Yes, very similar all year round. I didn't have winter and summer schedules. They were both the same. What I would say is that when I was running at my best, I was running fast. I would go out and do some easy runs, but even when I was on my own they would invariably end up getting faster and faster. If I felt really bad, then they probably wouldn't be quite so fast, but they were hard. They were usually pretty brisk sessions. You have to be a bit mad, a bit intense and a bit obsessive to get to the top level. I wouldn't want to be like that for the rest of my life. I wouldn't like to think that I became the sort of person where all my life was running, but certainly I would say that if you want to reach quite a high level, you have to be prepared to train very hard. Running has to be number one. It has to be top of your list, and it has to come before everything else. However, I think that when you are training very hard, a day off, even if just once a fortnight, should definitely be in the schedule, and you shouldn't feel guilty about it.

Did you take a day off before races?

I sometimes had a day off before a race or the day before that, as often when you are training hard you feel sluggish when you stop. You also need to learn to be able to take a day off and not feel guilty about it. If you feel guilty about it, then it is counter-productive. I think it is very important on the day you have off to potter about and do other things, and to relax. After a hard session, you should also make sure that you go home, relax and get something to eat. I think that is really important.

Were you also a top 10km runner on the road at this time?

I was running in the 33s. When I went to New Zealand, I ran under 33 minutes, but it was actually a five-point-something-mile race. It was probably equivalent to a 32.40 10km. I think that was in 1990. There were a lot of us about then; there were a lot of us running that sort of time. I doubt I would have been in the top 10 because there were a lot of girls running faster than me over 10km. You had a lot of really good track athletes about then. I don't know what position I would have been in, but I must have been there or thereabouts. I won one of those Liverpool Women's 10km races.

What was your attitude to the races you used in your build-up?

I always used to run them as hard as I could, and usually I was knackered when I was doing them because I was always in a build-up. I might have once run a race where I was meant to run at a set pace, but it didn't suit me. I wanted to go out and run as hard as I damn well could, which is what I normally did. They were run as hard as I possibly could in the middle of a very intense training phase.

So, you didn't get much chance to ease down for these races?

No, not often although, as I said earlier, I occasionally had a day off. I remember once getting out of the car and then leaning against it feeling absolutely shattered. I can visualise it now. I don't think that is healthy. You shouldn't go into races feeling that tired, and I invariably used to feel like that.

Did you use any form of mental techniques before or during a marathon?

Mental preparation was very important. It made a huge difference. In the early days of racing, I had my own mental strategy, which is probably best not repeated because it was about other people, and how I'd beat them into a pulp. I would psych myself up big time. Certainly, during a race my mental attitude was very strong, and I could focus really well. I would constantly be saying key words and key things to keep me going. I worked very hard on that. However, when I went to Alan, the mental preparation became a lot more refined. Alan put me in touch with a lady called Carol Schultz, who was a sports psychologist, and she gave me a bit more structure. Carol advised me to choose a piece of music that would incite me, and so I chose Queens' "Don't Stop Me Now." I rehearsed with it and then used it in one of my marathons, switching on to it at about 18 or 19 miles. I used the music with the words to strengthen my mental attitude. I would also focus on somebody in front of me, and as soon as I was getting close to them, I wouldn't look at them any more and would be onto the next person. There were lots of mental strategies I would use while I was running. I would never look at a marathon and think it is 26 miles. It would blow my head off. I would work in blocks or chunks. I would also have strategies in training about other people to make me work harder, which is probably why I trained so well on my own. Aggression is what got me going; I had to be quite aggressive, and it worked for me. So certainly, I would use mental strategies a lot in training to make me run hard and then in races to help me focus. It was definitely beneficial, and I would say that if someone wants to maximise their potential, then psychology must play a big part.

Did you do any other forms of training?

I used to swim quite a lot although I have to say that when I was on Alan's schedules I found it hard to fit it in. I used to be able to on Scobie's schedules, but I think it was getting a bit too much. When you start to train very hard and are doing a lot of miles, you can maybe go and do a little bit of a swim, but the trouble with me was I wouldn't go and do a little bit of a swim. I would go and swim as hard as I could for about a mile. I should have gone there to relax, but I couldn't seem to do that, and I stopped doing it before the Commonwealth Games. So, there was a spell at Leeds when I was probably going once or twice a week. However, once I got down to the good times, I did less. I might have gone once a week but maybe not even that sometimes, and some weeks might go by without me going at all. I went to the gym and did arm weights. I was only in there about 20/25 minutes though. I tried to do leg weights, but it was not beneficial. I can remember going to the track the next day, and it was impossible to run. So, I just did upper body stuff. If I wasn't training intensely, I might sometimes go and do leg extensions and the back of the legs but not when I was training hard. I would also go to the gym because it made me stretch. I was very lazy when it came to stretching. I have to say it was one of my worst things.

How often would you go to the gym?

About two or three times a week.

After easy runs?

Yes, after an easy run or sometimes at lunchtime, as I wasn't working. I certainly wouldn't go on a hard day. I also did yoga at one point. I did it when my mum died as I was in really quite a state, and I thought it might calm me down. I stopped doing it though because I didn't want to be hyper-flexible. However, it was something I should have kept going, and I keep saying to myself that I must get back into it. The breathing techniques are really good. I think the breathing that you learn in yoga would be helpful for running. It makes you use your lungs more. I think that is really important, and it certainly makes you stretch a bit more. It improved my breathing a lot and helped me, but it took me ages to get into it. I couldn't calm down; I couldn't switch off. I was dreadful. So, I was never particularly good at it, but it definitely did help me.

So, just to confirm about coaches – you had a brief spell with Frank, then you went to Brian and finally, Alan?

Yes, I was with Brian for about two years and then Alan. I really enjoyed being coached by Alan, but he went down to London and was really busy. I wanted someone nearby and was feeling unsettled, so with great heartache I pulled away from Alan and went to Dave Cannon for a while. He was great. Dave's schedules were steady and very simple, and it just so happened that at that stage of my life it was exactly what I needed. Anyone that looked at his schedules might have thought that you couldn't get fast on them, but he obviously did, and I still ran fast on them. They were not awesome sessions. I would just go and do things like 8 x 400m or 10 x 1 minute efforts at a relaxed pace, yet I still ran 55 minutes for 10 miles and 33 minutes for 10km. I obviously had the background though. Anyway, I was at a stage when things were complicated, and I actually needed that type of training at the time. I didn't go back to Alan after that simply because I was no longer competing.

Do you have any more thoughts about training with an elite group of women at Leeds?

It actually did me a lot of good training with them. There's no doubt about it. It really pulled me on. However, it was just becoming destructive. All three of us were training for London, and we all broke down. It was a sign that something was wrong. You obviously have to train hard, but there has to be a point where the person in control of the group tells you to calm down and not race. Otherwise, it is no good. You can't race every day; you just can't.

So, you did it for so long and then went on your own?

Yes, and I am really glad that I did.

Did you ever train with any guys or anyone else?

Well, my husband used to help me a bit and run with me, as he had been a good athlete at school, but I did an awful lot on my own. One of my best races though was when a bloke that I knew ran along beside me. He'd obviously decided he was going to go for it that day, and it helped me enormously. I ran a brilliant race. He paced me and was offering words of encouragement, and it made a big difference. Training on my own

79

though got me used to running on my own in races. I was used to running hard sessions on my own too.

Did you ever use altitude or warm-weather training?

No, I didn't. It wasn't for any particular reason. I just didn't think about it.

Did you work at all during your running career?

No, I didn't work. I was a hairdresser when I first left school, and then I set up on my own until I was 20. Just before my 25th birthday, I packed it in. After talking to Frank Horwill, I decided to concentrate on my running. I thought I'd give it a year and see if I could really get to the top. I also did it because I was getting run down quite a lot. So I stopped working completely and was just a housewife really; I was a runner and a housewife.

Were you married by this time?

Yes, I got married quite young.

Was your husband supportive of you?

Yes, he was totally supportive of me. However, in hindsight, it would probably have been better if I had stuck with a part-time job. It would have been good to have something to take my mind off of running.

Did it help your rest and recovery though not to work?

I always felt so guilty, and so I'd find things to do. In fact, I'd probably have rested more if I'd had a job. I knew people who had office jobs, and they had far more rest than I had. I'd get up and do my morning run, cook my husband's breakfast, pack his lunch and take the dogs for a walk. I'd then clean the house, do the washing, prepare the tea and bake bread. We never bought any convenience food; everything was cooked. Later, I'd do my second session. I didn't sit down much. I remember saying to Angie that I bet she thought I had it easy, but I didn't. Obviously, if I had continued working as a hairdresser, I would have been standing up all day, but if I had been in an office job or at college, I would have had far more rest. I do recall that I helped out at a charity shop for half a day a week, but it was only for a very short time. I also had a spell helping out in a gym for three half days a week when I was out of running due to illness or injury. It was for about three months. I really enjoyed it, as you can get quite lonely and isolated being at home alone. I missed the interaction with people.

Did you have any forms of sponsorship or financial assistance?

Nike sponsored me for clothing, but I didn't get any money. I think to get money you had to win a medal or something.

So, you didn't have a contract? Did you get any bonuses or incentives?

No, nothing. I only got clothing and shoes. I won a lot of money in Berlin, but I had to put that into a trust fund. However, you just needed to say that you wanted to buy stuff, and they'd send it to you straight away. I had no other money. My husband supported me entirely.

What about other prize money?

There just wasn't a lot of money around then. Plus, I didn't capitalise on the races where there was any. In hindsight, there were a lot of races I should have done, but I had this thought pattern that I shouldn't be money orientated and materialistic. It was silly when I was a full-time athlete and needed to earn money, but my husband was financially very secure, and it was probably the guilt complex again. I didn't want to look as though I was just going for the money. London had good prize money, but the depth of the women's road running was awesome when I ran there.

Did you ever get any appearance money?

Yes, I think I did actually. It was in London. It was nowhere near what it would be today though. I think it was about £500. If I had got a few like Berlin, I would have been OK, as that was a few thousand pounds, but you can only run so many in a year.

How many did you do in a year?

Two and that was quite enough! Marathons take so much out of you.

Did you have a special diet? Did you do the carbohydrate depletion/loading diet?

Yes, it was the worst thing I ever did in my life. It was dreadful. It made me ill, and I was shaking. It doesn't suit my body, as I get hypoglycaemic. I don't endorse it. I think the depletion stage of the diet stresses your body too much, and it makes you more likely to get a virus or something. I think that all you need do is to wind down your training and make sure that your diet has plenty of carbohydrates. I used to eat an enormous amount of food. I was hungry all the time. I'd always have breakfast, morning snack, dinner, afternoon snack, tea and some stuff before bed. I had a reasonably healthy diet, but I think I probably had too much carbohydrate. I think you need more protein, especially when you are training hard. Carbohydrate is important but not to the exclusion of other things. I would go out and have two bowls of pasta with tomato sauce all over it. I think there is too much emphasis on carbohydrate. You also need fats although not the saturated kind. I learnt the hard way. I cut out fats after reading a book in my 20s by the triathlete, Dave Scott, but I soon realised that you need oils in your diet. I also had a dairy allergy, which I

83

didn't realise until later and that has given me a lot of problems. It gives me catarrh and diarrhoea. I had a reputation for stopping in races.

Did you take any form of supplements like iron?

I took iron but as I had trouble absorbing the tablets, I had to have iron injections. You don't want to take iron all the time though because it is not good for you. I also took other supplements. I think they are a necessity if you are training hard. The vegetables you buy don't have all the goodness in them unless you buy everything organically grown and even then you are not guaranteed. When training hard, you need a multi-vitamin supplement. I used to take drinks like Staminade as well, especially after a long run. I found that quite beneficial at the time.

Did you drink that during marathons?

No, I couldn't drink. I was just hopeless at it. I don't know how I got away with it, and I wouldn't advise other people to do it. It would go up my nose or give me stitch. I did try to take drinks, but it would only be a very minute amount.

Did you drink a lot generally though?

Yes, loads. At one stage, I was drinking too much coffee and tea though, and I should have reduced that and drank more water. I was probably a bit dehydrated at times through not being diligent enough to take on more water.

How tall are you, and what was your racing weight?

I am five-foot seven, and I weighed eight stone one or two, except when I went to New Zealand and my weight went down to seven stone twelve, which was really thin. I still looked heavier than everyone else there though!

Did you need a lot of sleep?

I needed a lot of sleep; I needed at least nine hours, and I would often fall asleep. When I was training really hard, I would be in bed by half past nine. I can also remember having naps after lunch at one stage. It was probably in the build-up to the Commonwealth Games. However, I'd have an hour's sleep and then wake up feeling awful. Similarly, when I was training in New Zealand, I would often sleep after a race in the afternoon.

Did you have regular massage or any other therapies?

Yes, I had loads of massage, and it definitely saved me. My calves used to get very knotted and lumpy. When I was training very hard, I probably used to have a massage at least twice a week. My husband did it and was very good at it. If I hadn't have had that, I would have been in a bad way.

85

You've already mentioned that you had quite poor health. Did you also get many injuries?

I wasn't too bad with injuries although I did have them. I didn't go through my career without having anything. I had a few knee problems, and in New Zealand I had a heel problem or something to do with my foot like plantar fasciitis. It was bad, and it hurt, but I ran through it. It was mostly just niggly things. However, I got ill loads; I never went more than two months down the line without getting ill. It was a sign that my immune system wasn't healthy. I used to plough through it, but then I'd have to stop whether I liked it or not, and I'd always start back too soon. I often got colds, and they would go on for ages; I couldn't shake them off. This was not so much in the early days but certainly later on.

What do you think were the factors that made you and the others of the era so good?

I think the main factor was a strong determination and tenacity to want to get to the top, which overruled any other common sense. We were very strong-minded and strong-willed. I suppose you could say slightly nutty and obsessive as well although it is perhaps not a good thing to have to say. I, for one, was committed to get there. I was prepared to train very hard, and I could train hard. I couldn't do now what I did back then. No way could I put myself through any of it, and I don't want to. So simply, it is mental tenacity, determination, and the ability to train hard and not "bottle out" even when you feel absolutely knackered and when you really don't feel like going out for a run. It is being able to go out and still do it in all sorts of weather.

Paul Davies-Hale

PB: 2.11.25 – Chicago 1989

Highest World Ranking in the 1980s: 32nd

Marathon Achievements:

Winner - Chicago Marathon 1989

How did you become involved in athletics?

I ran cross-country at school when I was around 13 or 14, but I joined a club when I was 15. A guy who went on to coach me for a while in the early years was involved in schools' athletics in the area, and after I finished third in the county, he persuaded me to go along to the club at Cannock Chase. At that time, I was just doing football training.

What events were you doing in those days?

I did cross-country in the winter when I was playing soccer, and I'd do the 800m and 1500m, which fairly quickly progressed to the 1500m steeplechase, in the summer.

Did you do any road at this time?

No, I didn't do any at all.

Did you have much success at the junior level?

I made the English Schools' on the track for my county in 1977, which I think was at Hendon, but I don't recall making the final. I can also remember running in the English Schools' Cross-Country at Redditch when I was 16. There was lots of mud, and I think I finished about 200th. I was then about 60th in the youth's race at the National Cross-Country Championships in Leeds in 1978 and third the year after at Luton behind Dave Lewis, who won it.

So, you made quite quick progress then?

In that year, and once I started training quite hard, yes. In 1979, I finished third in the junior steeplechase behind Colin Reitz and that persuaded me to give up football and concentrate on athletics. I didn't have immediate success, and I had to train quite hard, but I was always at the front end of races really at that level.

How did you progress to doing marathons?

In 1981, I won the European junior steeplechase title and broke the British steeplechase record with a time of 8.29, a record that I believe still stands. As a junior, I also ran 13.35 for 5000m; I was reasonably good. In 1982, I went to the Commonwealth Games as a steeplechaser and then in 1983 I ran the Tipton 10. It was my first serious road race, and I won it in just under 47 minutes. However, I ran very badly in a 10km in Jarrow, which Steve Cram had got me to do. I think I just scraped in the top 10. I don't remember doing a lot on the road before that at all; we weren't involved in the road relays then or anything. So, I was really a track runner. I would train all winter for the track with the odd cross-country race and then perhaps in April I'd do a short road race. In 1984, I wanted to get to the Olympics, and so I didn't really race on the roads again until 1985. I got to Los Angeles and made the semi-final in the steeplechase. After the race, and before going home, I did a session with Steve Jones. I remember him saying that he wasn't going to have a rest at all, but that he was going straight into training for the Chicago Marathon. I struggled to think how he could go straight from running at that quality on the track to the 100 miles a week that he said he was going to be doing. However, as we now know, he ended up running really well and that was the beginning of his marathon career. I started to think that maybe I should do a few more road races and the year after, in 1985, I landed the opportunity, as I got a six-week open ticket to America. On the way there, I ran a 3000m race in Trinidad in around 7.53 and then went to Boston where I did the Boston Milk Race. I did really well, finishing third and running 28.18 for 10km. It was quite big money too. In fact, bigger money than I'd ever seen, and from then on I thought that I should definitely do more on the road. During the trip, I also won a race in Boulder, where I was staying for four weeks, and then one in Spokane. However, it was not until four years later, in 1989, that I ran a marathon because I still had ambitions on the track. It was always a bit frustrating for me that I never really broke through on the track. I was running pretty well, and I got down to 13.12 for 5000m, but it was on the roads that I had most of my success. In 1989, I had run the AAA's 5000m in about thirteen-and-a-half minutes, and Kim McDonald said that if I wanted, he'd try to get me into Chicago. They came up with a bit of money, which was ridiculous really as I hadn't run a marathon at that time, but it persuaded me to go. It was as good a reason as any. So, I ran it off of limited mileage and won it in 2.11.25, which is still my PB. It was disappointing that I didn't run any faster than that.

How old were you when you ran Chicago?

I was 27 years old. I was supposed to run London the spring after that, but I got a bad injury in the Stafford 20. I was running really well too.

So, your first marathon was your PB?

Yes, it was. In February 1991, I ran in Tokyo and finished 12th in 2.12. I was in good shape, but I was ill before I went out there. In fact, it was 50/50 as to whether I should even go, but as I was actually getting quite a lot of appearance money, I decided to run. I suppose it was terrible really, but I was earning a living from running. I had six days rest out there and was actually quite chuffed with the 2.12. At the end of 1991, I did Carpi and ran 2.11.50, which I had to run to get an Olympic place in 1992.

How long before a marathon did you decide to do it?

Before Chicago, it wasn't a typical thing because I had run a whole track season, and I was racing every 10 days or so. One week I'd run 3.56 or 3.58 for a mile, and on another, 62 minutes for a half-marathon. However, it was probably a good foundation. I didn't race for about four weeks before Chicago though, and I did a couple of weeks of higher mileage. For Tokyo, I planned and trained specifically for most of the winter from the end of October through to February. However, it just goes to show that an illness can throw everything out the window even after doing all the right preparation. The background has got to be there, which I suppose I had. I rarely had an injury all through the 1980s. I'd have a couple of weeks off at the end of the track season, but all the rest formed a base. In hindsight, I am now convinced that I may have trained too hard for races and that's why they didn't come off, but you just train with the knowledge you have at the time. Once I started going over 80 or 90 miles a week, then little niggles started creeping in. It is about finding your own line really.

What was a typical training week in a build-up to a marathon?

The biggest week I ever did was about 105 miles. I remember trying out lots of things when I was young, including running 115 miles when I was 18, but it totally knackered me. I only ever managed about four weeks over 100 miles; I never did over 100 miles consistently. It was more like 80 to 90. Every four weeks, I'd have a week where it would be light, but I'd still be doing 65 miles or between 60 and 70; I'd always do that. I'd do 15 to 20 miles on a Sunday and another long run of 15 or an hour-and-a-half midweek on a Wednesday. They were pretty steady although at times they got fairly quick, depending on if I trained with a couple of people. However, they never went a lot under six-minute mile pace and were mostly at about 6.20, I suppose. I lived over at Cannock Chase, which was quite undulating and there were forest trails. Some of the hills were quite steep and broke up my rhythm quite a bit. I am convinced that's why I stayed injury free; I was hardly training on the road at all. I could do a 20-mile loop and only cross a road once. It was lovely. I'd do the midweek long run there too. Generally, on Tuesdays and Saturdays, I did harder sessions. These would be longish reps on the road or track or even on the forest trails again over a measured strip. The road sessions would be the longer sessions like 4 or 5 x 1 mile, which was enough for me in the winter. I'd have a couple of minutes recovery and run them at 10km race pace or a bit quicker - something like 67 or 68 lap pace. The other session would be something different. If I went to the track every couple of weeks, I'd maybe do something like quarters or 1000m reps in the spring. The rest would be steady running. Towards a race, I would do a hard effort over four or five miles. Occasionally, I would go to Sutton Park and use the relay course.

It was like a time trial?

Yes, it was always a hard effort. I would warm-up and do it. It was in place of a race or not far off race pace. I'd do that every three weeks.

Did you do any specific hill training?

If I were doing track, especially when I was doing the steeplechase, I'd do a lot of hills and sometimes in place of track sessions. I'd do them on a hilly circuit in the forest or just up and down a hill.

93

Did you do any fartlek?

Occasionally. If I didn't feel like doing a structured session, I'd put a repeat alarm on my watch and do 30 seconds on, 30 seconds off or something like that. The two long runs were the key though really in my marathon training.

What was your longest run in a build-up?

It was about 22 miles. Having said that, before a couple of marathons I did 25 miles about three or four weeks before the race. I never went over distance. I know Charlie Spedding used to do that.

So, were you still a top 10km runner at the same time as you were training for marathons?

Yes, I suppose. Every year, or most years, I'd run the AAA's 10km on the track and do about 28 minutes. My best was 28.21 on the track and 28.15 on the road. I always felt that if I could stick with the track season long enough, it would help me on the roads.

How did you taper for marathons?

Two weeks before, I would do two hours and that would be my longest run. It would then all go down from there. On the Sunday before, it would be an hour, and then I'd perhaps do some easy fartlek of five or six miles on the Monday or Tuesday. On Wednesday, I'd do half an hour, Thursday 20 minutes, Friday 15 minutes and that sort of thing. I didn't rest totally, but I didn't do very much.

Did you do the carbohydrate depletion/loading diet?

No, I didn't. I just ate more. I remember going to Chicago and trying to keep up with Dave Long in the restaurant. I could hardly get out of the chair afterwards! The main thing for me was to get well stocked up three days before and that was it really.

Did you choose certain races to do in a build-up to a marathon?

Yes, a month or three weeks before, I'd try to do a half-marathon and perhaps a 10km before or after the half. So, five weeks before it might be a 10km, followed by a week off, a half and then another 10km or something along those lines, depending on what races were available. If I couldn't find a 10km, then I'd do a time trial.

What was your attitude to these races? Did you ease down for them?

Yes, sometimes I would treat them properly. However, if I had a series of three races fairly close together, I wouldn't be able to treat them all like big races; I would have to keep the training going a bit. I think it is a fine line. If you train right the way through, then it can hardly be worth going to the race because you'll be too tired on the start line. You may as well stay home and do a time trial or something. On the other hand, you can rest up too much. For the half-marathon, I would usually ease down. I've also done a 10 mile race and then run the course again afterwards as training. Whether that was a good thing or not, I don't know, but I'd talked to a few people and decided it was probably a decent thing to do as a long session, and it made me run depleted. I am not sure whether it would have been better to run it before the race though. The main thing is that I think it's hard not to get demoralised after running badly even though you've trained hard. The psychology of racing is the hardest part.

Did you use any form of mental techniques in preparation?

Not as such. I didn't have any meditation tapes or anything like that. I think we all go through routines that we get used to though, don't we? Sometimes we get worried if we are not eating the right thing at the right time, especially if we are in a hotel or something.

What about during the marathon?

I'd aim to treat it as a run for as long as possible, as opposed to a race. I'd try not to hurt and try to get comfortable. If someone went off at 4.50 pace, and I wanted to run 5-minute or 5.05 pace, then I would just stick to my pace. I wouldn't attempt to go with the lead pack. I suppose strategy-wise, I would just look at the splits. I would know in my own mind what I needed to do. I think it is actually a very individual race. In fact, it is a ridiculous event. I never enjoyed it. You can't enjoy it, can you? The first one I did was really for the money. It was as simple as that. Charlie [Spedding] said to me once that you need a really good reason to do a marathon. Whether it is for money or medals or whatever, you have to have a good reason because it is a long race.

Were you a full-time athlete?

I left school at 16 and didn't have a clue what I wanted to do. I did a plumbing apprenticeship for four years, but the firm I was working for had to make all the apprentices redundant, and so I started looking round for something else to do. At first, I decided to look for part-time work, as I was having some success at running. However, I couldn't get the right sort of work that I wanted. I was 19/20 and had just won the European Junior Championships on the track and some money was just starting to come into athletics, so I decided to make a go at it full-time with athletics. The last year or two of working, I'd also picked up a few injuries, which I attributed to the job. I was biking over to Cannock Chase to do a full day's work, squeezing in a short run at lunchtime, biking all the way back and then doing a session at night. I got a lot of training in doing that, but I felt that it might have been injuring me at times. I began winning some money in around 1984, and then I started on the roads in 1985. It seemed to suit me more not working.

Did you have any other forms of financial assistance or sponsorship?

Yes, I was with Puma when I started off as a junior and then with Nike from 1983 although I didn't have a lot of money from Nike at the beginning. At the end of 1984, I got bits of prize money off of the track. It was just creeping in. From the mid 1980s, my income, by and large, came from road racing. By the late 1980s, I could just about live off what Nike was paying me but only just, so the road racing was important to do. There were bonuses, but I didn't make a lot from that. Most of my money was from prize money, as there also wasn't much appearance money around then. In fact, they weren't really allowed to pay an appearance fee in the US at that time. The prize money was quite good. When you won a 10km, you'd get about $7000, and I was always in the top three. I did a 10km race in Europe where I won $10,000. However, no Europeans win these races now. There were some good Africans about in the 1980s but not to the extent that there are now. Now there are hordes of Africans, and they get themselves organised and are well coached.

So, you were able to live comfortably on the money?

Yes, it was not bad, not bad at all.

Did you do any other forms of training?

Yes, I had a big multi-gym in the garage, and I did weights about three times a week. If I were doing an easy five or six miles in the morning, I would do some weights afterwards for half an hour. In the early to mid 1980s, I also had a good circuit training session going on at a local school once a week. I think it helped on the track, but once I started concentrating on the marathon, I probably did less. I also moved house and had to get rid of the multi-gym because it wouldn't fit in the new garage. I think there is such a big imbalance in just running, and I feel it could help in terms of injury. I didn't do big weights; I just did mostly reps of 20. I very rarely did a pyramid or up to a maximum lift or anything. I used to do a bit of cycling too but not as structured training.

Were you coached throughout your career?

I was coached as a youth and for the first couple of years as a junior and then sort of self-coached after that really. When I started doing marathons, I had various bits of advice from people, and I'd talk to those like Max Colby and Alan Storey about things. In hindsight, I might have been better off with a coach and a more structured plan, but I might have run worse, you never know. It is something you definitely need when you are young because it is a big learning process, but at the end of the day, in terms of physiology and things like that, you can also read books as a coach does. It is probably more important on the track to have someone to watch you.

Did you mostly train on your own or with a group?

I ran on my own for 90% of the time. On a Sunday, I would perhaps run with a group, as well as occasionally on a Tuesday.

Did you ever use altitude or warm-weather training?

I went to altitude a couple of times. I recall doing a 22-mile run in 1985 when I was in Boulder, and I had to stop and walk at one stage because I was going dizzy. I also went to St Moritz in 1987. I organised the trip with Colin Reitz, John Solly and Steve Ovett. We had a month there. However, because there was the four of us, I think we probably trained a bit too hard. I enjoyed it, and it was a lovely place to go and run, but I don't know if it made any difference. I remember running a 10,000m to try for the World Championships, and I finished fourth in 28.25 or something. I probably did benefit but not to a large degree, and I am not sure if it is worth the expense. I only went warm-weather training once in the early 1980s, but I never made an effort to do that. I went to train with a friend on the sand dunes at Southport for a change of scenery at one point, and I also went to the Pyrenees once for a few days just to have a look and see what it was like to train.

Did you have a special diet or take any supplements?

I took multi-vitamins but not a lot though. I also took iron tablets at one stage although I don't think I ever had anaemia, as I had tests done at various times with the Olympic team. As far as diet is concerned, I didn't do anything special. I just used to eat a lot of carbohydrate and try not to eat too much junk. I couldn't do my morning run without a decent cup of strong coffee though, and I'd drink water and juice after every run.

What about electrolyte drinks?

There weren't many around then, so I only took them on the odd occasion. I think Isostar was about in the late 1980s, but I didn't go out of my way to buy it. I'd just have water and juice.

What about during marathons?

I had a bad experience in Barcelona. I had a terrible stomach from a drink out there. It was Max or Maxim or something like that. In Chicago, I just drank water. I drank at most of the feed stations, especially the early ones, even if it was just a mouthful.

Did you drink alcohol while in training?

Not a lot and usually only at weekends.

What is your height, and what was your racing weight?

I am 1.74 m or five-foot eight-and-a-half and around nine stone two.

Do you have any ideas as to why you and the others were so good in the 1980s?

Perhaps the talent isn't coming through from the shorter distances now. If you haven't got the 5km and 10km runners running decent times in depth, then that is probably going to transfer to the marathon. The publicity surrounding the marathon in the 1980s created a lot of interest, and you were just getting club runners working that bit harder to run 2.16 and make teams. You could also argue that in the 1970s you had a lot of interest in the distance races on the track with the likes of Brendan Foster running well. Nowadays, everything is competing with football. It is such high profile. As well as this, you've got 11 year olds that are obese, and all they are talking about in the changing rooms is what computer games they are getting at the weekend. It is frightening really. If kids see heroes on television, it is bound to inspire, isn't it? However, these days there are fewer role models, and it is more difficult with the influx of Africans. The Africans I was running against weren't running the outlandish times they are now. When I was a junior, Henry Rono was the world record holder with something like 13.05 or 13.08. You knew you weren't going to be a lap behind, as even as a junior I was running 13.35. You thought that a high level was obtainable, but now they are running four-minute mile pace nearly the whole way, so it is going to seem impossible to some.

Jim Dingwall

PB: 2.11.44 – London 1983

Highest World Ranking in the 1980s: 50th

Marathon Achievements:

5th - London Marathon 1983

How did you become involved in athletics?

I was fairly young. It is difficult to put a time on it, but I can remember back to things like Sunday school sports and primary school athletic events when I was well under 10 years old. However, I wasn't taking it seriously then, and I didn't become involved competitively until I was 13 and at secondary school when I did open athletics. One of the biggest influences would have been my mother, who certainly encouraged me. The sports teacher at school was also influential. When I was at school, there were several inter-school competitions and lots of sport on the curriculum. I think that is one of the fundamental differences between then and now. You were expected to take part in at least some sort of sport, and athletics had a strong tradition in my school. So, I was very much guided by the P.E. teachers.

Do you think that you had natural talent at that age?

A little bit. I wouldn't say colossal, but I'd imagine I was in the top 20% of the population, if not the top 10%. So yes, there was a bit of talent there. It is nice to have a bit of success, and if you are reasonably good at something, it keeps you interested and encourages you that bit more, especially when you are young.

When did you actually join an athletics club?

Not until I was 21/22 because I was getting plenty of competition at school and university. At school, I did things like cross-country leagues, and I was also representing the school in national championships. I then went to Edinburgh University where similarly the environment was conducive to athletics and distance running. I ran winter cross-country and road races, and then went on the track. I did university competitions as well as national and district championships through until the end of June. In those days, I was fairly happy to have a more laid-back July and August. From 13 to 15 years of age, I did as much sprinting as I did distance running. I have the 1964 Scottish Schools' gold medal for the 110 yards sprint relay. So I was doing quite a bit of sprinting and quarter miles and that sort of thing, as well as cross-country in the winter. There was no indoors then – we are talking about the 1960s - so if you did any running in the winter, it was cross-country.

Which club did you join?

I joined Edinburgh Athletics Club.

Did you have any other successes at junior level?

Yes. After that sprint relay gold medal at 15, I moved up distances, and in 1967, or it may have been 1966, I got a bronze medal in the mile at the Scottish Schools'. I think my best in the Scottish Cross-Country Championships was as a youth in the mid 1960s when I came eighth. I was reasonably good. I wasn't blazingly fast, but I was in the top end. I also finished eighth in the National.

Were you doing a lot of training then?

At the beginning, I didn't really train at all other than once or twice a week on school pack runs. However, from about 1964 to 1967 – I was born in 1949 – I would run 20 to 25 miles a week or something like that. So, I was starting to run about four or five times a week and distances from a couple of miles up to six or seven. I went to university in 1967, and from then on I increased the mileage a little bit. I would have been running up to 30 or 35 miles a week by 1970.

How did you eventually come to do marathons?

In the period between 1967 and 1973, I moved up to being a middle-distance runner and was running 1500m and 5000m. I guess I preferred long-distance training, and I liked running through the countryside. However, I did find my sprint ability useful, as I could outsprint almost anyone. I ran my first marathon in 1972 but that wasn't really on marathon training. High mileage training was in vogue at the time with people like Dave Bedford, Ian Stewart, Ian McCafferty, Lachie Stewart and Ron Hill all running 100/120 miles a week. It became the norm. Even as a 1500m/5000m runner, I was doing 80 miles a week in the early 1970s, including 20 miles every Sunday. I had moved up from 35 miles a week in the late 1960s to running 60, 70, 80 miles a week, and so I felt almost able to dabble with the marathon. I ran the Preston to Morecombe race in 1972. I just ran steadily and did 2.27. I think there was a difference between 1500m runners then and now. Your average 1500m runner, Frank Clement, for example, who was much the same age as myself, would have been running 70, 80, 90 miles a week. This was what was expected of a 1500m runner. You would do 20 miles on the Sunday and probably 15 miles on the Wednesday, and then your speedwork on the track or your fartlek would go on top of that. It was therefore an easy transition to at least take part in a marathon. I was running 3.45 for 1500m and 13.50 for 5000m, and so at that stage I was better at the middle distances. However, I had the mileage background to dabble in the marathon. I always had a fascination with long-distance running. This went right down into my personality, and also my background of loving the countryside and the walks with my mother as a child. I enjoyed wandering over the hills for two hours on a Sunday; it gave me great pleasure. This was before the marathon boom, but there were lots of role models, such as Jim Alder, who had won the Commonwealth Games, Ron Hill, Don Faircloth, Jim White, Bill Adcocks, and lots of others who all did high mileage and ran marathons. So, I at least wanted to have a bash. Quite a lot of my friends in Edinburgh had also done marathons. There was a good nucleus of people who wanted to run long distances, and so there was a lot of talk about marathons and who was doing what.

How old were you when you did your first marathon?

I was 23 years old, but I wasn't taking marathons seriously at that stage. I was still very much a track runner who just did it as a bit of a laugh.

How many marathons did you run before you did your PB?

Approximately 25. I certainly did a few.

How long before the serious marathons did you decide to do them? Did you plan them meticulously?

Fairly seriously, yes. In those days, competing in the marathon at the Commonwealth Games, the Europeans' or the Olympic Games had a significantly higher prestige than it does now, so I suppose the first marathon I thought of trying was the AAA's Marathon at Rotherham in 1976, which was the Olympic trial. It was a long shot that I could make the team and, of course, I didn't then or at any other time. However, I certainly planned to run that marathon in Rotherham fairly seriously, and I trained specifically for it for some months prior, in fact, probably from the winter before. The same would have applied when I was trying to get into the teams in 1978, 1980, 1982 and 1984. I was probably thinking about it from October/November of the previous years. I would need a bit of a break from the track season, and after that I would start getting into the long runs and building the base over the winter. I would then sharpen up in the spring in order to run well in the summer. You are probably looking at eight or nine months ahead of when I was hoping to do well.

Can you outline a typical week of training in a build-up to a marathon?

A typical week would have been about 90 miles. Some weeks I might have done a bit more and some weeks a bit less but 90 miles a week was fairly typical. I never ran more than 130 miles in a week. I would do a few weeks of 100 and then ease off again. It would usually be 14 sessions, consisting of one run on a Saturday and Sunday, three on a Tuesday and Thursday, and two on the other days. From Monday to Friday, there were two sessions a day where I used to run to and from work, which was four miles. That was from 1974 to 1983 when I lived in Falkirk. On Tuesdays and Thursdays, I would also do a 10-mile run in addition.

Was that run hard?

I was never a particularly hard trainer really. I liked to run with people, so I'd run with my club mates up at Falkirk. I might work slightly harder than them on a fartlek session or whatever, but I was more interested in the social side of it and running along with them. On Mondays and Wednesdays, I would quite often extend the four miles home after work to anything up to a half-marathon, and some of those would be hard sessions. I might do the half-marathon at 6-minute miling or a 10-mile fartlek with fairly hard bursts in it, say a 5.15-mile or something like that, and then at a weekend I would

109

race. I raced virtually every Saturday because in those days races were on Saturdays. On Sundays, I'd do a long run of 15, 20 or 25 miles. I liked to do the occasional fast one as the marathon approached, and so I'd do a couple of 20 milers at between 1.53 and 1.58. I'd maybe do one seven weeks before and the other, a month before the marathon. The rest of the time, it was just a social saunter with club mates where you'd spend two-and-a-half to three hours on your feet. You can't thrash it out every day, and it was also dependent on what Saturday's race was. If I had done a 10-mile race, then I was not going to go out and do a hard 20 miler on the Sunday.

Did you do any track interval sessions or shorter reps?

I was always a fairly enthusiastic fartlek man, so a normal Tuesday night session up at Falkirk, which even went back to my days at Edinburgh University in the late 1960s/early 1970s, was a 10-mile fartlek and that was always pretty hard. I'd do 12 or 14 bursts where I'd thump something in between 300m and a mile. I didn't do very much track work after I abandoned serious track racing really, which would have been in 1978/1979. I always got a lot more pleasure out of doing fartlek on the road or the country than I did doing reps or intervals on the track.

Did you do specific hill sessions?

Quite often the Tuesday night sessions at Falkirk would involve repetitions on a hill. It would just be the standard stuff like bursting up a hill and jogging down, but I didn't do a lot of hill work really.

Any time trials?

The nearest I got to time trials were the occasional brisk 20 milers that I would do as the marathon approached. I also sometimes used to do a half-marathon home from work on a Monday night when I would try to go inside 6-minute miling but still not flat out. On a good day, I might do 5.50-miling feeling quite comfortable, and on a bad day, 6.10 and struggle a bit. I would probably do four of these in the 10 weeks before a marathon to get me used to running at something close to race pace. I was doing that as the second session of the day and when I'd maybe done a 20 miler the day before, so although it is not as fast as race pace, I was running with heavy legs.

Were you also a top 10km runner at this time?

Well, I was never that brilliant. My 10km PB was 28.45. I did more road than track 10km races. While there weren't that many runners in Scotland running 29 minutes, there were still a few like Nat Muir, Allister Hutton, Laurie Spence, and John Robson, as well as a

111

few other respectable performers, so I couldn't just turn up at a road race and walk round and win it.

So, you were still pretty classy at 10km?

Yes, and even down to 5km. Up until the mid 1980s, I still retained a lot of my speed from my sprinting heritage. I could hold my head up with very good club men and the bottom end of the international market. However, a top-class class international would obviously thrash me.

How did you taper for a marathon?

I didn't taper to any great extent. I would keep running fairly hard until about five days before the race. I would be quite happy to go out and do 15 or 17 miles on the Sunday before although maybe not terribly hard. I'd just shuffle out. I might also still do a 10km fartlek on the Tuesday night but not thrashing it. I had experimented with easing down through the 1970s, and as a track runner, but not found it very successful. In fact, if anything, I ran worse after easing down for a week or 10 days before a race rather than if I just rode up and ran. I'd even go out for a four-mile steady the day before, and I still do now when I dabble in the marathon.

What races did you do in a build-up to a marathon?

Given the geography and race availability in Central Scotland throughout the late 1970s and early 1980s, what I did was governed more by the fixture list than any well thought-out plan. If the local race was a 3-mile road race, I did a 3-mile road race. If it was 10 miles cross-country, I did 10 miles cross-country. I would then build my training in around the races. If in the build-up to a marathon there were quite a lot of short races, I would do more of my hard 20 milers and half-marathons in training, and vice versa. If there was some significant race opportunity to do, such as the Balla to Clydebank, which is 12 miles, then that would do as a fairly long, brisk workout, and I wouldn't do the half-marathon on the Monday night. I'd do a 9-mile steady or something like that instead. I think it is important if you are going to run a marathon, to get your body used to running reasonably quickly for a reasonably long period of time. You can't expect to run a good marathon if all your training is very short stuff or if all your long stuff is very slow. Somehow or other, you have to get in races or training runs at well within a minute a mile of what your race pace is going to be in order to get your body used to cruising along and so that you can run for an hour or two at something near race pace and not fall apart.

113

Did you use any form of mental techniques in preparation?

I think a lot of it is almost at the subconscious level. I am a scientist by training, and so I guess a lot of my preparation is very factual. I got a lot of reassurance from things like I'd drunk plenty of water before the start, that I'd tied my shoe laces tight, that I'd run in the racing shoes before, that my shorts didn't rub, that I'd put Vaseline on my nipples, and that I had a sun hat if it was hot or a woolly hat if it was cold. So there was a lot of practical reassurance in making sure I was ready for all eventualities and that I was as physically prepared as I could be. I think that was my main mental preparation. It was just from a practical angle.

What about during the race?

This would be pretty similar really. Before the gun went, I would have some sort of idea as to what was a realistic time. So, if I reckoned that 2.15 was ambitious but not ridiculous, then I would work out the even pace for 2.15 – whatever that is – 5.15-miling or something – and then I would spend a lot of time thinking about the speed I was running at. If I was going too fast, I wouldn't necessarily slow down, but I would relax and not work at it at least, or if I was going slower, I would be questioning whether I was taking it a bit too easily.

Did you mainly run the race to your splits? Did you not take much notice as to what other people were doing?

Yes, to an extent and probably more than most. This is not to decry the benefits of running with a pack. In fact, you are often better off running in a pack even if it is going slightly too fast or too slow for you; as long as it is not dragging you away too much from what is comfortable. So, I might run with a pack that is going 10 seconds a mile slower or faster than I wanted to be going. However, if that went on for a significant amount of time, I'd have to ask myself whether it was sensible to stay in the pack from either angle. Either I'd be in danger of becoming exhausted for going too fast and pay the price later on or not getting the maximum performance I was capable of because I was sauntering along with a pack that was going a bit slower than I could do. You have to have the courage to get out in front and do it. I certainly spent a lot of time thinking about the speed I was going at and things like keeping out of the wind, keeping out of the sun, going around the shortest corner, not tripping over water hydrants and anything that would physically make life a little bit easier.

115

Did you do any other forms of training?

Not really. I was virtually running and nothing else. I had a fairly demanding full-time job, and any spare time I could have for sport was devoted to running.

Did you work full-time throughout your running career?

I gained a PhD in Chemistry at Edinburgh University in 1974 and then started working 40 hours a week, or thereabouts, for BP Chemicals in Grangemouth. I wouldn't say I was one of the most ambitious research chemists that BP ever had, as I had a slightly nine to five type attitude, but I certainly did work nine to five and probably a bit more now and then. I had to get up at seven o'clock to run to work, and then I'd leave work at 5 o'clock in the evening to run home again.

When you did three times a day, did you run at lunchtime?

No, that was in the evening as well. I would run again at 7.30 with the group. I wouldn't usually bother getting changed. I would get in at a quarter to six, put a tracksuit on and have my tea, and then go out again at 7.30.

So, you actually had something to eat as well?

Oh yes. If you are running three times a day, you need to do a lot of eating.

You didn't get stitch or stomach trouble?

No, I have a good stomach. I had a big breakfast too. I'd have a bowl of porridge and three or four slices of toast, and within five minutes I would be off running down the road.

Did you ever consider becoming a full-time athlete?

Not in those days. I did as much of my good running in the '70s as the '80s, and there wasn't the income around then. In the 1980s, you could probably make a semblance of an income out of running if you were good enough, but in the 1970s it was just not an option. By 1985, I had more or less become a club runner. I had no international ambitions after 1985.

Did you have any sponsorship, such as clothes and shoes?

Yes, I had plenty of shoes and so on. I had Adidas, Nike, Asics and Puma.

Did you have any money contracts with them and bonus incentives?

Yes, I got some bonuses for running in some races or doing well in races. I wasn't good enough to be paid by them though.

What about prize money or appearance money?

By today's standards, no. The total amount I probably got in prize money, appearance money and any other kind of money would have been £6000 or £7000. That would have been the lot I made in my career.

So, you couldn't live comfortably on it then?

No! Not a chance.

Were you coached at all?

I was self-coached. I had lots of advice from all sorts of people though. There is nothing I like more than sitting down in a bar with a Donald McGregor, a Ron Hill or a Jimmy Alder and talking about running. You learn a lot from these guys. It is just inspirational. Distance running is not a complicated sport, and I think motivation and the incentive are vastly more important than the niceties of coaching. I mean, what coaching is there in running? Maybe I missed the trick. I think it is relatively straightforward. In a nutshell, the more you train without overdoing it, the fitter you get. You can do fartlek, track, road, cross-country, repetitions, hills, races or whatever. These are subtleties, and I think it depends much more on the individual. If you enjoy hills and track running, then you do hills and track running. If you prefer doing fartlek and cross-country, then you do fartlek and cross-country. It really is less important than being motivated and willing to get out there and train hard. People have been successful with very different regimes. If we are talking specifically about marathons, you clearly need to do quite a lot of long-distance running. In the middle distances, it is more open. You can be a good middle-distance runner with high mileage steady running and just a little bit of sharp stuff, but you can also be a good middle-distance runner with hardly doing any long-distance running at all and making it all high quality stuff on the track, roads or in the parks. You can clearly not run a good 26 miles unless you occasionally run a 20 miler or thereabouts.

Did you do most of your training alone or with groups?

Most of the to and from work stuff was on my own although sometimes I would have colleagues who would run with me. It was mostly 50/50, but I think groups help enormously. I think that is why my motivation isn't what it was in the 1970s and 1980s because I do 80% of my running on my own now. It is tremendously important to get motivation from other people, and other runners with their ambitions are a source of that. I am sure it is beneficial to run with people. While it may take longer to arrange a rendezvous to go at set times, and you may have to compromise on the sessions you are doing, there are enormous benefits of running with other people. It is no coincidence that a lot of good distance runners have come out of areas where there were a lot of good groups. There are the odd people like Priscilla Welch, who can run on their own in Shetland, but they are pretty rare, and you will see a lot of good distance runners coming out of Gateshead or Birmingham where they have good team mates. I certainly acknowledge my running colleagues, both at university and at Falkirk, as a major source of inspiration.

Did you ever use altitude or warm-weather training?

No, I never went altitude training. I did have a couple of holidays in the Canary Islands a month before the London Marathon, but they were very "Mickey Mouse." If you only have your annual leave, you are fairly limited. I think for altitude to do you any good, you have to be there for several weeks or months, and so it wasn't an option for me.

Did you follow a special diet or take any supplements? Did you do the carbohydrate depletion/loading diet?

I dabbled with the depletion/loading diet a couple of times, but I never ran successfully on it. It upset my stomach or digestive system, and so I abandoned it. As a scientist, I made sure I did it properly, but it made me physically sick and anxious, and it also gave me diarrhoea. So after that, I just had a fairly standard diet and simply made sure that I had a high level of carbohydrates two or three days before the race. I didn't take any supplements at all, not even vitamins or iron. I had a healthy appetite.

Did you drink a lot of fluid?

Yes, I drank everything in sight, alcohol included. I ran my 2.11 after having had four pints the night before, but generally it was lots of tea, orange juice and water. I'd always go to the start line with a 2-litre bottle of water and drink it constantly.

What about during the race?

It wasn't so easy in the 1970s and 1980s because there were much fewer feed stations. In the first two or three marathons I ran, you would get a drinks' station every five miles, and the drinks would be in a china or plastic cup. You'd be lucky to get a couple of mouthfuls down.

What about electrolytes?

Electrolytes were coming on the scene in the mid 1970s, and I did dabble with them. I drank something called Dynamo and also Accolade. I was getting into the electrolytes in the late 1970s, but I packed them in after the Commonwealth Games in 1978, as I threw up at about 16 or 17 miles. I think I was drinking them too strong. So from 1979 onwards, I stopped with the electrolytes and just drank water.

What is your height, and what was your racing weight?

I am 1.73 m, and I weighed 63 kg.

What factors do you think made you and the others in the 1980s so good?

One of the most important things is the greater affluence in the 1990s. Nowadays, young people have cars and get driven around, and they don't get much physical exercise. My generation grew up having to walk everywhere, and if you were really well off, you might get a bike to cycle. We spent a tremendous amount of time walking to and from where we had to go. We walked to school, we walked to the shops, and we walked to our relatives and to our friends. We also played in the streets and were on our feet running around all the time. People have a much easier life these days. As well as getting driven around, they take part in fewer sports, and there are a lot more options. I didn't have a TV when I was young, and sport was one of the few outlets, particularly distance running, because you didn't need a lot of cash or equipment. Nowadays, people have money to go off to McDonalds or to the cinema or to the disco. There are loads of things and even if they decide they want to go into sport, they have vastly more opportunities. There is not nearly so much sport in school though and that is linked to it too. Teachers also have a hard time delivering the basics of

the national curriculum and there is much less inter-
school sport. The other major factor is the rise of third-
world countries in distance running, particularly the
African countries. When I was young, the vast majority
of the good distance runners in the world were
Northern Europeans or English-speaking white people.
I am not making any racist or derogatory comment
when I say this, but when the majority of the runners up
the front in the World Cross-Country Championships or
the Boston Marathon or the London Marathon are
African or South American, it doesn't provide the same
role models for British youngsters or any European
youngsters for that matter. It isn't just a British problem.
You can see the same decline in Scandinavia, Germany,
the USA, Australia, New Zealand and Canada. We have
seen a movement in athletic powers in distance running
from Northern Europe and white Commonwealth
countries, such as Australia, New Zealand and Canada
to Africa and Southern Europe, with a few Latin
Americans and Middle Easterners thrown in. So, the
role models have gone and that has had a knock-on
effect with sponsors, television and press coverage.
When Ian Thompson and Ron Hill were doing well,
they were headline news every weekend, but this is not
the case now. Now it is all football, or at least, it
certainly isn't athletics, except for the wilds of Channel
Four or something. Top runners in Britain are still very

good, but there are very few of them, and the depth has gone.

Paula Fudge

PB: 2.29.47 – Chicago 1988

Highest World Ranking in the 1980s: 46th

Marathon Achievements:

Winner - Columbus Marathon 1985

5th - London Marathon 1986

4th - London Marathon 1987

17th - Rome World Championships 1987

3rd - Chicago Marathon 1988

What is your background in athletics?

Basically, it started off at junior school where we ["we" meaning Paula and her twin sister, Ann] were running around a field. We then took part in the district sports' doing things like throwing a cricket ball, hurdles, 80 yards and high jump. Eventually, we went on to senior school where we played out in the field at lunchtime throwing a discus. Some girls came along and asked if we'd like to try down at the local club, and it went from there.

Was that Hounslow AC?

Yes, Feltham as it was originally called. We started off doing the 80 yards, 150 yards, long jump, shot put and discus because there were limits as to how far you could run, and in the intermediate age group it was 150 yards. At 16, we moved up to doing the 880 yards. It wasn't until you went into the seniors that you could run any further. From then on, we gave up all the other "side bits" and concentrated on track and cross-country.

No road at that time?

No, although there were the road relays, of course, but it was just a mile for youngsters. We moved up to the 1500m as we got older. Ann gained an All England title, but we weren't that good, and it took about three years before things started to move forward. We had changed coaches by then and began working a lot harder. We weren't natural or anything; it was something we really had to work at. The road running started in the early 1970s, and I did the Walton 10 when I was about 20. However, the marathon came a lot later. In fact, it was 1985 before I did my first one. I'd had a daughter by this time, and I wanted to do a marathon before I retired. Ann had also done one, so I thought it was about time I did.

How old were you when you did that first one?

I was 35.

What was your greatest achievement?

The 1978 Gold medal at the Commonwealth Games over 3000m.

What was your PB?

It was set in the same year. I went to the European Championships and ran 8.48.07. Winning the National Cross-Country was also something I'd wanted to achieve because Ann had already won it, but it took me another five or six years after that. I wanted my name on the cup. The 5000m world record I set in 1981 with 15.14.51 was another highlight, and I did the World Championships in 1987 over the marathon distance.

What were your PBs for the other road distances?

I did 53.44 for 10 miles in 1985 before my first marathon and 32.44 for 10km. I also ran 49.43 for 15km when it was the World Championship in Monaco. I didn't actually do a decent half-marathon until 1988 when I was 38 and that was 71.37. It was three years after my first marathon. It took a long time to come down from 72-and-a-half.

How long before a marathon did you decide to do it?

We had a six-week build-up and that was it, but we were basically ticking over for other races anyway. We'd just make sure that we did a two-hour run and, if necessary, a two-and-a-quarter-hour run three or four weeks before, so that we got in the distance.

So, what was a typical training week in a build-up to a marathon?

It actually didn't change that much other than putting in a bit more mileage. We were always doing about 70 miles a week, and so we just did a few extra runs, such as doing a five-mile run after a nine-mile run in order to keep the strength and the distance there. Our coach felt that we didn't need to put in a lot more than that. I think we went up to 100 miles once and that was when we went warm-weather training. We were training near enough twice a day every day anyway. The only things I can remember changing for the marathon were the long reps where we would do something like five by five minutes. These were our longest reps and that was it really.

Did you train twice a day throughout the week?

No, we trained twice on Monday, Wednesday, Friday and Saturday. The other days we just trained once.

How many quality sessions did you do a week?

If I raced abroad - because I was going to France a lot at that time to race cross-country - I used that as a hard training session and didn't ease down or anything. So, I was doing three quality track sessions a week, as it were.

Did you go to the track the other two times?

No, we went on the grass or road. After we had our children, we actually stayed off the track because of the bend running and the potential for injury.

What was the other session you did apart from the long reps?

I think it was short recoveries. It was four sets of 5 x 200m, and we'd do them hard in 35 seconds with 20 seconds recovery. It was something we did for years and years, and even now I do them to get fit again.

Were the long reps always 5 x 5 minutes, or did they vary?

No, it was usually five-minute reps.

So, your training was pretty structured?

Yes.

You said your long run was two hours. What sort of distance did you cover?

I don't know. We just ran for time.

Were the long runs quite fast?

Yes. Bernie [Ford – Ann's husband] would also come along as well, so they would be quite high quality. We'd start them as we meant to go on, but if one person was going through a bad patch, say up a hill or something, we'd help each other out.

Were they on the road or grass?

They were a mixture. We used to train at Virginia Water a lot.

Were all your training runs quite brisk?

Yes.

Even your morning runs?

Yes, it didn't really matter. We were so used to getting up and out that they were done just as fast as the other runs. We'd done a paper round when we were younger, and we also ran to work, so we were used to it. Most of our runs were at about five-and-a-half-minute miling.

So, not hanging about then?

No. It's like the 200m reps; they are something we did with Conrad [their coach] very early on and whenever

129

we'd been injured or had a break, the short recovery session was the thing we used to go back to. It is surprising how quickly it gets you back into it; it brings on the runs. If you were to just go out and plod round some 400m reps, you are not getting your speed. They were hard, but they had to be done.

Were there any easy days?

Friday was usually the easiest day when I'd only do two five-mile runs, or if I was racing on the Saturday, a five and a three.

So, you never had a complete day off?

I never had a complete rest day unless I was ill. However, I'd sometimes just do one run on the Friday if there were a big race on the Saturday. On occasions, we'd do a five miler in the morning and then the Southern League Cross-Country in the afternoon. It was mostly quality running although the distance was there as well. In fact, I can't understand why people want to do 120 miles a week for a 10km race. Why? Some people are trying to do quality and a lot of mileage. They can't take the two together, and then they wonder why they break down. We have always found doing 70 miles for 3000m to be plenty. When we decided to do marathons, it increased to 80/85 miles, but we did have many years of running behind us, and it was a natural progression. We had the strength anyway.

On the whole, your training was the same as usual then?

Yes, it was the same as usual. It was just that instead of doing 6 x 800m for the track, we'd do five-minute reps or 5 x 1 mile. We had the schedules written out for us by our coach, or we'd just ask him for some advice by that stage. I'd sometimes say to Ann that I wasn't doing something, and we'd throw it out. There were two-and-a-half-hour runs in the schedule, and we agreed that we didn't want to do those if we were going to be running for two-and-a-half hours in competition. We just did it once to see what it felt like, and then we did quality runs of two or two-and-a-quarter hours.

So, you never ran the marathon distance in training?

No. We'd do about 20 or 22 miles and that was it.

Were you still a top 10km runner at this time?

Yes, because my mileage hadn't increased too much, and I still had my speed.

Did you have set races in a build-up to a marathon?

I used to do the Fleet Half-Marathon before London because that is when I wanted to do one, and it fitted in. In the lead up to Chicago in the October, I did the Great North Run, as it was in July back then. In fact, doing a PB there confirmed to me that I should aim for Chicago rather than the Olympics. It was the decision made. I didn't plan any other half-marathons. Two weeks before a marathon, I'd like to a 10km just to get some speed into my legs and that was my last race. I'd only do something like a track race if there were one coming up for the club. That's all.

How did you taper?

We used to keep the pattern the same because it was what our bodies were used to, but we'd just not do as much. So, instead of doing 5 x 5 minutes, we'd do 4 x 5 minutes, and if we were doing 4 x 6 x 200m, we'd cut out a set completely. We'd also reduce the runs on the twice a day sessions to maybe five and three miles, and the long run would come right down to an hour-and-a-half. The Sunday before the race, we'd do about 10 miles, and on the Thursday perhaps half a dozen 100m strides. The intensity would also be more relaxed. I am sure that I used to go out and do a couple of miles on the Saturday just to keep my legs moving. You get so used to running every day that to suddenly stop can make you feel sluggish.

Did you do the carbohydrate depletion/loading diet at all?

We used to do that when we were younger for track races and found it absolutely rubbish, so we didn't bother. What is the point of doing it if it is going to ruin your training and make you feel both mentally and physically bad? All we did was eat more carbohydrate, not drain it. We ate more from the Thursday onwards.

Did you have a special diet or take any supplements?

No, just a normal proper diet or, at least, what I'd call a proper diet. I have been anaemic since I was 15, so both of us have been on iron religiously since then. Vitamin C was probably the other thing I used to take regularly and maybe ginseng although that was only in 1986 and 1987 when somebody recommended it to us. I probably take more now than I did then.

Did you generally drink a lot?

We were probably the world's worst at drinking, and we never used to drink a lot of water. It was always tea and coffee. When I was 21, I had a kidney infection, which worried me, and then I should have drunk more. However, I probably worry about it more now than I did then.

What about electrolyte drinks?

There were no electrolyte drinks around then.

What about in marathons?

I used to drink water. When we did long runs, there was a point where we could stop off to have a drink, and I had a little hand thing I'd take just so we could get used to it. I took a drink at most feeding stations in a marathon, as I think you need to. However, I didn't drink anything in races up to half-marathon in case I got stitch.

Did you use any form of mental techniques before or during races?

No, nothing. I wanted to do it and that was it. I was just focused on that. All that worried me was making sure that I had done the training that was relevant for the race.

How did you cope with any bad patches?

In one London Marathon, I got stitch at 18 miles. I was running with Ann and just got so carried away with the atmosphere that I was probably running faster than I should have been. Fortunately, she went off, and I managed to sort of plod through it. I was just determined to finish. In Columbus, it was freezing cold at the start and then boiling hot. I was out in the lead, and my thoughts were that I just had to finish. It was getting hotter and hotter, and I was getting weaker and weaker. I think you just get to a certain point in a race when you are out in the lead, and you say to yourself that you are not going to lose it, and you just keep going. This is the reason that you need to do the two-hour long runs and maybe the five-minute reps; you need to be able to learn to concentrate. I can't understand going to a sports' psychologist. If it is something you want to achieve, why do you need anybody to help you?

Did you do any other forms of training, such as weights?

I never did weight training. I used to do circuits as a 12/13 year old but that was all. I did general exercises like sit-ups and press-ups. I probably do about 50 to 60 sit-ups a day. I can't see what you are going to achieve as a distance runner doing weights.

You mentioned a coach earlier. Were you always coached?

Conrad Milton was my second coach from when I was about 16/17 years old. That was when I thought I had to do something different. Before then, I had a general club coach. We were told if you wanted to achieve anything, you had to train twice a day and up your runs. We were doing 10 miles then anyway, but it was a case of having to push it up even more. After Conrad, there was no other coach. For the marathons, we just went to him for advice really, as by this point I felt that if I couldn't do it, I didn't want to waste his time. We knew enough by then anyway. It was just a case of what rep sessions we thought we should do. He gave us a schedule, but we adapted it to suit ourselves and did what we thought was right.

Did you do most of your training with Ann?

Yes, mostly with Ann. Even when we both got married, we tried to get together for track sessions. She'd come down here, or I'd go up there. Well, I say track sessions, but they were on grass. We also tried to get together for a long run as well. When my children started school, we didn't get together quite as much. We didn't have the time. I did go out with a guy over the back for some other runs as well. Until about seven years ago, I had someone to train most of the time, but then Ann moved to Nottingham, and the guy got injured. For the last three years, I have done most of my runs alone.

Did you work full-time?

I worked full-time until I had my children. From 1978, I used to get two afternoons off a week in order that I could do rep sessions with Ann. That was the only time I got off. I worked in an office from when I was 16 years old. I'd get up in the morning and run to work or around here, and then I'd go to work. After work, I'd go out again.

Did you get time off to go to championships?

Sometimes you'd get the leave, and sometimes you'd have to take your own leave or lose pay.

What happened after you had children?

I had Rachel, and then I left work. Robert [her husband] was doing shift work then. He would have her for one of the sessions, and if I was training twice a day, a neighbour would have her for the other, or she'd go to my mum. They helped out.

Was it easier for your training not to be working?

For the first couple of years, it was not so bad because I was at home and didn't have to go places. However, once you have two children, it changes. I'd have to take one to school and then still have another one to worry about. I used to go out at six o'clock in the morning. The only reason I got back into my running was that I found I got back into it really easily. Whether it was because I was more relaxed, I don't know. So, I decided to plod on back and see what I could achieve. Robert didn't mind. I got back to representing Great Britain and going abroad again, and I made the World Championships. When I went to races, Rachel either came with me, and we paid for her, or Robert was here with her. She was never left with anyone. We didn't dump her off with anybody at all.

It still sounds quite a demanding schedule though?

It was a good distraction. I did my training, and then I had someone to look after. Although it was hard work, it was also relaxing. My sister managed to work four hours a day. It is just a regular pattern really. I am in such a routine during the week.

What sponsorship or financial assistance did you have?

It took a long time before I was able to get anything. After I broke the world record at 5000m, I approached Adidas, who I was with, about getting paid, but they refused. So I walked off and found somebody else who would actually pay money to sponsor me, as well as give me clothes and shoes. I was with Nike, and so was Ann. However, later they stated that they would only carry on sponsoring us if we did a marathon. I told them to get stuffed whereas Ann said she would do one. After that, I was looking around for someone else, but I was more or less sponsored throughout my running career.

Did the contracts offer you a lot of money?

Reebok were probably the best. When I did my first marathon, I was actually wearing all their kit. After that, they started paying me a salary every month for about three or four years. When I got closer to retiring properly, all these bonuses were coming in. However, there was no point, as I was not going to achieve them. The sponsorship then dried up. Unfortunately, it wasn't there when you needed it.

Did you have anything else like Sports Aid?

Yes, Sports Aid occasionally, and we got meat sponsorship for a while. Also, when I worked at Marconi around the corner here, they asked the employees if they'd like to contribute something. Every so often, I got some money from them. However, it wasn't much, and it soon dropped off. By the time you worked out your travelling expenses and all that, there wasn't a lot left.

Did you get prize money and appearance money?

Yes, the first one I did, which I won, I got prize money. However, it went into a trust fund, and I had to give receipts to draw out the money. I think it is a lot easier now. In the 1980s, I also started getting appearance money, but obviously a lot of it was undercover at the beginning. It then became more publicised as to what people were receiving. My husband wasn't even earning a lot of money, so it just helped out and meant we could have a few luxuries. My dad said we were the wrong side of 30, but I didn't really care as I had achieved a lot. We were quite lucky as we both earned money. We've set up a pension fund for when we retire, so that we will be comfortable. It has helped to look after our future. When I did Chicago, I missed out on $10,000 by one second. It hasn't bothered me. It bothered everyone else bar me. I went under 2 hours 30, so I don't care.

What was your racing weight, and how tall are you?

I weighed eight stone. I am five-foot six. Before I got to be any good, I was always over eight stone. Ann only weighs seven stone, and she is five-foot five.

Did you get a lot of sleep and rest?

Just the usual eight hours at night. I would go to bed at ten o'clock because I was getting up at six o'clock. I just accepted the pattern of life as it was. I would be up at a certain time to get ready for work, go to work, train in the evening, go to bed, and then I'd be up the next day.

So, there was no chance for an afternoon nap then?

When I had my second child, I sometimes did. She was colic, and so if I was tired, I tried to sleep with her in the afternoon but not other than that. We are women, aren't we? We just get on with it.

Did you have regular massage or any other therapies?

No, not really. I only had a massage when I went on a trip. It was the only person I could get it from.

Did you suffer from many injuries or illnesses?

No, not really or at least no more than is usual. I didn't have much time off with injuries although I had six weeks off back in 1985 or 1986 when I had a foot operation. I had a piece of bone that they originally thought was floating, but when they opened it up it was still attached. Every time I went round a bend in a race, it was agony, so I managed to get it taken out. I had to get back properly from that with physio and rehabilitation, which I had never had before. I had to learn to walk again after having my foot up for 10 days. It really shocked me. However, I managed to get back from that and do the London Marathon. It happened in the February, and I still only ran three seconds slower than I did the year before. Before I fell pregnant for Rachel, I had a knee problem. I had no idea what it was, and so I thought that was the time to take a break. It was like my whole body was collapsing and that went on for two or three months, which is probably my longest break.

You and Ann were notorious for running right the way through your pregnancies, weren't you?

Ann was the one that ran right to the end with her two, but she had a break afterwards. You have to. I ran up to four weeks before mine. I couldn't do any more. I did it for as long as I could, but I found it too uncomfortable. I got back four to six weeks afterwards. You have to be careful though, as you need to wait for your ligaments and back to return to normal. Once I started training again, I got back very quickly. It was great. However, I had a urinary infection at one point, which stopped me getting to the World Championships. That really dragged me down, and I was a bit up and down for six months.

Do you have any ideas or thoughts as to why you were all so good in the 1980s?

I can't say that I really know, other than the fact that probably the girls that were running then had years of background training. That is all I can think of. I think we also had good coaches who knew what they were doing and who got it right. Coming up through the distances helped, and you also had to fight to get into a team because there were always five or six of us who were brilliant.

Julia Gates (Armstrong)

PB: 2.36.31 – London 1986

Highest World Ranking in the 1980s: 75th

Marathon Achievements:

Edinburgh Commonwealth Games 1986

How did you become involved in athletics?

When I was six years old, I thought I was a runner. I remember making my dad time me running around the garden, and up and down the playing fields. I was also doing athletic things in the Brownies and was very competitive. However, I really got involved when I did the Farnham & District Sports' at 12. I didn't join an athletics club, but I started doing some training on my own in the summer. I'd go for runs of about three miles and take myself off on little journeys. I was allowed to do things like that in those days. I'd walk the dog for miles, go off on long bike rides, and get off the bus from swimming a few stops early and walk home. I was always keen and endurance minded. When I was 14, I made the Surrey Schools' 100m. I came first in the heat, second in the semi-final and fifth in the final, and I ran a PB of 13.3. The following year, I did exactly the same in the 200m, coming fifth in the final and running a PB of 27.5. At the age of 15, I decided that I wanted to get better, so I joined an athletics club. The only club nearby was Haslemere Border, but it was an all men's athletic club. However, they let me join, and I became the first woman in the club. After joining the club, I got a coach, who told me that I was obviously more suited to distance running. So I started doing the 800m, 1500m and 3000m on the track as well as cross-country. From there I went right the way up really. I always wanted to run, and I decided that I would like to run for England. I still enjoyed sprinting and thought I was quite good at it, but when I was 16/17 I got to the Surrey Schools' over 800m and won it in 2.14, which was obviously quite fast. I then ran 4.26 for 1500m aged 17 and 9.27 for

3000m aged 19. Unfortunately, I missed the English Schools' Championships because I had tonsillitis and also had a trauma with my coach about travelling with the team. He'd wanted me to travel with him, but they wouldn't allow it. On the country, I was second in the Inter-Counties as an intermediate, sixth in the trial race as a senior, fourth in a home countries' international, third in an international - where I met Nigel [her first husband] - sixth in the Inter-Counties, won the Southern Inter-Counties and was fourth in the actual Southern. I had a terrible run in the National Cross-Country though and came 17th. I was traumatised because I thought I was going to make the World Cross-Country team. My car had broken down on the way up, and I'd had a rotten journey. So all in all, I was pretty successful on the country. I never ran as well on the track though as I wanted. I got to be an international on the country, but what I really wanted was to be an international on the track. However, I think I trained too anaerobically. I'd come off the winter so fast, get all my PBs in May and then just get slower as the year went on. My mum died when I was 16 and that obviously had a profound effect on me. I threw myself towards my coach and my running, which sort of sustained me until I was 19 really. I put all my emotions into my running. Unfortunately, I also became anorexic at 17. My coach said to me that I looked a bit heavy and could do with

144

losing some weight. I was about eight-and-a-half stone, which was quite slim for me, but I dieted and got down to seven-and-a-half stone. My whole psyche turned at that point.

How did you work your way up to doing marathons?

Well, I was obviously an endurance runner. I was running 18 to 20 miles on a Sunday at the age of 15 and 70 miles a week at the age of 17. I even wanted to run a marathon when I was 16, but we decided it was not a good idea. When I was 19, I met Nigel in Spain while running for England and along with Grenville or Graham Tuck – I can never remember which one - we went for a 15-mile run. Everyone was going for an 8-mile run, but we went for 15. They went at about six-minute miling, and I was hanging on. However, I did hang on, and at the end Nigel asked me if I always ran at that pace. I lied and said yes, and Graham or Grenville said to me that I could be a future marathon runner. Someone else also told me at 15 that they thought I could be a good marathon runner. So it was obviously apparent. Nigel and I then started going out together for about three months. I'd had my bad run in the National Cross-Country and went to stay with him the following weekend. I was really pissed off because I thought I was going to make the World Cross-Country Championships, and so Nigel suggested that I run the Bath Hilly 10 while I was down there. Unbeknown to us, Kath Binns, who had won the National, decided to run it. No woman had ever broken 60 minutes on the course at that point, as it is so tough, but Kath ran 57.45, and I ran 58.48. It made me realise that I was a road runner. After that, I split with my coach and went to Loughborough University. However, I dropped out after only two terms because my eating disorders had gotten out of hand by this stage. I went there, and I was broken. I had no stability, and the grief over my mum hit me hard. So I then went to Bristol and tried to start nursing, but once again I dropped out. I was very lost, very depressed and very unhappy. I kept hanging on to running, but my weight was going from seven-and-a-half to ten-and-a-half stone. I then met Nigel again, and we became friends. For a year, we just met everywhere. We went to lunch, and we went running together. The following year, I asked Nigel to coach me and basically he managed to stabilise me. First, I wanted to do a half-marathon, and then I decided to do the London Marathon. So I ran the second London Marathon in 1982 on just 50 miles a week, weighing nine-and-a-half stone. I ran 3.02. I just did it, and I could do it because I always just had that natural endurance. I certainly wasn't fit, or at least really fit, and I certainly wasn't lean.

How old were you when you did this first one?

I was 23.

How many marathons did you run before you did your PB?

I think it was about five. I had a lot of illness. The following London, I did 2.54, but I was really wiped out and fainted at the finish. I then did Bristol in 2.54, and finally I got my act and health together and ran 2.47 in Dublin although even there I had an infected tooth; every mile was agony. I got to 20 miles in 2.01 and thought I was going to go under 2.40, but then I just went. I never used to drink in those days either; I never took any water or glycogen on board and so that probably didn't help. I was disappointed with that because I thought that I was fit enough to run a decent time, especially as I had come fifth in the National 10 Miles Championships. After that point, I didn't do another marathon for two years and went back to run on the track. I got down to 4.27 for 1500m, 9.27 for 3000m, 2.11 for 800m, and I did 9.20 in the Gaymers' Races, so I sort of got my track speed back. I also came sixth in the Inter-Counties. I then decided to do another marathon in 1985. I got my half-marathon time down to 77-something and opted for the Dublin Marathon. I put my mileage up again, but I only did 80 miles a week. I ran 2.41 completely on my own, as it was a women's only race. If I'd actually had people around me, I think I was worth a sub 2.40. I also took some sugar on board, which I found to be OK. Just as I was recovering from

Dublin, I was asked to run for England three weeks later in Tokyo, but I said I couldn't cope with that. Instead, I decided to try to make the Commonwealth Games because I had London and then six months to train for it. So I tried to put my mileage up to 100 miles a week. I did 100 miles a week for about six weeks and just knackered myself in the process. I kept getting illness after illness. I could cope with 80 but not 100. In the 12 weeks leading up to London, I averaged 69 miles a week, and I did my 2.36 off of that. I was also lighter at eight stone nine. It felt easy although I had sustained a back injury before it. I was doing 20 x 400m with 30 seconds rest on the track, and I felt it go. Mind you, I never bothered with much stretching in those days. Anyway, I felt it go at 23 miles in the race, and then I could see how people didn't finish marathons. However, I did finish, and I got selected for the Commonwealth Games. Leading up to London, I ran PBs of 15.51 for 5000m, 26.22 for 5 miles, 33-and-a-half for 10km, 55.08 for 10 miles and 72.48 for a half-marathon. I was kind of disappointed that I didn't run 2.32 as I had wanted, but Brian Smith said I'd done very well to run a PB that day because everyone else had run slower due to a headwind. So I started building up for the Commonwealth Games, but it was such a stress because for the next three months I was virtually limping on one leg while training. Then, even though I was in pain and limping, for some silly reason I put my mileage up to 90 a week. Despite the injury, I was getting really fit, and I went on this thing to Europe where I did some fantastic running. But I got more and more stressed, as I was by then virtually pulling my leg behind me. Just before the Commonwealth Games, I really wrenched it during a race, and so inevitably I dropped out of the marathon itself at 20 miles. I shouldn't have run. Nigel and his brother were there, and Nigel told me to stop running. So I came back from that, sorted my back out with some treatment and yoga, and in 1987 I ran 2.41 in New York. All was fine, and then I got a virus, which went all the way through until 1988. I was ill for 18 months or so, and I couldn't really do very much. I then carefully pieced myself back together and managed to run 2.41 again in 1992. I was very careful; I had to learn to train within my body.

How long before marathons did you decide to do them? Did you have a meticulous plan?

Well, I always had a plan, but I didn't make half the ones I planned. I had a five-year gap between marathons from 1987 to 1992 when I was planning to run one but kept getting ill or injured. I had that weird leg problem and then a virus, followed by the leg again. I kept thinking I was going to be doing a marathon and then not doing one. However, I very much decided on them and planned for them. I would decide in

December to run London in order to have a five-month build-up.

Can you outline a typical week of training in your marathon build-up?

I ran 70 miles a week for 12 weeks and tried to do three sessions a week although I could never really manage three. One session I really liked and would always do, as it suited me, was 10 x 300m. I would do them in 56 off of 45 seconds. I really liked that session. I also used to do a fast five-mile run on a Monday night in around 30 minutes. However, that would often go if I didn't feel very good or if I had raced. In fact, if I had raced, I wouldn't do a session until the following Saturday. Another session I used to do on Saturdays was 6 x 1 mile on a cycle track. Actually, I don't know exactly how far they were, but I'd do them in 5.45 or something. They weren't very fast, and I'd have two minutes recovery. Sometimes I was just too tired to even do two sessions, and so I'd only do one. I had a lot of problems with tiredness. I kept trying to do three but failing. I remember being able to do it once for three weeks. I can recall doing the fast five-mile run, the 300m session, and something like 6 x 1 mile or 6 x 800m, or I went to the track and did 20 x 400m between 75 and 78 seconds with half a minute rest. I couldn't do that now. Essentially, I remember doing what I could and often having to miss sessions, so it probably averaged out to two a week. My steady running was very slow; it was eight-minute miling. I did a 20 to 22 every Sunday, which Nigel did with me, and it was also at eight-minute miling. We used to be out for three-and-a-half hours; it was just jogging really. Before the Dublin Marathon, I did a similar build-up, but I just did things like 8 x 400m with two minutes rest. I would do them in 67 to 70 seconds and that would be my only session of the week. However, I also did things like 10 x 3 minutes with a two-minute jog or 20 x 2 minutes with a one-minute jog within a 10-mile run. Those worked and suited my mentality at the time. I would try to do two or three of those a week, and before I did my 2.41 I did a lot of those sessions. I also did a few tempo runs based on a heart rate of 160bpm, which came out at 6.30-miling or something like that.

Did you get to a track much at this stage?

When we were in Bristol and Bath, I would go to the track and do things like 8 x 400m. I have always mucked about with my training really. I've done sessions of 5 x 1000m but that never really worked for me. I'd do them in 3.06 to 3.08, but they never made me a good runner. They just made me think I had run a good session. In fact, I found that I was much better doing 3 x 1000m or even 2 x 1000m quick because drawn-out training doesn't really work for me. It is very odd, as I am a marathon runner, but I need to train like a 5000m

151

runner. I think I am better off doing 1500m and 3000m type sessions. I thrive on things like 6 x 300m or 8 x 200m, as well as 2 to 3 x 1000m and tempo runs. I didn't get so many injuries then. I think my injuries came through doing too much mileage. I tend to find I am better doing one long run like a 20 or 16 miler. Before the 1992 marathon, I didn't even go further than 16 miles, or maybe I did one 22 very slowly. I think I am a marathon runner, so I can just run them. I don't really need to do all those long runs. I am an endurance runner in my build. Marathons don't actually damage me; it's the training that damages me.

So, to sum up your training week...

Sunday was a long run. Monday, if I hadn't raced and wasn't too tired, was a five-mile tempo run and Wednesday was my 300m or 800m session. I messed around with it, but it was my short reps. Tuesday and Thursday would be a couple of easy five milers or ten miles and a five to seven miles. There might even be a rest day/half day in there. On Friday, I'd run five miles and on Saturday I'd do the mile reps or whatever. If I were racing at the weekend, I'd do something on the Wednesday like the 300m reps and then nothing until the Saturday after. I was slimming all the time and so that also controlled my training. I liked to be eight stone three then. Being light seemed to make my training light somehow. I used to feel different, and I didn't want to keep pounding away. I can't explain it, but I just felt that I needed to do more quality sessions and be more "race horsey." When I was light, it made me be more pure in my training. When I did the mileage, I ate more. It has been hard for me to separate the food away from the running. Although my eating disorders weren't drastic, I was very over disciplined.

Were you a top 10km runner at this time?

Yes, I was. I was ranked in the top 10 in the country. I did 33-and-a-half, and I was regularly running 34 to 34-and-a-half minutes. I could also run 15.51 for 5000m.

How did you taper for a marathon?

I seem to remember doing my last long run, which would be a 20 miler, three weeks before, and I'd go something like 60, 50, 40, 30 miles per week. I could never be bothered to train in the week of the marathon really. Two weeks before, I probably did a 16-mile run. Once, I remember going on the track the week before on the Saturday to do some 300m reps, and I couldn't run. I did one in 60 seconds and thought it was crap. So I threw away my watch and just plodded through the rest of the session. I had just lost it, and I jogged the rest of the week. I felt terrible; I always felt dreadful. Marathon running is a really weird thing. I'd often feel terrible for the first three miles of the race as well because I'd feel heavy and fat with all the water on board. It is a horrible feeling; it is a funny event.

What races did you generally do in a build-up to a marathon?

I would plan the races that I was going to do, but because I was so good, the races took so much out of me. The faster and fitter I was, the more I damaged myself. I ran my 72.48 before London, but I was completely ruined. I also ran the Rome Half-Marathon one year and came second. I ran 74 minutes or something like that, and then I was invited to run the Rome Marathon a few weeks later, but I was just too knackered. I was probably only running 50 miles a week then, and I ran the half-marathon off of that. So, as races took so much out of me, I would race less frequently. Before Dublin, I decided not to run a half-marathon at all. However, I did do the Marlborough 10km the week before in 34.04.

Did you use any form of mental techniques before and during a marathon?

I am interested in the power of the mind. Running a marathon is an emotional thing, as well as a mental thing, and I think it is fundamental. While I think visualisation is useful, it isn't useful if you don't really believe in it. Ultimately, affirmations and visualisation work when I believe in them, but they don't work otherwise. For me, my running is an expression of me being healthy. When I am really healthy, I run reasonably well. In 1992, I lay in bed every night visualising coming over the bridge, and it worked for me. I have been a searcher all my life, and running has been the medium through which I have searched. I think my intensity and awareness on one level are ultimately going to make me live a healthier and happier life, but it also means that I am too aware and too sensitive, and things hurt me too much. I am too much of a little flower. Despite my outer impressions of being jokey, quite relaxed and quite chaotic, I am incredibly in control and organised. Mental preparation is something I have been aware of, but I don't believe in strategies as such. I do breathing exercises and yoga breathing; I do this thing where I breathe in and breathe out and then say, "What the fuck!"

What about during the marathon?

I go mile by mile. It is like life in a way as you go through many emotions, and if you acted on most of them, you wouldn't get there. You might get too elated and go too fast as you are running over Tower Bridge with lots of people cheering you on, and then you might slow up when alone around the Docklands where you can get bored and miserable. You can get frightened if something begins to hurt; you can start panicking that you haven't done enough long runs. You just need to learn to relax while you are running and not think that you might have to stop. You go up; you go down. You love the crowd; you hate the crowd. You think it is going well; you think it is not going well. You can get emotional too. When I went by my sister, I felt tears. It is a very emotional event and, of course, your blood sugar is going up and down. I think you just have to have a natural endurance runner's mind, and I think I have got the mind for it. I can concentrate very well. It all goes in a flash; it goes very quickly really.

Did you do any other forms of training like weights?

I did weight training. I always weight train once or twice a week. My strength is my strength. I've got these muscles [pointing to her thighs], and they are not going to get any smaller, so I might as well have them strong. I used to do light weights and nothing too dramatic. When I was younger, I did heavy weights because my coach was keen on them. I'd do 20 reps and sometimes go round twice. I did free weights like cleans and bench press, as well as lat pull downs, sit-ups, press-ups and jump stuff with dumbbells. Since 1986 and my back problems, I have also done yoga, and I go on the exercise bike when I am injured. I don't really like it, but it's OK when I am injured.

Were you coached throughout your career?

Apparently, I am un-coachable. I had Tim and then Nigel, and that has been it. I think I ran well with Tim despite his coaching. Nigel just got to know my body really well and how I worked. Actually, it was difficult for him to coach me because I always wanted to do more, and I also had a lot of health problems. When we split up, it was frustrating because I was starting to run really well, but it was not appropriate for him to carry on coaching me. He found that I could cope with a lot of anaerobic work and that I thrived on getting fast, and as I mentioned earlier, that I have to do it in 1500m type sessions rather than drawn-out 5000m type ones. We also found that it was perfectly fine for me to run at eight minutes a mile on steady and long runs and that if I tried to go any faster, I just got tired. I jog, and it works for me; I just go running.

Did you mostly train on your own or with a group?

I trained on my own or with Nigel. Occasionally, I trained with a group, but essentially it was on my own except when I was younger and with Haslemere Border. I would be too embarrassed to run with anyone else; anyone my level would run much faster than me. For instance, when I came to this area, I couldn't train with Margaret Lockley. I was a far better runner than her at the time, but I couldn't do any running with her. It was

157

horrible. I hated it. And she couldn't do any rep training with me because I'd be at the end before she'd begun. In the end, we agreed just to go for lunch. I hated training with her; I hated running at six-and-a-half-minute-mile pace. It felt horrible. Conversely, I felt uncomfortable going miles ahead on rep sessions.

Did you ever use altitude or warm-weather training?

Not really. I would have liked to.

Did you work throughout your running career?

Yes, I have always worked. I seem to remember doing fewer hours at one stage but not in 1986. When Rachel was with us for about 18 months, I didn't do so many hours then, but I don't think it necessarily helped my running, and it was still shift work in my own gym. We opened the gym from 10 A.M. to 2 P.M. and from 5 P.M. to 9.30 P.M. We didn't run in the afternoons, as we tended to shop or watch television, but we'd take it in turns to run in the evening. So, I was working a full eight-hour day. Even when Rachel was there, and I was working fewer hours, I still had full responsibility for the gym. Essentially, I have always worked, and sometimes I have done mad levels of work.

Did you have any forms of financial assistance or sponsorship?

Not really. I made some prize money, and I had kit sponsors like Etonic and Reebok, as well as Nike briefly. However, the Nike and Reebok shoes didn't suit me that well. There was no contract money. I got reasonable amounts of prize money at that level, and I won a car in the Dublin Marathon.

So, it wasn't enough to live on?

No, it just supplemented my salary.

Did you have a special diet or take any supplements?

I've always used supplements; I am a complete crank. I take them because I have a weak system. My coach in my younger days was also very keen on supplements and so that is when I first knew about them. Later, when I was 23 or 24 and suffering with all my eating disorders, I went to a herbalist, and he said my adrenal system was low and that I had candida. So, I started taking various things. Because I was always overdoing the undereating, I'd go on a lot of carbohydrate binges. I was always up and down. It took me a long time to discover that it wasn't actually the carbohydrate I was craving but the fat, as when I went on a binge I would have the top of the milk and biscuits, and butter, cheese and peanut butter. I used the Cambridge Diet as a supplement because it was a high protein meal replacement. I found that helped me not to binge. It seemed to me that if I ate enough protein and fat, then I didn't crave the carbohydrate as much, and I felt well and could maintain a stable weight. Big blocks of carbohydrate also gave me an upset stomach, especially too much bread.

So, did you bother with the carbohydrate depletion/loading diet?

Yes. I used it before my 2.36, and I almost didn't run. I had the most awful diarrhoea. I went to the toilet about nine times the day before. I felt fine on the depletion phase though because it was high protein. However, at this stage, it just hadn't clicked that I could keep my weight stable and that I felt OK on a high protein diet. I thought it was the nutrients that were making the difference. It also became obvious that I needed the fat. My best pre-race meal was actually a burger and chips, not pasta. A cheeseburger or a bacon and cheeseburger with lots of mayonnaise on my salads worked well for me. I ran my 55.10 for 10 miles off of that meal. A high carbohydrate diet doesn't suit me; it doesn't suit my mind as I get depressed and unbalanced.

So, what supplements were you taking?

I generally always take adrenal support ones because, according to my kineologist, my adrenal system is never up to scratch. So, I take those and a liquid multi-vitamin thing, which is supposed to be absorbed better by the cells. I also take vitamin C when I think about it although it does tend to upset my stomach.

Did you ever get anaemic?

Yes, I used to years ago. I used to take Ferograd C a lot, but now I don't seem to need it. I don't get anaemia any more. So I have been a complete junkie, but I think I've needed to be. My eating disorders have steadied out, as even up to two years ago I was still binge eating and starving, and I was still taking laxatives.

Did you generally drink a lot? What did you drink during marathons?

I never drank in my early marathons, although I did in my best one when I drank Excel or something every three miles. I didn't drink a lot during training because I was weighing myself the whole time. I only started drinking a lot more water when we came here 10 years ago, but I still didn't really want to start drinking until I had weighed myself. I was dehydrating myself whereas now I drink about 8 to 10 pints of water every day. I drink loads. Back then, I would only drink coffee a couple of times a day; I don't remember drinking water at all. I started drinking water in marathons in Dublin when I ran 2.41. I was leading the race and had the radio cars and everything all around me. I was fading a

161

bit at 16 miles, and a guy on one of the cars asked if I was OK. I asked for some sugar and water. I drank it, and it worked really well, so I drank from then on.

What is your height, and what was your racing weight?

I am 1.71 m or five-foot seven, and I liked to weigh eight stone seven to eight stone nine. I think that is what my body likes; it likes a fat percentage that is just that bit healthier.

What factors do you think made you and the others in the 1980s so good?

I think it was just the standard. In order to be good back then, you had to break 2.40 for the marathon. A time like 2.36 was considered good, and so I did that. I didn't rate anything slower. There are also no young runners now. Apart from Paula Radcliffe, where are they? There are fewer runners, and there isn't much encouragement for sport these days. When I was at school, we had P.E. every day and double games on a Friday, but now children have half an hour a week or something. We had encouragement to do sport and to join clubs. I also think my generation's parents weren't so child-centered; they were more themselves-centered. Children were largely seen and not heard and given a huge amount of discipline. In addition, we had values of self-discipline and striving. I used to walk my dog eight miles when I was eight. I would take it out on my own across the common to the local village, buy some chocolate and Lucozade, and walk back. I always did that. Television was rationed, and there wasn't daytime TV. There was "Watch With Mother" and the test card, and it was black and white anyway. Plus, there was always homework to do. As well as this, everything was more outdoors. I had a big garden, so I was lucky on that score, but we also had some fields nearby, and I used to climb trees, run and cycle. I would run around the village at night when I was 15 because I wanted to go running so much. It was pitch black with not a street light in sight, but I would run round and round because I just had to run. My dad was also very much a believer in personal discipline and in not giving us too much. We had duties at home, and I was brought up on the idea of having to earn things. I had to earn my riding lessons, so I did the garden for three hours every weekend. I have a huge amount of personal discipline. It was instilled in me. I had to go to church every Sunday, and I belonged to a church group, which I loved actually. I even went to a school where they said, "If you got an Ordinary Level, you got an ordinary brain." You were expected to get nine of them and do A-levels. However, there is a negative side to this. It can make you overdriven and lead to illness, as in my case.

John Graham

PB: 2.09.28 – Rotterdam 1981

Highest World Ranking in the 1980s: 4th

Marathon Achievements:

3rd - New York Marathon 1980

Winner - Rotterdam Marathon 1981

4th - Brisbane Commonwealth Games 1982

2nd - Rotterdam Marathon 1985

4th - Edinburgh Commonwealth Games 1986

How did you become involved in athletics?

Like all boys in the West of Scotland, I wanted to play football for Glasgow Rangers or Glasgow Celtic, so I had a footballing background. My father was also involved in football, and therefore I was always fit. I then participated in the Boy's Brigade and the school cross-country teams. My father thought it would be quite good to strengthen my legs for football, and it was ideal training in the winter. I joined Motherwell YMCA's running club – the harriers club – and they met on a Thursday night. I ran on the Saturday using someone's number, and I actually won the Scottish Championships. However, I promptly got it taken off me for running under someone else's name. I realised then that I had a natural ability to run, and it just went from there. I was also very fortunate because one of the guys in the club, Bert Mackay, helped me with my career. He was instrumental in my sort of philosophy of running from when I was 14-and-a-half/15 right the way through until I left Motherwell to go to America when I was 21. So for the first five or six years, we all grew up together at the YMCA. Bert coached five internationals, and we had a twelve-man squad. Allister Hutton was a main rival for me, and he beat me in the Scottish Championships by five seconds, but he was a little older than me – about 18 months – so he was in the last year of the age group, and I was in the first. Our paths crossed many times, and he eventually took my Scottish marathon record off me at the Commonwealth Games.

So, cross-country was the first thing you became involved in?

Yes. In those days there weren't very many tracks around and not many facilities. I think that is a problem nowadays, as there is too much pressure on kids because the season just runs and runs. We had cross-country in the winter, road relays in March/April time and track from May to August. You then went back to the cross-country and road again. We had different types of running, and your training was geared to that. Basically, if you got a good winter under your belt, then you always ran quite well on the track and that was installed in you from an early age. It was very important that you had a good October through to February when you did all the slog and hard work, and put the miles in. You then sharpened up, starting in March and going through to May. We did a lot of grass work, golf course work, hills and stuff like that, which kids don't seem to do nowadays. Hill work was very instrumental in my training. I did a lot of hills at one point. We then started going to the track, but we only went there once every 10 days or something like that just to sharpen up and do really fast sessions. Most of the work done at that age was on the grass, road and cross-country.

Did you race on the track?

Yes, I was successful from a very early age. My Scottish youth's record still stands, and I hate to think that no one has beaten it. No one is getting anywhere near it now. The guy that won it this year did 9 minutes 10 seconds. My record is 8 minutes 27 for a 16 year old and that was set on a cold morning at 10 A.M. at Grangemouth with the wind howling. I think the track was very important to me, and I really got into it. I met guys like Nat Muir, Allister Hutton, Frank Clement and Laurie Spence - all the good Scottish runners of that era. I was very aware at that time that you needed international competition; that you needed other competition to what you were getting domestically. I managed to get down to run in England - in Carlisle - which doesn't sound very exotic but at the time that was international competition. So I mixed in with other guys, and I also met a lot of friends through Birmingham University like Kevin Steer and Barry Moss, who had world bests at 3000m. It gave you a wider horizon rather than just being the top guy in Scotland. When you get out into the big pond, there are a lot more fish, and the competition is good. I enjoyed it and wanted more, which is what my coach's psychology was. I would come back and train just that little bit harder each time.

Were you training hard even at that age?

Yes. Well, I have always trained hard. All I did when I was young was eat, sleep and run; that was it. I was very fortunate in those days, as like a lot of other guys, I could run to work and run home. I could do most of my mileage in the wintertime. I was doing 70 to 75 miles a week, and Bert introduced me to twice a day on some of the days. I was 16 and very young, but I wanted it; I really wanted to do it. I was also very aware that Bert was putting a lot of time into me. He would pick me up every day from work at five o'clock at the corner of the road, and we'd then go to his house. He was like a father figure to me in many ways. I just got on with him, and we'd go training every night. He was 35/36 when I was 16, and so he was just going over that hill. I was at

167

his heels all the time. Within one season, I improved so much that I was just way ahead, and then he started coaching me more rather than running with me. I was running very hard. The main thing was that I would always run for an hour-and-a-half on a Sunday, and it was reasonably quick. In fact, I did more than that sometimes. I remember when I was 15, I won the Midland Senior Boys on the Saturday, and then they took me out for a two-and-a-half-hour run on the Sunday. That was part and parcel of it. There was nothing scientific about it. All the guys did that on a Sunday.

How did you progress from there to doing marathons?

Money! I just remember getting pissed off at some stage when some guys I thought I should've beaten beat me. I was doing the steeplechase at the time in the UK Closed. It happens to most runners; to get beaten by people you think you shouldn't. I did the steeplechase for about two seasons. The first priority was to try to get into the Commonwealth Games team in 1978, which I managed to do. I wasn't fast enough over 5000m, and I wasn't yet strong enough over 10,000m, so I went for the steeplechase. Within three of four races, I managed to run 8.39, which in those days was quite good. So I was fortunate, and it gave me another string to my bow. I then just decided to train really hard and that was when I started training full-time. I was doing something

168

like 10 miles and 5 miles on a Monday; 10 miles, 5 miles and 10 miles on a Tuesday; 15 miles on a Wednesday; 10 miles, 5 miles and 10 miles again on a Thursday; 10 miles on a Friday; fartlek on a Saturday and a long run on a Sunday. I was doing about 125 miles a week. In fact, I even did 140 miles for about four or five weeks. However, in general, it was just over 100 miles a week. I did the Stafford 20, and the Nuneton 10 where I ran 47.52. It was the first time anyone had broken 48 minutes on the course. People like Ian Stewart, Dave Black, Ian Thompson - people of that ilk - and Steve Kenyon, Andy Holden, Alan Rushmere – all local guys – had run it and never got anywhere near it, and I suddenly run under 48 minutes on it. So, everybody started telling me to go for the longer stuff. I knew I wasn't going to make it as a 10,000m runner because I was never going to be able to run 25 laps of the track, and I wasn't fast enough. Also, at that time, I was starting to run with Dave Moorcroft. I knew the sort of training Dave was doing, and I couldn't get anywhere near him. There were lots of good guys around then like Dave Black and Bernie Ford. Ian Stewart was also still hanging about running 27 minutes, and there were others, such as Steve Kenyon, Charlie Spedding, Hugh Jones, and Mike Gratton – a lot of tiers of guys. You'd just have to have an off day, and they'd have you. It was very competitive at that time. I mean, 50 minutes was

169

nothing; it was just a benchmark. Most of the 10 milers were won in 46 or 47 minutes. So, I eventually did the Stafford 20 and ran 1 hour 39 minutes there, which at that time was the fastest in Britain. The British Board must have seen some potential in me after that race because they gave me a trip to do the Olympic trial for the Spanish and Italians in Laredo in Northern Spain. It was my first marathon, and I won it in 2.13.21. After that, I went to Milton Keynes in 1980 for the Olympic trial. I decided to follow Ian Thompson because I thought that he must know what he was doing. He'd been a marathon runner for a long time and had a point to prove, as he'd missed out on the previous Olympics. I thought he was the guy to watch. In fact, he did go on to win it. Unfortunately, I had overtrained and had come down with flu the week before. I was stupid. It was just one of those things you regret. I felt obliged to run as there was a lot of pressure involved, and I didn't want to let anyone down. Maurice used to stand outside in shitty conditions with a whistle and time me, and there was the club as well. However, at the end of the day, the wisest thing would have been for me not to run.

How old were you then?

I was 24. I was one of the first guys to take the marathon as a sport almost in its own right at that age. I felt the most important thing was to have a change of pace. A lot of marathon runners are carthorses, and no disrespect, but they don't have a change of gear. The really great runners, who I have had the privilege to run with, had a change of pace. That is the difference between the good ones and the really great ones - the guys that win the Olympics. When I went to Spain, they couldn't understand why I wasn't going to the Olympics. Looking back, it was probably my best chance of going because one of my friends, the big Dutch guy, actually got the bronze there, and I know if I'd been running with him, we would have had a good tussle. But that's in hindsight. I enjoyed it; I loved every minute of it. So I ran in Laredo, and I won. I could have run under 2.13, but I think I had my arms up for the last mile! I just wanted to win the race.

How many did you run before you did your PB?

It was my fourth. After the Laredo Marathon, I phoned Nike, who I was trying to organise a contract with at the time, and tried to get some money out of them. I ended up going over with them to do a marathon in Eugene, Oregon. It was in August/September time, so I didn't have much time between them. I came eighth in 2.15.04. I did a stupid thing though. It was the first time they'd had a pace maker in the race, and nobody had told me. They had just brought me over to make up the field really and, of course, being young and inexperienced I went out with the guy thinking it was a race. Basically, I blew up. Dick Quax of New Zealand won it in 2.11-

something, which was the ninth fastest time in the world at that point. I came back feeling a bit bruised by the experience and thought - right, I am going to train harder. I just ticked over for New York in October though, and I suppose that was my big breakthrough on a world scale really. I came third in 2.11.46. So in June, August and October of 1980, I ran three good marathons in 2.13, 2.15 and 2.11. They were all quite close together. After that, in 1981, I went down to New Zealand and had a problem with my Achilles – a bursa. It swelled up, and I had to drop out of the race. However, I came back from there in the January and then ran Rotterdam in the May where I did my PB of 2.09.28.

Did you meticulously plan for your marathons or just do them as they came along then?

Everything was planned, in the sense that I would know what I was doing. Generally speaking, I put myself down for two marathons a year, which looking back was maybe a mistake. I could have done more, but I wanted to do the big ones. I only did the big ones because I couldn't get excited about the other ones. They were also the two major points of the year for me because I was a full-time athlete at the time, and I had to make money. I had a mortgage, and so I had to make that decision very early on. They sent me over to run the Cascade Run in Portland, Oregon and that was the first professional race. The British Board sent me a fax saying that if I ran, I'd lose my amateur status, so I couldn't run it. It was something like $15,000 for first prize. However, it sort of opened it up to me. I realised how much money the guys in the USA were making. I went to stay with Alberto Salazar a few times and was lucky enough to train with him. I knew what sort of cash he was getting, and I thought I'd like to get as much as that. There was a big differential between what a marathon runner and a track runner could get. However, I suppose at the end of the day, if you counted the whole season as a track runner, they probably got exactly the same or maybe even more than us. We were on good salaries though at the time; it was a good living, but I think it all changed.

Who were you running for by this time?

I'd moved to Birmingham in 1979 and was running for Birchfield Harriers. If I may diversify a bit – I think one of the main problems now is that big clubs like Birchfield have lost their club runner base since the jogging boom in the early '80s. I always had guys to train with down there. If I went down there on a Tuesday or Thursday night at six thirty, there were always four of five guys to run 10 miles with at a good pace, but they don't have that nowadays. They all have their individual training, which amazes me. I think that is one of the problems, and I think it has fragmented the club system. I think the clubs are fun clubs now. The standards are so low, and anyone who comes through thinks they are really good and that they don't have to try any harder. Why should they? I suppose. The professional runners around now have also got too much on. There is too much pressure on them and too many races, championships and everything else. I used to run a half-marathon, a 10 miler and a 10km. That is how I planned it in a build-up to a marathon. I would pick a half-marathon, and I would know that if I could run 64/64-and-a-half minutes, I was near enough ready to run close to 2.09/2.10. I packed in running when I was running 2.12 because I thought it was ridiculously slow!

Were you always a full-time athlete when you were running well?

Yes, I was full-time. I think having a part-time job is good as well, say maybe 20 hours a week or something just to keep your mind off of it and to stop you getting obsessed. I was never obsessive. I enjoyed life, and I think the people that are really obsessive are crap anyway. Some people say they are going to do this, and they are going to do that, but they never do. I think there is a lot of that about nowadays. We all got on really well in our era, and without blowing our own trumpets, we were all really good blokes. We all ran hard, but we also got pissed and had a good time as well and that was the way it was. It is sad to see that

that doesn't happen so much now. We would talk to other people about our training and enjoy ourselves.

What was your typical training in a build-up to a marathon?

I kept it simple. Bill Adcocks told me that when he was fit, he did more 10 milers. I certainly incorporated that into my training. I did a 10-mile and a five-mile run and incorporated pace. My ex-father-in-law, who had never done any sport in his life, said that surely the simplest thing is to run all your training at five-minute miling, and if you think about it, he is probably quite right. So I actually tried to run at my optimum near enough most of the time. I could do distance and speedwork at the same time with no ill effects. I did get flu and viruses a bit, but I never had any problems with my legs. On Monday, I would do 10 miles and 5 miles and then on a Tuesday, which was one of my big days, I'd do 10 miles, 5 miles and 10 miles. The 10 miler at night would be at the club, and it was fast, as I was running with people like Richard Partridge and other good quality guys. On Wednesday, I would run one-and-a-half to two hours and then rest, and on Thursday it would be back to doing 10 miles, 5 miles and 10 miles. On Friday, there would be another 10 miles and then nothing until Saturday morning, so I was having 24 hours recovery. I did a big block of work Monday to Friday – 100 miles - and then it was up to me what I did on Saturday and

Sunday. Saturday was normally a race day or I did fartlek in Sutton Park and along the canals. The canals in Birmingham are brilliant. I don't know why anyone would want to go warm-weather training. The best place is where your routine is. A runner needs routine and consistency. It is boring, but you will find that most runners run the same trails all the bloody time. You just get on with it. You don't even look at your watch because you know you are doing certain times, and I didn't even count the miles that much. It was as much time on my feet. When I was living in Four Oaks, I had a lap around Sutton Park from the house, and if I got to Streetly Gate in 60 minutes, I knew I was going well. Eventually, I got to Streetly Gate in 58 minutes, then 57 and then 56. At that point, I extended it back up to the hour, so that it was time on my feet. Therefore, I was actually doing more miles for the time I was out. I didn't realise it at the time, but I was extending my training, and my threshold was going up all the time.

Did you do any sessions on the track?

Well, I met John Anderson. I believe in John, and he is a great person, and I very much wanted to work with him. However, I am not sure it was the right thing for me. When I ran 2.09.28, I went away for 10 weeks and did my own training, and then he sharpened me up. I wanted to believe what he said about speed and pace being very important, but the unfortunate thing about marathon running is that it is completely different from any other event. I think people can be born marathon runners. It has been proven in the past that people can have crap times over 10,000m, 5000m and even 10 miles but still be great marathon runners. As an example, Ian Stewart could run round the 12-Stage Road Relay in 24.50 odd. I could never run as fast as that, but what I could do is run 26 minutes back to back, and he couldn't do that. It is also like Jim Brown up in Scotland. He must have run god knows how many sub 47 minute 10 milers, but ask him to do 48 or 49 minutes going through in a marathon, and he couldn't do it. He couldn't do 50-minute ones. People talk about their legs getting heavy at 15 or 18 miles and things like that. I think people are either naturally a marathon runner, or they are not. However, I think there are a lot of 5000m and 10,000m runners who don't realise that they are marathon runners. I think that is what has happened now. Ian Stewart used to say to me that if you really want it, you will do it, and I think that is true. I still think that today there is scope for people if they really want it. Looking at standards now, there is no comparison. I just don't think they train hard enough. I have beaten most of the Kenyans of my time and people like Shakanga. We were never frightened of them, and when I got on the start line, I felt I could beat anybody. Some lads I see coached now seem to fall between two stools. They do the sort of sessions I used to do, but they don't do them as fast, and they get a longer recovery. They are not actually doing quality work with short recovery, and neither are they doing longer units with longer recovery, so they are not getting pure quality or pure strength work. It is in between, and I think that is what is going on with a lot of running now.

How far was your long run?

The longest run would be about four weeks before the marathon, and it would be two hours fifteen/two hours eighteen minutes. I didn't really do that many long runs. I tended to run for more like an hour-and-a-half fast, and then maybe I would go out again at night and do another five miles. I preferred to do that; I preferred a sandwich effect. I was never frightened of the distance; I was never frightened of finishing it. I always thought that on Tuesday and Thursday with my 10, 5, 10 miles I was covering 25 miles anyway, and between that I had a good hour-and-a-half to two hours on the Wednesday where I worked really hard.

How did you taper for a marathon?

Just how I felt really. I used to get in and out of the hotels quickly with no hanging around. That was the best scenario or you are just panicking.

Did you do the carbohydrate depletion/loading diet?

Oh no! Basically, I just thought that was a lot of crap. I don't believe in it at all. I sort of semi tried it once, and I couldn't hack it. Before Rotterdam, I had bacon, eggs and sausage, and I used to love flat coke. I think you just need to be sensible and eat well, and you have to look after yourself and taper a bit. All I would do is cut back on some quality sessions and instead of the 10 and 5 miles, I would do two 5-mile runs and then a 10 and 5 miler would replace the 10, 5, 10 miles. So I used to cut back a bit. The week of a marathon, I would have done 100 miles, including the marathon. Some people believe in only doing 50 or 30 miles, and some don't do anything the last few days, but I didn't believe in that.

Did you do any other forms of training like weights?

Loads of pints of beer and some stretching! I have dabbled with a lot of different things over the years, but I never really did anything else. I did a little bit of stretching. I did steeplechase, so I had to be a bit flexible. I think stretching is good for you, but a lot of people overstretch, which can cause some problems, such as muscle tears. My philosophy was that if you are going to be running fast in training then you are going to be stretching your legs naturally anyway. John Anderson believed in that a lot. If you are running fast, then you are OK because you are doing exactly what

179

your legs are supposed to do. You don't want to be doing any jerky exercises or those where you put your leg on a barrier and things like that. The faster you run, the better you get because you are stretching yourself more. Every other day, I was doing a fast session, so I was doing it the natural way if you like. I don't know of many marathon runners that did a lot of stretching, or if they did, I never saw them.

Did you do most of your training alone or with others?

I was very lucky. I always had a lot of young guys to train with, and young guys are often more enthusiastic. I also had older guys for doing a good, steady long run with on a Sunday – the club runs. I had training partners the whole time. I had Richard Partridge, who I trained with for about two years, and a guy called Pat Morrison. There was also Shane Wagstaff at the club. I had several guys to train with - all heroes basically and all talented, although some of them never did it in the races. I remember running with Shane a week before the New York Marathon, and he took me apart on a 10-mile run. I was about three minutes behind him, and I was trying really hard to catch him. However, a week later I ran 2.10.46 for 5th place. I thought I was going to run crap, but it just goes to show that when it comes to it, and you have that singlet with your number on, you are a different animal. I was very competitive. I wouldn't let anyone in the club beat me.

Did you use any form of mental techniques before or during a marathon?

It was just basically shitting yourself that you are going to be the next one off the back of the group. I don't know; I can't remember much about it. I just remember enjoying myself. The closer it got to the start line, the more I enthused about it. I enjoyed the battle to see who was going to come out first. It didn't matter who it was, which was perhaps occasionally a problem. For example, in 1986 at the Commonwealth Games, I should have paced it, and I could have won the silver medal, but I wanted to win; I wanted the gold medal. I knew Rob de Castella was ready to get beat, and I was proven right a couple of months later in New York. I knew he wasn't infallible, and I knew someone could beat him one day. Unfortunately, it wasn't me. At the end of the day, you just go and run, and you do your best. I've always had that philosophy generally in life. There's no point getting depressed. I've been in a situation where Grete Waitz has passed me in the marathon, and you'd be a bit down. You'd lie in the bath and think that you'd ran shit that day, but after you'd had a few beers and a talk with the guys, you'd forget it. You'd then look forward to the next race and put that one behind you because there is no point dwelling on it. You can't change anything. I never had any motivational tapes. I didn't need anything like that. I occasionally used to sing to myself. I'd get a famous tune in my head and sing it because it stirs you on. Generally speaking, it was just concentration, and you don't remember much, especially in the good ones. When I dropped out of New York one year at the 14-mile mark, I didn't have a clue where I was, and yet I had done the race four times before! I had run up that street four times but because I had been totally focused and running well, I'd never noticed where I was. I also never thought about the money until I had finished although that was nice as well.

You said that you were a full-time athlete. Did you have a contract and bonuses with Nike?

Yes, I had a four-year contract with Nike and bonuses. I had bonuses for a Scottish record, a British record, a world record and everything else. It was performance related as well, so if I was in the top 10 in the world, which I mostly was, I got a bonus. I also got a bonus for being in the top 15/20. I was never outside of that for quite a few years, or maybe just in 1984 when I ran 2.15, but the rest of the time I would have been.

Did you win a lot of prize money and receive appearance money?

Yes. I didn't go anywhere unless it was for cash. In fact, I was the first pacemaker in the marathon. In 1983, I paced Rotterdam, as Jos Hermans asked me to come over. They wanted me to run the actual marathon, but I couldn't because I had already planned to run Stockholm, as I was getting a good deal there. So I said I could go over and run to halfway. They offered me money to go and do it. I think it was $5000, so that wasn't bad.

So, you were comfortably off?

Yes, fortunately. My wife had a good job as well. Looking back, I suppose I could have saved all that and got a part-time job, but my philosophy was that I was good at something, and so why not get paid for it? No one really did that at the time though.

I believe there wasn't much money in the UK at this time. Is that why you went to the USA?

Yes. They opened up a track in Scotland, and they brought up Ray Smedley to do the mile with Rod Dixon. They offered £50. I couldn't believe it - £50! In New York, nine or ten months later, I was third and got $18,000, which was worth about £12,000. So there you go, £50 to $18,000 – a hell of a difference! I thought they'd made a mistake and meant $180. I had to go right back to the hospitality tent and have a few pints of Guinness! I managed to buy my terraced house outright. However, there are times when you don't run well and don't get paid, but that's sport in general. I certainly never had the big deals that Steve Jones or

Charlie Spedding got. I never had the big wins like London, but I did OK. It is the last thing I think about now. I was privileged and very lucky to have been able to run against all the greats. I ran against Carlos Lopes when he broke the world record. In fact, I ran in two world record races, as I was 10th when Steve Jones set a world record in Chicago.

Did you ever use altitude training at all?

I went to Boulder once, but I didn't like it. I am quite big, and I think it has been documented that big people don't do so well at altitude or in a short period of time. I was there for six weeks. I certainly did some fantastic track sessions though, as due to the thinner air I was running faster. However, the long runs were dreadful, and so I don't think I got a lot of benefit out of it. At the end of the day, Nike were paying for it, so I went. However, as I said before, the best place for me was the canals.

Did you have a special diet or take any supplements?

I did early on when I was a youngster. I took multi-vitamins and vitamin C. I was very much into that. In fact, we went in for ginseng and bee pollen because it was all the rage then. They are all fads. I was very lucky at the time because my wife was a good cook. I also enjoyed cooking. I always ate a balanced diet although I did eat a lot of garbage as well. You can do that when you are running. I ate my fair share of curries, and cod and chips. Basically, I could eat anything. I didn't see the point in having a special diet. I did what I did, and it got the results. I could do 20 miles on a piece of toast, a Mars Bar and a bottle of juice. Some people couldn't do that but that was the way my metabolism worked.

Did you use electrolyte drinks?

Yes, I did. However, I thought water was the best thing.

In the marathon too?

Yes, I drank water. I tried everything. I worked for Sportif Perform for a while and had all their stuff, but at the end of the day, I think that a good, sensible diet, and plenty of juice and water are enough. I kept drinking plenty of fluids. Many people don't realise they are getting dehydrated.

What is your height, and what was your racing weight?

I am just under six-foot, and my weight was between 10-and-a-half and 11 stone - about 10 stone 10 really. I weighed 10 stone 2 once; I can't believe that now.

What do you think are the factors that made you and the others in the 1980s so good?

We trained hard, and we played hard. We really enjoyed it. I look at guys nowadays, and they come into the club and are dead pensive. They hardly laugh or have a good joke. They come training, and then they go home. We used to sit and have a few beers after, and chat about things. It was generally sociable. I used to like to think I was accessible to anybody. I wasn't like I am John Graham and don't you come near me. I trained with everybody. Some of the guys I talk to nowadays seem a bit stuck up. Unfortunately, that is the way the sport has gone. A couple of years ago, I was training with a group of guys doing some fartlek, and it seemed that nobody wanted to take any of the efforts; they seemed frightened to take an effort. I thought - come on, we are all out here to do some work, you know! You are only cheating yourself at the end of the day. Certainly, we had a lot of good guys around at that time, and we raced against each other every Saturday. There were also a lot of good club athletes, who could beat you if you were just a bit under the weather. They'd give you a fright and keep you on your toes. That is what it is all about at the end of the day. It helps keep things in perspective and brings you back down to earth. A lot of the so-called good athletes now train themselves and don't get involved in a club, and I think that is a problem. They've got their agents, and they've got their races all planned and everything like that. Andy Holden and I used to do a fartlek or a steady run together on a Saturday morning and then go and do the relays or cross-country against each other in the afternoon. The

Birmingham League Cross-Country was the standard of the Scottish National. In fact, I only won two! The first time was when I was 16, and then they put me in the senior race, and I came 14th. Ian Stewart won it, Andy Holden was second and Ray Smedley was third, and then there were people like John Wheway and Dave Black. It was a who's who of British athletics. Unfortunately, that isn't happening now, and it's sad. The kids are just not coming through. I think there is a lot of variety now in sport. Before, it was just football or running. It has all changed, and a lot of kids talk about their Sony PlayStations and spend hours on that. I also think people just don't train hard enough.

Mike Gratton

PB: 2.09.43 - London 1983

Highest World Ranking in the 1980s: 14th

Marathon Achievements:

Bronze - Brisbane Commonwealth Games 1982

Winner - London Marathon 1983

What was your background in athletics?

Like most people, I started in school. My father was in the army, and so we ended up going to Germany. I was in a boarding school, and we had to do various sports. One of the things we did was an inter-regional, which

187

was similar to the county championships in the UK. They also had the British Forces German Schools' Championships, and when I was around 12, I was asked to do the 800m. I finished second in about 2.10. The following year, we came back to England, and I joined Folkestone Athletic Club. I did the 800m and 1500m and came seventh in the English Schools' 1500m final. I progressed from there really, moving up to the 5000m as a senior and winning that. I also started doing some road and cross-country.

What times were you running?

About 1.53 for 800m, 3.50 for 1500m, 14.20/30 for 5000m, and I also did 50.1 for 400m. When I went to college at West Sussex Institute in Chichester, I was still basically a 1500m/5000m track runner. I joined Brighton & Hove and went over there on Tuesday nights to train with Carter, the Bristow's and all that lot. The first year I was back in Canterbury, I stayed with Brighton & Hove because I was still hoping to get back into track & field. However, due to an injury, I couldn't get up on my toes. I couldn't sprint, as I didn't have the strength at that time in my muscles and tendons.

What was the injury?

When I left college at 22, I couldn't get a job as a teacher straight away, and so I worked on a building site. While I was working there, I got run over, and my left foot was broken. It put me out of the sport for about six months. On my return, I just did lots of road running and got involved with Invicta. Invicta were basically a road running club and didn't have a track & field team at that time. They were training for the Paris Marathon because London hadn't yet started, and I just got caught up in it. I also eventually lost contact with Carter and the guys at Brighton AC, which was breaking up anyway. This was in 1979, and it was really the start of my road running career.

So, did you get back to doing any track later in your marathon career?

Yes, I got back on the track again some years later when I started running 10km and did quite a lot of it actually. I also ran my personal bests for the longer distances – 3000m upwards - when I was training for the marathon. So, I did 8.01 for 3000m, 14.01 for 5000m and 29.01 for 10km.

How old were you when you did your first marathon?

I was 25. It was the Paris Marathon in 1979. I was 11th, which was a Brighton club record.

Did you do many road races before the marathon?

Not a lot actually because of the accident. I was run over in July 1978, and it was through to December before I could start running again. The Paris Marathon was in

May. I didn't do very much. I did the National Cross-Country for Brighton and finished around 120th, and then I think I did something like the Tonbridge 10 in 51/52 minutes in the March, followed by the 12-Stage Road Relays. I had quite a lot of background though because even when I was at Brighton doing 1500m and 5000m, I used to run with Bob Heron a lot. He was a 2.17 marathon runner and was training for London to Brighton in those days. So I was in the habit of running for two hours on a Sunday even when I was training for the track. I think the reason I became better later on in the marathon was because I got my speed back.

How many marathons did you do before you set your PB?

I think it was 13. I did the Paris Marathon in 2.21, the Poly, which I won, in 2.19, was fifth in Harlow in 2.19, and then I did the Olympic trials in 1980 where I was 12th in 2.17. After that, I went to Poland and ran 2.17, followed by the Dutch National Championships. I blew up there and ran 2.21. I then went to Kosice and in my first proper international I ran 2.25. I thought I was going to run 2.12. I think the next one after that was London in 1982 where I did 2.12. I got the improvement I was looking for. I am sure it was 13.

It seems like you did quite a few in quick succession then?

I did three a year right the way through from 1979 to 1983 but progress was pretty steady. It went 2.21, 2.19, 2.17, followed by 2.16 in 1981 in the AAA's Championships, and then I had that "hiccup" with 2.25 in Kosice. I then ran 2.12 in London, 2.12 in the Commonwealth Games and 2.09 in London. So, I was just gradually hacking away at it and making progress.

What would you say was your biggest achievement?

The Commonwealth Games in 1982 is something people tend to overlook. I wasn't a complete outsider, but there were a lot of 2.09 marathoners in there. There were people like John Graham and Rob de Castella, and it was a really tough course. Plus, we ran it at eight in the morning. By the time we'd finished, the temperature was sky high. So I think that my 2.12 there was worth a PB or a 2.09 at least. The Commonwealth Games was a proper race back then, and unlike this time, the top boys competed. Kanga and anyone who was anyone in the Commonwealth in the 1980s were in that race. I was only 10th or so ranked in the starting field. There were lots of people there with better claims than me. It was also a hard race, with John Graham and Rob de Castella running at 2.07/2.08-pace early on.

How long before marathons did you decide to do them?
Did you have a plan?

Initially, I just took them as they came. I didn't plan to
do the Paris Marathon at all. I just started to get fit and
ran much better than anyone expected in the National
Cross-Country, as I had only been running for about
eight weeks or so. I was staggered, and everyone else
was surprised too. I think I was probably one of the top
Brighton finishers that day. After that, I thought I was
going alright, and so I might as well go over with them
and run it. I think the next one I did was the Poly
Marathon in July. I did a planned build-up for that and
won it in 2.19 on a really hot day. I was about three
minutes ahead of the next guy. Chris Brasher was there,
and he did a big report in The Observer, who I think he
was writing for in those days. It was called something
like "One Foot In The Door To Moscow" because the
next year was the Moscow Olympics. I think it was at
this point that I realised I should be a marathon runner
and that it could be my career. I made gradual progress,
but obviously I didn't get to the Olympics. I ran the
AAA's Championships in Milton Keynes, which was
the trial, and only finished sixth or seventh, so I didn't
make the team. However, I ran a PB of 2.17. The
following year, I was third in the AAA's in 2.16 behind
Hugh Jones and Andy Holden, and I thought that if I
were going to go any further, I'd have to find a coach.

So at that point, I asked Cliff Temple, who I'd known for years, to look at my training and try to help me plan it properly. We didn't change very much, but we thought about putting things in the right places and doing certain things at certain times of year. It was more tweaking really.

Can you outline your training in a typical build-up to a marathon?

Through the winter, I would have averaged 120 miles a week with up to two-and-a-half hours on a Sunday morning and another half hour or so on a Sunday afternoon.

How fast were the long runs?

They were always quite quick. They would be 5.30 to 5.45-miling. We knew exactly how fast because we used to run over parts of the old Faversham Half-Marathon course, and there were quite a few mile markers painted on the road. They were hard sessions and included good marathon runners, such as Nick Brawn and Merv Brameld. Some people thought they were too fast, but you have got to learn to run fast for long periods of time. I think most people train too slowly now. The morning run would have been a very easy five miler. I was teaching in those days, and I used to run to school with Martin Knapp, who was a lecturer at the nearby university. So, we'd do five or six miles in the morning and then on Monday night we'd always do a hill session. The hill was about 500m, so quite steep, and we'd usually do it 10 or 12 times. I don't think I'd run it quite so steep now though because it actually caused me some injuries. That was a hard session. The whole of the main group, people like Ian Stewart, who was a 3.53 miler, and some other really good people did that session. It was a sprint up and a jog down with usually a three miles warm-up and three miles warm-down. On Tuesday, it would normally be something like 25 x 300m with a 100m jog recovery or 20 x 400m. Most of it was quality training. On Wednesday, I did 13 or 15 miles.

What was the pace of the 300m and 400m reps?

They were at 10km race pace or faster, but as I got fitter towards the spring, the 400s would be in 67/68s and occasionally faster than that. The 100m jog was normally in 45 seconds to a minute.

How about the pace for the 13 or 15 miler? Was it easier than the Sunday long run?

Yes. It would have been six-minute miles. Also, I was a P.E. teacher, and we had sixth form games on Wednesday afternoons. We'd do mixed hockey or something like that for about two hours, and I would always join in.

So, you would have been quite tired after that?

Well, I think you get used to it, and I think it helped. It gave me upper body strength. On Thursday, I usually did long reps or fartlek. Friday was an easy day.

Were the reps on the track?

No, we rarely went on the track. It was usually on a grass field. We had a 1000m field at the University of Kent laid out because we didn't have a track. It was dead accurate. It was around three cricket boundaries, and there was a white line painted out permanently with every 100m marked. In the summer, we used to drive up to Bromley to use the track there, and in the middle of the winter we did the reps on the road. We used to have a circuit at the University of Kent, which went round what is now student housing. Each side was about 400m and each end piece about 150m. So, you could sprint down one side and jog the 150m in a square.

How long were the long reps?

They would vary from probably 800m up to 2000m, or if the weather were really horrid, we'd go out and do seven or eight miles fartlek.

How fast were they?

It is difficult to say. In the summer, when we were doing them on grass, probably 2.45 pace. However, in

195

the middle of winter on the road, we probably weren't going quite as quickly as that. I guess they were still inside three minutes though. They would be faster than 10km pace with about two minutes recovery, and we'd do six or eight of them. Friday was just a couple of easy five-mile runs and Saturday, in the winter, was usually a race because there was the Kent League, the National, the Southern, the Inter-Counties, etc. There was not much in the way of rest, but then it never seemed to make much difference. You just tended to build into it. I used to do a track season, which would mean lower mileage, and then I would go straight into heavy mileage from October onwards. It was different and quite distinct. I did 120 miles a week right throughout the winter. The highest week was 140 miles, and the lowest about 60 in the week before a marathon.

So, there was quite a lot of quality in there?

It was mostly quality. The easy stuff was just the mornings. Most of the evening runs were hard and nearly always with people who were good runners like Ian Stewart, Nick Brawn, James Webster and Gary McCall. If we went out for a group run on a Tuesday instead of doing track, it would start out steady, but by the end it would be absolutely flat out. It used to be like that with the Gateshead people in the late '70s/early '80s and also at Coventry and Tipton. You'd just get a group of people together of around the same age and

196

ability, and they'd all came through at the same time. In 1981 to 1984, I did 2.09, Nick did 2.11, Merv did 2.13, Andy Girling did 2.15 and Martin Knapp did 2.17. Nowadays, I am involved in coaching, and there is so much protectionism. You don't often see people training together as groups any more.

Did you train any differently for 10km or other events?

Well, basically there were two seasons: summer and winter. In the summer, I would mostly train for 5km and 10km, so we would cut down the number of reps. We'd do 10 or 12 x 400m in 60 seconds or faster, and if we were doing 1000m reps, we would maybe do six with much longer recovery, and they'd be in 2.40 instead of 2.55. I'd cut out the midweek long run as well. However, there would still be a 20 miler every Sunday. I kept the long run much of the year whether I was training for the marathon or not because that is your background training.

Did you ever run over distance?

No, I didn't ever deliberately run over distance. It would only happen occasionally if I got lost or something. I used to aim for two hours ten. There was a psychological reason for doing that because that is what I was aiming for.

Were you a top 10km road and track runner at the same time as being a top marathon runner?

I was a top runner on the road. I did 29.01. I was better on the road than I was on the track. I had a psychological problem with the track. I used to sort of drift away in the middle of the race and then come back strong at the end. I never got the track performances out of me that I thought I could, given that I had quite good speed over 800m and 1500m. My best on the track was 29.09. I would never be deadly competitive. If I did the AAAs, I would always be in the second group. However, there were people like Brendan Foster, Ian Stewart and Mike McLeod around at that time, so it was tough. Having said that, they should have dragged me round to faster times. I could never get on it. I'd start with the lead group but then for some reason with six or seven laps to go I'd drift back to the second group. I couldn't keep the rhythm going. Someone like Bernie Ford, whom I was competitive with on the roads, would almost lap me on the track. Nine times out of ten he would beat me although only by a few seconds usually.

How did you go about tapering for a marathon?

I didn't really taper much. I would probably do a fast two hours ten minutes or 22/23 miles two weeks before and keep a normal week's training going. I'd then drop down to about 13/14 miles or an hour-and-a-quarter/hour-and-a-half on the Sunday the week before. The week of the race, I would cut down on the intensity in the first half. So instead of doing hills, I would do a couple of easy runs on the Monday and then do 10 x 200m on the track in racing flats with a 200m jog recovery on the Tuesday. They would still be around 30 to 32 seconds, so I was keeping the tempo there. I also used the diet.

The depletion phase as well?

Yes. It would end on the Wednesday, and I'd do a couple of runs that day, the second one being an eight or nine miler. Thursday, Friday and Saturday would only be 20-minute runs just to tick over.

Do you think that the diet helped?

I did then, and I never did a marathon in the early days without it. I really only had two bad ones: the one in Holland in 2.21, which was a step backwards, and the one in Kosice where I did 2.25. Kosice was because I went off too fast. I thought I was a 2.12 marathon runner. My next marathon was a 2.12, so I was, but I just got it wrong that day. As I never ran a marathon without the diet, I can't say whether it helped or not. It was just something I did. Every marathon I did the diet, and I always did the depletion phase. I did it properly.

What races did you do in a build-up to a marathon? What was your attitude to these races?

Well, I was running PBs all the time. The first time I targeted races and built up very carefully was for the Commonwealth Games in 1982. I had an intense period of racing where I did five races in two weeks. I did the Oxford 10km and was second to Bernie Ford in a PB of 29.01, followed by a half-marathon in Gravesend in 65 minutes. I just ran at the pace I wanted to run for the marathon. After that, I did the AAA's 10 Miles at Reading, which I won in another PB at the time of 47.40, and then another couple of races leading up to Brisbane. We were there for a month before the Games, and there were no races, so I concentrated my entire racing into that one spell. I then had four weeks to get over jet lag and prepare for the Games. For London in 1983, I did the traditional cross-country season right the way through. I made a mess of the Kent Cross-Country Championships though, only finishing 7th or 8th when I should have won. I don't know why; it just didn't happen. I then finished 5th in the Southern Cross-Country, which was my best ever Southern, followed by 29th in the National. Again, my best ever performance. The week after, I did the Tonbridge 10, which is quite a tough course, and I ran a PB of 47.11. After that, I went to Rome with Bernie Ford to do a half-marathon although it turned out to be a 28km. I went through

200

21km – half-marathon distance – in a PB, but Bernie ended up beating me by about 10 seconds. Lastly, I did the Southern 12-Stage Road Relay the week before, which was five-and-a-half miles in those days. So, I very carefully chose races leading up to London, and they were fitted in and planned as part of the training.

Did you use any form of mental preparation?

I didn't do anything deliberately, so no, not really. I personally think that if people have reached that level in the sport, then they are pretty self-motivated anyway. You get nervous because you have to be nervous, but you control it. You don't need to focus your attention too much because the target is there, and you are working towards something. It is not something you have to build yourself up or get psyched up for. I've always felt quite cool actually. I think on the day of a race I am quite nervous. I show that by talking too much, and I chat to people while warming-up. In the days leading up to the race, you are thinking about it all the time, but I didn't go through a mental routine where I tried to psych myself up or anything. I don't think you need to in a marathon because you've got a long time for things to unfold whereas on the track you've got to get it all out in a shorter space of time. If I wanted to relax, I went down the pub.

What about during the race?

During all the good marathons, I'd focus on tactics and how the race was going. I'd also concentrate on split times and catching groups. In London in 1983, I actually talked to people during the race to sort of reassure myself we were doing the right thing. I remember asking Dave Cannon, who was an experienced runner, what sort of schedule we were on because I was quite a long way down the field for someone who was going to end up winning it. He said 2.08/2.09-pace. I was actually 40th or 50th. After that, I concentrated on moving through groups until I got to the lead group. I then stopped thinking about times because it became a race I was involved in. Actually, from 18 to 22 miles I slowed down because I was running with runners who were slowing. That is why I made a move and broke away at 22 miles. So, I just thought about what was going on around me all the time, and I did notice people on the side of the course. I didn't get tunnel vision or anything. I always found it a source of being more relaxed when someone shouted my name, and I acknowledged them, especially when you are going through the motions at a pace that is slightly slower than your maximum.

Do you think you actually hit the wall in your two bad marathons?

Yes, I think I did. I ran much too quickly early on and blew up. Also, for the one in Kosice, I'd done the first part of the diet before travelling, and then when we got there I couldn't carbohydrate load as I wanted. There were lots of potatoes and stuff, but I was living for three days in a hotel environment, and it wasn't so easy. So on that occasion, it was probably the diet that I got wrong. I am sure that is why I hit the wall. I was capable of running the pace, but I didn't have the energy levels there to keep it going. When the race is going wrong, you feel every ache and pain. However, when it is going well, you are pretty aware of every movement around you and concentrating. Afterwards though, you almost can't remember what happened during the race at all.

Did you do any other forms of training like weights?

I used to do a lot of weights. I think that was a legacy of being a track runner. By the time I was a marathon runner, I used free weights once a week but leading up to that, and certainly while I was at university, it would have been two or three times a week. I did squats and free weights. We didn't have multi-gyms or anything like that in those days. Later on, when I stopped teaching, I realised I had to do something for my upper body. I was the type of P.E. teacher who used to join in, and so I was getting all-round fitness from that. However, after winning London and leaving teaching, I had to deliberately go back and do something for my upper body. We organised a circuit training session at a college in Canterbury where we used ropes and beams and things. I don't do any now, and I would probably benefit from it.

Did you do all your training with a group?

On average, out of 14 sessions a week, 10 of them would have been with people. It was either one person, for example, running to work with Martin Knapp, or with a group in the evening. On an occasional Sunday, when I was doing a fast, long run and other people didn't want to be involved, I would be on my own.

Was Cliff Temple your first coach?

He was the only coach I ever had. He coached me from 1981 until 1984/85. The formal coaching then stopped, and we just used to talk about things. He was involved with coaching Sarah Rowell and Shireen Bailey as well. When he was going to things like the Olympics as a journalist, we wouldn't speak for virtually the whole summer, and then we'd just talk about the build-up to the London Marathon or something. I used to listen to everybody though, and in the early days of the BAAB - as it was then – I went along to squad meetings. I was in the England B squad in 1980, and I used to go to every squad session and listen to everything said.

Did you ever use altitude or warm-weather training?

I used warm-weather training but that was only by accident. I just happened to get invited to a half-marathon race in Puerto Rico, which was in February, and you used to be able to extend it to ten days or two weeks. It certainly wasn't a deliberate plan to go warm-weather training. I never went altitude training. I go now it's too late!

Did you always work full-time?

I was a full-time teacher virtually my entire marathon career. I became a full-time athlete after winning London, and it didn't work. My performances went backward. I don't think you are so active. You just need to do other things, and I think it makes a difference. I had a couple of years after winning London when I just thought that I would be a runner to see if I could get a world record or whatever, and it didn't happen. I think I trained too hard and too often. The mileage didn't change but the quality and intensity did. I also got involved in training with milers and did more speedwork. I was training with Ian Stewart, who did 7.43 for 3000m that year, and so the whole speedwork thing went up a gear. It was great! I could probably have done a sub 4-minute mile at that point, but it was

205

no good for marathon running, and I finally started getting a series of injuries that put me out of action.

Is that when you changed careers?

Yes, I didn't go back to teaching.

What sponsorship and financial assistance did you have?

I was with Nike. They started sponsoring me for the Commonwealth Games in 1982 but that was just kit. I then got some money after the Commonwealth Games when I was building up to London. It lasted for a couple of years, but the money just wasn't there then. Winning London was my biggest payday and that was probably about $10,000. I got $2000 for being third the year before, which is nothing. Luckily, I was still teaching.

Did you ever get appearance money?

Yes, I got appearance money - not the year I won the London Marathon, but later. However, after the 1984 Olympics, Nike got into trouble because they were paying bonuses to all their medal winners. More Nike runners won medals than they had anticipated because of the boycott of the Eastern Bloc countries and so their budget went down. They then put most of their top marathon runners on kit only contracts. So, there was no money coming in from Nike in those days. I went to Brooks for a few years, but they didn't have any money either. There were performance-related bonuses, but you had to work for them, and the amount of appearance money was nothing like what it is now. You were talking $2000 - £3000 to go to a race. The prize money was reasonable. As I said, winning London in 1983 got me $10,000, but there were no time bonuses. You live in your time period, and you can't change that. In Bill Adcocks' time, I wouldn't have got anything!

Were there any other forms of financial assistance?

I got a small amount of money from the Sports Aid Foundation, which amounted to maybe £100 a month. There was no lottery funding or anything. I didn't get anything from the BAF. They put me on BUPA but that was all. You had to earn the money. You had to go out and race, and you had to do some silly things as well. I ended up doing the Great Race from Glasgow to London because that was the only way of earning money that year. It was a 21-day race with 20 stages, and there was £10,000 to do it, but it completely wrecked me for ages. Some people, such as Paul Evans, came out of it really well. In fact, that was the making of him. However, it was not good preparation for a marathon. I caught a cold during it, and by the time I had finished I was absolutely knackered. So, having to earn a living out of races was detrimental to performance.

Apart from doing the carbohydrate depletion/loading diet, was there anything else special about your diet?

No. I used to take vitamin C out of habit, but otherwise I just used to eat loads of pasta, rice, potatoes and stuff. I had no particular diet, just what you would normally eat.

Did you drink alcohol?

Yes, just the normal amount. After training, we would normally go down to the Royal Dragoon in Canterbury and have a few pints.

Did you use any electrolyte drinks?

There was a forerunner to Isostar called Accolade around, but I only took it if someone gave it to me. I wouldn't go out and buy the stuff. I used to live on tea and coffee actually. I'd have a pint of water after training. You do it out of habit. You are thirsty, so you drink.

What did you drink during a marathon?

I didn't drink anything at all. I didn't drink because I got bad stitch from it the first time I tried it. It was in the Commonwealth Games in Brisbane. It was a really hot day, and I'd actually put water bottles out on each table. I stopped to take a drink at the first couple of stations, and I got stitch. So after the second station, which would have been about 5km, I didn't take on any more.

I ended up overtaking people through the race. I didn't find that I slowed down because I hadn't drunk.

Even in hot climates?

There were occasions like the Manila Marathon in the Philippines, for instance, where I drank because it was survival, but in London in 1983 it rained almost from start to finish, so I didn't need to drink in that. I seldom drank in races. I just made sure I was fully hydrated beforehand. Plus, if you do the diet and are drinking lots of liquids during the loading phase of it, then you should be well hydrated anyway. Anything else you are drinking is going straight through you.

What is your height, and what was your racing weight?

I am five-foot ten-and-a-half, and I weighed 10 stone 12. I never used to monitor it particularly closely. I've never been fanatical about that sort of thing. Your performance is much more important. You know when you are going well, so why psych yourself out because your weight has gone up two pounds or your pulse rate has gone up three beats or whatever? If you are running well, you are running well and that's all you need to know. I think all the people around me who I trained with were pretty normal people. I don't know anybody who was worried about their weight. They just went out there and did it.

Did you get a lot of sleep and rest?

I've actually had a very unregulated life. I've always lived a bit like a student. Basically, I'd go to bed late and wake up to go to work. I'd go to bed at midnight and wake up at eight o'clock and that was fine; that was what I was used to. As a family, we still don't have a routine, and we do a lot of travelling. I think people who get too much into a routine worry when it gets broken, and then they can't cope with it.

Did you have regular massage or any other treatments?

No, it just wasn't available. I would now. There were times after a hard track session when I could have done with it because it would have made the next day's run easier. In the long-term, I think I got my back injuries because I wasn't properly looked after. At the time I was performing well, my body was just recovering extremely well. However, at the point when I ran 2.09 and started running much faster in races, I think the stress on the body became much more. Your fitness can take you to a point where you are actually running as fast as your body can take. So after I had run 2.09 and other PBs, I was pushing myself to the limit and that is when I started getting injuries like sciatica. I could have done with some regular treatment then.

Did you suffer with a lot of injuries and illnesses?

The worst injury I had was when I got run over, and I was out with a broken foot. I used to get colds the same as everybody else. However, when I was training hard, I found them more difficult to shake off. Mind you, like most runners, I wouldn't rest; I just carried on. I never had any real problems until after the London Marathon in 1983, and then the intensity of what I was doing started to cause injuries.

Why do you think you and the others were so good in the 1980s?

I think it's like the Coe and Ovett thing, which spurred on Cram, Elliot and others. Once a band of people are doing it, and it becomes almost normal, then everyone else seems to be able to do it. There were people at the time that were not natural runners, yet they ran very fast times. It was because everybody could do it. People didn't have a mental barrier to running 2.12. They just thought that is what you have to do. They just thought that you have to go out there and run 5-minute miles for as far as you can. No one really worried about hitting a wall. I think a lot of athletes nowadays have built up a mental problem about the marathon. It has almost become a daunting thing whereas in the 1980s people just went out there and did it. You ran 120 miles a week, and you did it. I think people are planning too much,

211

and they over prepare. People go out and run with heart rate monitors all the time but that's not how it is. There is something about doing a training run with a group where you might plan for it to be a steady run, but it ends up being flat out. The Kenyans do that. I think what we did wasn't that scientific. We had people around like Dr Humphreys, who pointed out why you had to do the long run and why you had to do 25 x 400m or whatever, and we built those things into our schedules, but it wasn't planned as tightly as it is now. I think there is scope for experimentation and just going with your head a bit. They just don't go for it sometimes now. They should run more as they feel. You might have a few bad ones, but you find out things.

Caroline Horne

PB: 2.37.26 – London 1985

Highest World Ranking in the 1980s: 87th

How did you become involved in athletics?

I was a little bit of a tomboy when I was younger, and I had a fair bit of natural stamina. However, I started off doing hurdles and high jump because I was actually quite tall for my age. When I went to secondary school, they wanted someone to do the 800m in the town sports', and so I thought I'd have a go. They made me run round the school field just to see what time I could do. I ran a bit quicker than someone else – 3 minutes 20, I think – and was picked to go into the heats. I was second in my heat in 2.50 and then third in the final in 2.47. By this stage, my sister had also been going to the local athletics club for a few weeks, so I went with a friend from school, and we joined as well. That was how it all began really.

Which club was that?

Bournemouth. I did cross-country and track, but when I first started we weren't even allowed to run 1500m, let alone 3000m. I only got to the English Schools' Championships on the track in my last year because the 1500m came in. I came fourth and ran about 4.42. I'd been doing 800m up until that point. When I started off, I was not very good, but I persevered. There was a group of six of us in the club doing distance running at that time, and I was the only one who stuck with it. Later, I got together with Conrad Milton from Hounslow, and he really helped me. He brought me on from being a very average club runner to winning the English Schools' Cross-Country Championships at Guildford in my final year.

How did you get together with Conrad?

They used to have an athletics course every Easter at Bournemouth, which coaches used to come down for, and we would work really hard. Conrad was one of the coaches, and I was very impressed with him. He coached me up until the London Marathon although I have to say I wasn't so happy with his marathon coaching. However, he did a huge amount for me and was very motivational. I was always better the further I ran, and so once they brought in the 3000m I moved up to that. I was also good at cross-country because it was longer. I won the British Students' Cross-Country in my first year at college and was third in the World Students' Cross-Country.

Which college did you go to?

Chelsea College at Eastbourne. However, after that initial success, I put myself under a lot of stress in the second and third years, as I was trying to catch up on some of the work I hadn't done. In fact, I wasn't very well in the last year. I then started working at Crawley Leisure Centre. It meant doing shifts, so I also found that difficult. I lost interest in athletics for a bit, got married to a guy I was working with at the leisure centre and moved out to Lingfield in the countryside where there were no streetlights. I still wanted to be a good runner and never stopped completely, but I couldn't motivate myself to do the training. It was only when I split up from my husband that I really got back into running, as I found it helped me get over it. Actually, I have found that a lot in life. When things are down, it is a constant; it is something that is always there to cling on to. I was about 25/26 years old, and by this time I had joined Crawley AC. In 1984, I did PBs for everything on the track. I ran 2.16 for 800m, 4.30 for 1500m and 9.30 for 3000m. I was also running 34 minutes or low 35 minutes for 10km. I had started doing the odd road race over 5km and 10km by then although there still weren't that many road races for women. In fact, I only ran two half-marathons before my first London Marathon, which is why I found the marathon a bit daunting, as I had more or less gone straight from a track background.

So, what made you go for the marathon?

It was Cliff Temple who initially put the idea into my head. I was chatting to him after the Hastings Parkland Races, and he said I ought to have a go at a marathon, as there were opportunities at the distance. Therefore, the next day, whereas I would normally have run 12 miles, I went out and did 16 or 17. I didn't find it a problem at all and felt fine. So I thought that maybe it was a good idea. Then Conrad also started pushing it. I wasn't going to run my first one until the following year because I wanted to have a good cross-country season that winter. However, after coming off of a successful track season, I started having problems with my Achilles. I couldn't do the speedwork I wanted to do, and so I thought I might as well go for the marathon then rather than wait. I didn't have a proper preparation

215

for it though, as I had lost a lot of time due to the injury and then the flu. In fact, I only did five weeks of specific training with higher mileage and three long runs, but because I had a speed background it got me round. Mind you, I probably didn't recover as quickly as I might have. I was really disappointed with the race itself, as I had all sorts of problems. I had a difficult menstrual cycle leading up to it, and my legs felt really heavy. I felt dreadful all the way. Anyway, it did point to the fact that speed is important. Well, it was for me. I've tried doing what other people have suggested in terms of doing a long run every week or every other week, but I don't think I need that. I need to keep my speed high. If you know that you can run a mile in a much shorter time, then running a minute a mile slower for 26 miles isn't such a problem. If you keep slugging out the high mileage, you just get tired, and you don't produce the results. I tried running high mileage this year and even went part-time building up for London, but I was running crap because I was just too tired.

How old were you when you ran your first marathon?

I was 28, which is probably a perfect age to run one.

What would you say was your biggest achievement?

Probably running that marathon and also doing 33.07 for 10km the week before. I was really chuffed about that. I would have said the English Schools'

Championships, but at that stage it didn't mean anything. It probably does retrospectively, but I had it drummed into me that the schools' championships didn't count and that it was only when you got to the seniors that things mattered. Plus, at the end of a long season, I was absolutely shattered, and I didn't really appreciate it at the time. You always think you are going to do better.

How long before a marathon did you decide to do it?

Normally, I would say a 10 to 12-week build-up, but it didn't work out like that for the first one. I decided to do that marathon around Christmas time. However, I didn't really get training for it properly until mid February or the beginning of March because of the injury problem I had, so I only had about five weeks of preparation. You can look at the following [she picks up her training diary]: 21 miles, 28 miles, 63 miles, followed by flu and down to 30 miles. I then ran the National Cross-Country in Birkenhead, and Crawley won the team title. I had an awful cold, but I had to run it. I still came 23rd. I then did a 16-mile run, which was my first medium length run - 21 miles, 32 miles – I was having trouble with my knee at this point and having enforced breaks. I won the Hastings Half-Marathon and then went out to Portugal. I did my highest ever mileage there of 114 in a week. I think I only topped 100 twice. I was stupid though really and was asking for trouble. I came back on the Thursday, didn't do much on the Friday, and then ran the Hastings Parkland Races on the Saturday and the Worthing 10 in 57.10 on the Sunday. I felt diabolical. It was crazy, and I could have easily got injured again. When you are young, you can get away with things like that. I then did a 23-mile run, followed by a few more weeks of training and a 10km in Battersea. I went through 5km in 16.08 although I don't believe that split, as it would have meant I slowed up quite a bit. It doesn't look like a marathon runner's preparation, but in a way I was doing a lot of work and then having a break, albeit enforced. I was getting a couple of hard weeks in and then an easy week, which is what some coaches advise anyway. When I ran my second best marathon at the World Cup in Athens, I had an almost similar build-up. It wasn't quite as bad as that, but I had a few problems in between, which meant I had to take a rest. John Allen, the physio, said to me that I'd probably have a flyer because of the break. I think athletes are terrified of easing off because they get obsessed about mileage. You can be really stupid. You can look back in your diary, and you can see it. However, at the time you can't see it, and you won't ease off because you become obsessed with mileage. This year, I was putting in loads of miles, and I was actually really consistent. I did 10 weeks where I averaged about 75 miles a week, which I had never been able to do, but I was running tired all the time. I didn't have a day off and I wasn't freshening up. Up to three weeks before the London Marathon, I hadn't had a day off since the beginning of December. I could point to some athletes that were doing things like 120 miles a week and still not breaking 2.40. I would be seriously worried if I ran 120 miles a week and hadn't broken 2 hours 40. I don't know how people can do that sort of mileage and work full-time. I fall asleep at work as it is on what I do. They reckon once you go past 70 miles a week, there is a law of diminishing returns anyway and that you don't get much back for the extra mileage. Maybe some people have to do long runs every week or every other week because they haven't got the background, but I've gone wrong listening to people saying that you must do that. I don't think it is a problem for me. I can go out and run for two hours even if I've only been running 10 miles a week. I will feel tired, but I can do it. I could go out and run for two hours one week and feel bad, but then I could go out and do it again a couple of weeks later and feel a lot better. I pick up on stamina very quickly. I think it pays to keep your legs quick.

What was a typical training week in a build-up to a marathon?

Every other week, I'd maybe do a long run. I went up to 23 miles. I remember reading that Charlie Spedding thought it was useful to go out and run 27 miles about seven to eight weeks before a marathon in order to know you were capable of doing more than the distance. I tried it once when I did three-and-a-quarter hours, but I don't think it is necessary. Generally, it would be 20 to 22 miles, with 23 or 24 miles the maximum. I didn't find it a problem. In fact, I found it quite relaxing. On Monday, I'd do a couple of four-mile runs to and from work to make it easy, and then on Tuesday it would be long reps although not necessarily on the track. I had a two-mile road circuit around Maidenbower where I'd do things like 3 x 2 miles. However, sometimes I'd do the club session at Crawley. I think the key marathon session for me is 5 x 1 mile, and it was the sort of thing we'd do at the club. I wouldn't do it every week, just when it fitted in with the schedule. There would then be another session of something shorter like 400m or 800m reps, or fartlek on the Thursday. We'd also sometimes do 4 x 4 x 400m on the track at the club just to keep the legs ticking over. Other sessions would be things like 8 x 800m or 6 x 1000m, and when we were out in Portugal we'd do 600m rep sessions as well.

At what sort of pace were you running them?

It is difficult to say on the road because it wasn't exactly a mile we were running over, but when I did them on the track they were around 5.20/5.25 at my best. In between the sessions, I'd do two steady runs: 10 miles in the evening and 4 miles in the morning. If I were racing, Friday and Saturday would just be steady runs, and if I weren't racing, I'd do a long run on the Sunday. Sometimes, I'd do a hill session on the Saturday as well. It was a 400m hill, and I'd do that 10 times with a three-mile warm-up. It ended up being quite a long session. On average, I would only do two quality sessions a week. Sometimes it was three, and if I had a race, it might only be one. If I didn't do hills on the Saturday, I might do a run or two runs. It just depended on how it all worked out and on what I had done the week before.

How often did you race?

I raced reasonably often. I'd mix up half-marathons, 10km and cross-country, but I would train through some of those races and not ease down. They just became a good workout or training session, if you like. One marathon I trained for, I did quite a lot of 10km races as sort of fast paced training sessions. However, it is always a bit difficult psychologically, as if you are any sort of racer you can't line up at the start and not try to run your best, and you tend to get disappointed if you don't run well. You are also running harder than a training session, so you do have to be careful with that.

So, what races would you do in a build-up?

Five weeks before my first marathon, I did a half-marathon in 76.08 at Hastings, which is a tough course, and then I went to Portugal. On my return, which was two weeks before London, I did the Hastings Parkland Races and the Worthing 10 in the same weekend. I then did a 10km the week before London where I ran 33.07. In fact, I did two races the week before. I did the Easter Monday Road Races at Feltham, which was a two-and-a-half-mile race, and then the 10km later that same week.

So, it was quite intensive?

Yes, but I wouldn't do that now. I was new to it all then, and Conrad didn't think there was anything wrong with it. After that, I just had a really easy week although I had a panic with my knee. I had trouble with my knee on and off. I had so many little niggles. However, I had a high dose of treatment on the Friday, and I didn't feel it in the race.

Would you say that your marathon training was similar to your usual training then?

Yes, pretty much although I pushed the mileage up a lot higher and did a longer run. For me, it was important to keep the speed going. The stamina part was never a problem. I never had a problem with the long runs.

222

Were your runs quite fast?

I guess I never used to hang around. I didn't think they were that fast, but people used to say that my steady runs were pretty quick. I did quite a few short, fast runs. I had a three-and-a-half-mile loop, which I'd do fairly often, and I'd always do it quite hard and fast. It was probably well under six-minute miling and more like a tempo run. I used to reckon that my long runs weren't that slow but that my easy runs weren't that fast. I really think you can run a good marathon on 60 miles a week, especially coming from a track background. It gives you such an advantage. I am not a very fast track runner, but I am faster than a lot of road runners. I also think that gym work has helped me a lot in the last couple of years. Before I ran London last year, I had an iffy sort of preparation, and I knew I wasn't really ready for it. I'd missed quite a few long runs. However, I still jogged round in 2.44 feeling quite easy. It probably worked because I had missed time! However, what I did notice was that with the gym work I was quicker on the track than I had been in years. I can only put that down to the weights and the difference in strength. That was why I probably felt so much more comfortable in the race because I was running at a much easier pace.

Were you also one of the top 10km runners at the time of your marathon best?

Yes. In fact, I actually ran the fastest 10km in the country that year. There were a couple of people who ran faster abroad though, so I was about fourth overall in the rankings.

How did you taper before a marathon?

Normally, I did a two-week taper. The first of those weeks, I might do 50 miles and then go down to 30 to 35 miles for the week before. I'd usually have a day off on the Thursday or Friday. I preferred not to have the day off before the race, as I liked to jog in order to stretch my legs. The longest long run would probably be three weeks before, and then two weeks before I might go down to 17 miles. The week before, if I wasn't racing, it might be 10 miles.

Did you do any speedwork the week before?

No, I just did steady running really.

Did you bother with the carbohydrate depletion/loading diet?

Yes, I did actually. I did it a couple of times, and it seemed to work reasonably well. I did it for the first one and then before Athens. The trouble is you do feel pretty dreadful after the bleed out phase. I did it because Conrad suggested it, and because back then it

224

was the thing to do. I don't know if it does anything physiologically, but I think it is the difference between how rough you feel the first few days and how good you feel when you start on the loading phase. So, it is more of a psychological thing than anything, as you get this sudden boost of feeling good.

Did you use any form of mental techniques before or during a marathon?

Not really. I think the trouble was the first time I ran I had so many problems, and I was very nervous about it being my first one. I was worried about the period and how rough I felt, and I was worried about whether I was going to get everything right. I didn't even really think about mental preparation. Since then, in a couple of races where nothing has gone wrong and the preparation has been good, I've had the time to be calm and think about it. With a first marathon, all you can think about is whether you'll get round and what it is going to feel like.

So, you weren't thinking about tactics for the race?

Well, no. I was thinking about whether I could do it even though I was an experienced athlete. I found it a very big problem trying to think of running that far and that was all I was thinking about really. I was lucky though, as the first year we were still running with the men, so there was a lot more company. Also, after a mile or two, I was tagging along with Ann Ford and Annette Hoddinott. Annette had run marathons before, but neither Ann nor I had. I got to about nine-and-a-half miles and thought they were going a bit quick. I didn't want to stay at that pace, and I knew Ann was fitter than me, so I had enough sense to back off the pace a bit and let them go. As it happened, I passed Annette at The Tower. She finished over a minute behind me, so it was the right decision. I actually overtook two people in the last three miles. When I got to 20 miles in 1.59 dead, I thought that if I didn't tie up, it wasn't going to be too bad. In fact, I ran 38.26 for the last 10km. When you get to 23 miles, you start feeling it a bit because you've still got a few miles to go. By that stage, your legs are tired, and your head is tired. Once you get to the last mile though, you know you can manage; you just know you can do it. If you haven't run one before, I think there is always this doubt in your mind that your legs might cramp up or whatever. Last year before I ran London, I had a mental block about getting through the 11-mile mark, which is crazy really as 11 miles isn't that far into the race, but I'd had two really bad runs in the previous two London Marathons and dropped out in another. So I decided to tell myself to stay calm and that all I was going to think about was running 11 miles. I got to 11 miles and then just concentrated on getting to 13 miles. When I got to 13, I concentrated on getting to 15. I didn't think about the whole lot. I just told myself that all I had to do was to run to the next point, and then I could decide whether to carry on. By concentrating on running in chunks like that, I ran really relaxed. It also probably helped that I was running on my own because I ran 18 miles of it without seeing anyone else. It was only in the last mile that I felt really tired, but I was short of long runs, so I shouldn't have been able to cope with it that easily. I think that is the problem with the women now running separately from the men because it is so easy to get carried away with the elite field. It has taken me 10 or 11 marathons to learn how to run the race. What taught me to run a good marathon was when I was in Athens. I was so frightened of the course, as the first 13 miles are undulating and then it is literally uphill to 20 miles, that I religiously wrote down my times on my hand and stuck to them. Even when the other British girls went off, I let them go, and I ran at the pace that I was going to run. It worked, and I ran the most comfortable marathon I have ever run.

What time did you run there?

I ran 2 hours 43. When I got to 20 miles, I couldn't believe how easy I felt. I thought I'd cracked it then and that I knew how to run a marathon. I actually ran negative splits. I ran 37.20 something for the last 10km because it was downhill.

Do you think that having the men around you in the London Marathon helped?

Yes, it did. Last year, I ended up with a gap of three minutes in front and two minutes behind from eight miles onwards. I didn't see anyone until the first men went past me. In a way, I didn't mind that though because I was running really relaxed. When I ran the Great North Run three or four years ago, I ran 11 miles on my own, and I ran a good time because I just ran it at my own pace. I think it is so easy to get carried away running at someone else's pace. I think you have got to run blinkered in a marathon unless you are a very experienced marathon runner and can race it, and I don't think there are really that many people that can race a marathon. You need to know how fit you are and be a very good judge of what time you can do. You need to split the race down and run to get to that time. You also need to do lead up races to know what shape you are in. Otherwise, it is really difficult to get it right.

Did you do any other forms of training like weights?

Well, in the winter, we did some sort of mobility work and stretching. I also did a little bit of circuits with the club, but I wasn't really doing any weights then. I only swam when I got injured.

Was Conrad your only coach?

He coached me up until London that first year, but he didn't really know enough about marathon training. One of the sessions he used to put on the schedule was 8 x 1 mile, and I actually did it once. It worked out a 13-mile session by the time I had done the warm-up, the jogs in between and the warm-down. In a way, it just ended up being a fairly hard 13-mile run. It was too much. I've done stuff with Pete Bennett down at Crawley, but I haven't really had a coach since then. As Conrad said, a coach should really make himself redundant anyway. You don't really need a coach to set sessions and stuff like that. You just need a coach to back you up and tell you when to take a break. Most athletes do not need to be told to train harder. They just need someone there to tell them to back off.

Did you mostly train on your own or with a group?

At that time, I was mostly training on my own. However, on the Sunday run I would occasionally do part of it with some other people. For instance, if they were going to do 10 or 12 miles, I might do that and then continue on my own. In fact, I sometimes ran with Debbie Peel when I trained for the marathon. Once, I remember running on my own for 10 miles, then running with her for another 8 and then doing 4 miles on my own again. It did help to have someone to run part of it with you.

What about your sessions?

Some of the sessions I did with the club, but it depended on what I was doing. It also depended on whether Conrad had set me something although I didn't always stick to what he had given me. I was mostly running on my own, but maybe once or twice a week I'd run with someone else. The trouble is if you do your long run with someone else, you are running at someone else's pace. Plus, running on your own does teach you mental toughness, particularly for women's races where you can easily end up being on your own. You could easily fall apart if you weren't careful.

Did you ever go warm-weather or altitude training?

I never went altitude training, but I went to Portugal for warm-weather training a few weeks before my first London Marathon. There are two benefits to it. First, you are having a break and are able to train all the time without having to think about work. Second, you are able to train with other people. When I went, we had Annette Hoddinott and Rosemary Ellis, who were both training for the marathon, so we had a little group. We also did some of the morning runs with the track runners. It was really nice for me to do sessions with other people, and it actually gave me a bit of a guide as to how I was going. For example, running against Annette, who had done marathons before, and seeing that I could cope with the long runs just as well, if not better, helped give me confidence for the race. In fact, when she went off in the actual race, I didn't panic because I knew how I felt and what her fitness levels were. If I hadn't have trained with her, I wouldn't have known that.

Were you working full-time at this stage?

Yes, I worked 8.30 A.M. to 5 P.M. on flexi-time. I'd stop off and do sessions on the way back from work, as I would pass by the track.

Did you have any sponsorship?

Yes, I had some help from Etonic. After that, I went to Reebok, but it was just kit and shoes, and it didn't last long.

Did you get any other financial help?

Well, I actually got some money from Evian and that is how I managed to go to Portugal. Evian backed women's running at this time and sponsored some 10,000m track races in order to promote the event for women. I won the overall prize money of £1000.

Nothing else?

No, I was never that good, and there wasn't even prize money about for races then. It was mainly prizes. The money started coming later. In the London Marathon, I came 10th, and the prizes only went down to 8th. My dad sent me £50 though, which was very sweet of him. I earn more money now. On the little I've been doing this year, I've earned £1000.

Was there anything special about your diet?

I was actually bulimic. I suffered with it for 12 years. It was only when I started training for the marathon that I realised how bloody stupid I was. I was OK when I was out in Portugal, and I felt so good about that. I told myself how ridiculous it was to be training for a marathon and throwing up, so I didn't at all out there. I threw up three times the night before the race though because I felt so full. I used to feel really guilty if I felt full up. I went to a doctor a few weeks before the London Marathon and was referred to a psychologist, but it took me until the end of that year to get over it. Even when I wasn't doing it any more, I'd still have panic attacks if I ate something that I didn't think I should have. It is really weird. It is like being an alcoholic. I had the problem because I was never as light as you are supposed to be for marathon running, and I always felt conscious of the fact that I looked bigger than everybody else when I stood on the start line. You have this distorted image of yourself when you look in the mirror. It was the carbohydrate loading that made me feel fat, but the idea is to take on extra water, so you are always going to feel a bit fat at the start of the race. I was struggling with it virtually every day for years, and you get neurotic about it. You get this idea that there are good foods and bad foods, and everything is black and white. There is no in-between, and if you get tempted to eat something that is bad, it triggers off a chain reaction. You go out and buy foods like cream cakes and foods that you don't even really like just for the sake of it. If I put on weight now, I just do something sensible about it and lose weight. At that time though, I don't think there was so much emphasis on diet and carbohydrates. I don't think people had gone into those things quite so much.

Did you take any supplements?

I took iron tablets because I had quite a few problems with anaemia. After I got over that, I felt that I should be able to run a lot better. However, I made the classic mistake of thinking that because I'd run a marathon on limited training, if I doubled my mileage, I'd run better. It didn't work that way or, at least, it didn't work for me. I decided that I wasn't going to do lots and lots of long runs and massive mileage because that didn't suit me. Instead, I decided I was going to keep the speed up.

I think you have to have the confidence to go with what's right for you and not necessarily what is right for someone else. I think it is difficult to set yourself up to say that is what you are going to do when you know how far the race is and how painful it will be if it goes wrong, but it has been quite painful when I have theoretically done the right training.

Did you generally drink a lot? Did you drink much in the marathon?

I didn't really drink much in the marathon and most of my long runs were done without a drink. The first time I tried it was in Hastings, and I didn't realise how difficult it was to even pick up a drink, let alone sip it. On my last long run before London, I practised by doing loops and picking up a bottle that I had left on the doorstep. I wanted to practise running with fluid in my stomach. However, on race day it was quite cool, and I only took three drinks on board. I didn't take on anything after about 18 miles. I didn't feel that I needed it.

Had you hydrated well before?

Yes, I think so. I was staying with Rosemary Ellis, who had run marathons before, so she was trying to get me to drink more. I just drank water, not electrolyte drinks. The other thing is I often have to go to the loo a lot, so I was petrified of being stuck and not being able to go to the toilet before the start of the race. I am very conscious of the fact that I probably don't drink anywhere near enough.

What is your height, and what was your racing weight?

I wasn't that light. I weighed eight stone four to eight stone six, and I am five-foot four. Ideally, I would like to be eight stone for a marathon, but I've always had trouble getting down to that.

Did you get a regular amount of sleep?

Yes. When I was training hard, I never had any problems sleeping. I always slept like a log. I tended to go to bed relatively early, especially as I was working. I used to go to bed around ten or eleven o'clock and get up at seven o'clock. So, it was a typical eight hours. Sometimes, if I was training at the club and had come home early from work, I would have a 40-minute nap before going out. You feel worse when you wake up but better for it later on. I did that a few times, and it helped.

Did you have regular massage or anything like that?

No, I had nothing like that back then.

Did you suffer from a lot of colds, injuries or illnesses?

Generally, I don't get too many colds. I had a lot of niggles but nothing that really went on for a long time.

I've always been fairly mobile even though I haven't stretched an awful lot. I used to do some warming up exercises though before I ran, and I think that helped a lot in making sure I didn't get injured.

Are there any key factors that you think made you and the others of your era so good?

I think possibly the fact that there were things like Avon, who sponsored a squad for women marathoners. They were trying to encourage women to get into running, particularly marathons. Brian and Joyce Smith spearheaded that, and I think it was quite a big thing. The marathon captured the attention and imagination of a lot of people at the time, and there were maybe more characters around then like Grete Waitz, Ingrid Kristiansen and Rosa Mota. People like that just inspired you. Ingrid was my heroine. I even called my budgie after her. Joyce Smith was also an inspiration to many people, especially because of her age. There was just a lot of publicity surrounding the marathon and marathon runners at that time. The other thing, of course, is that you are now losing the base of the pyramid. In that period, there were a lot of people into running and coming into the sport – the running boom – and so you had a much wider base to the pyramid. There were also more youngsters coming through the track system and then moving up whereas now there are a lot fewer. I don't know why. It isn't just the marathon, is it? You don't see middle or long-distance runners or 20 to 30 year olds coming in and running well on the roads. You are also not getting people like Veronique Marot, Sarah Rowell and Priscilla Welch, who just came straight into marathon running. They came in at that end of it because there was this charisma about running a marathon. I don't think there is so much charm about it now. Another thing is there weren't so many 10km and half-marathon races back then, and now you have these women only 5km races. It will obviously seem far more achievable for a woman to run a 5km race than a marathon. I just think there was an appeal, and there were a lot of us at that time. The main marathon that women run is London, and since the women have run on their own, the British women's times have gone down. It took me a long time to learn how to run a marathon. People tend not to like feeling too easy in the early stages. They think they have got to be running harder, and I think this is where they go wrong. They are not disciplined and go off at six-minute mile pace when there is no way they are going to keep that going. The elite women's start is too hyped up, and the tension is too much. You have to be blinkered and not look at anyone else. In 1987, I ran the first 10km in 35.50. I promptly blew up and dropped out. I was nowhere near the front or anything, but I just got totally carried away with it. I was ahead of Angie Hulley and

237

people like that. I tried really hard that year. I was so nervous for it because I got an invite, and I was staying up at the Tower Hotel. During the race, I had to dive in the loos and lost about a minute-and-a-half. When I came out, I panicked because all these people had gone past me, and I ran two miles at about 5.20-pace. I dropped out by the hotel. I just got carried away with the atmosphere; I was really stupid. There was no way I should have been running at that pace. I think having the men around in races sometimes helps calm you down, and you are not just trying to hang on to a certain woman or group of women; you are just running at the right pace for you.

Hugh Jones

PB: 2.09.24 – London 1982

Highest World Ranking in the 1980s: 4th

Marathon Achievements:

Winner - Oslo Marathon 1981

3rd - New York Marathon 1981

Winner - London Marathon 1982

Winner - Stockholm Marathon 1983

2nd - Chicago Marathon 1983

12th - Los Angeles Olympics 1984

3rd - Beijing Marathon 1985

2nd - London Marathon 1986

5th - Stuttgart European Championships 1986

3rd - London Marathon 1987

5th - Rome World Championships 1987

Winner - Stockholm Marathon 1992

Winner - Reykjavik Marathon 1985

How did you get into running? What was your background?

It was via cross-country running at school. My first ever race was as a boy scout when I was 11 years old. I won it easily. It was an under 13's race, so I knew I had some sort of potential.

Had you done any training?

No, just running around the streets, which I think is probably quite productive training but completely informal. I didn't really do much about it until about six months later when I went to secondary school, and then cross-country became part of the scene. On a wet afternoon, you were sent off around the games field or wherever. From there, I went through the class to the year, then to the lower school and then to the borough schools. In a matter of three months, I was running around Hainault Forest as first reserve for the London team, and I was still two years under the age group.

Had you joined a club by this stage?

No, and it stayed that way for about four years. I only used to race once a week, and I never trained in any formal way until I was about 15. It was at this point that a student teacher joined our school. He took the running club and got me to join Ranelagh Harriers. I then started to train a little, but it was mostly all steady running. By the last year of school, when I was 16/17, I probably managed about 40 miles a week. However, it didn't get any higher the whole time I was at university, and it didn't get any more purposeful either.

Were you doing any track at this time?

Yes, I did track racing from fairly early on. I joined Polytecnic Harriers about six months to a year after I joined Ranelagh Harriers because Ranelagh only had a road and cross-country section. I ran in the British League and did 1500m in about 4.20-something, which is as much as I've ever been able to do really.

Did you do any road races at this stage as well?

Yes, I did a bit for Ranelagh. I did six-mile road races and that sort of thing.

Did you do the English Schools' Championships?

The highest I placed in the English Schools' was 42nd, so I wasn't any great shakes really, but then I wasn't doing the training. I left school at 17 and took a year off before going to university. I worked to earn money and then went to South America for six months. I didn't do any training there at all, and it took me a little while to get back into things when I came back to start at Liverpool University.

So, how did you get into marathon running?

It was so obvious that endurance was my thing. At university, I ran cross-country all the time, but towards the end I also did a bit of track. I did some 10,000m races. Up until that point, I'd been running 5000m in the British League.

What sort of times did you run for the 5000m and 10,000m?

Well, I came through a bit in 1976. I won the Southern 10 Miles Championships at Shaftesbury, running about 49 minutes, and I also started doing some really long training runs of over 20 miles, which I had never done before. A couple of years after that, I was doing 5000m in about 14.30. My best ever was 14.04, and my best 10,000m was 28.49 set at the AAAs in 1978. After 1978, I didn't do much track any more. When I ran the 28.49,

Brendan Foster lapped me, and I was probably about 15th in that race, which was no great shakes. It would have got me some B-International vest against Finland at the end of season or something. The year I set my track bests was also the year I ran my first marathon. In fact, it was before I ran those bests. I did it on probably about 50 miles a week of training.

Which Marathon was it?

The Duchy of Cornwall, which is a tough one. However, I won it quite easily.

What time did you run?

I did 2.25 and second place was 2.28 or something. I didn't take it too seriously and did no specific training for it. The next one I did was Sandbach in 1979. I ran 2.20–and-a-half there, but I misjudged the pace quite badly and wasn't too pleased with it. I had trained specifically for that one. Alan [Storey] had been my coach for a year previously, or at least, had advised me quite a bit. When I decided that I wanted to get a decent marathon done, I went to Alan to ask him to give me some ideas on how to rearrange my training, and leading up to that marathon I had trained quite consistently.

Who helped you before Alan? Did you just do things on your own?

Pretty much on my own. There was a teacher at school, who got me into it, but his main input was enthusiasm, and he didn't really coach me.

What about at university?

No, I didn't really have the time. I just went out and ran at lunchtime. I did as many miles as I could fit in at lunchtime and that was it.

So, you weren't doing many sessions as such?

Not really. I just occasionally did a bit of fartlek if the others were doing it. Alan offered me a lot of insight into how to go about training for a marathon even though it didn't show in that second one I did.

What came next in marathons terms?

I did the Moscow Olympic Games trial at Milton Keynes. However, I got bad stomach cramps at 23 miles when I was around eighth, and I slowed up a lot. The last three miles, I was just jogging, and I kept stopping and trying to stretch. Anyway, I came 14th in 2.18.56, which was still an improvement, but I knew there were three minutes to spare. I was disappointed because previously that year the training had really come through. I think it takes a while to build up to marathon training. Your body has to get used to it in order that it

243

is productive, and you are actually absorbing it. In the spring of 1980, I had come through to international level at cross-country. I was 8th in the Inter-Counties, 7th in the National and 40th in the World Cross-Country, so I was disappointed not to run well in the Moscow Trial. I didn't have any ambitions of making the team, but I thought I could do well and run 2.15.

How many marathons did you run before you did your PB?

London was my ninth marathon, and I ran 2.09.24. In, 1981, I won the AAA's in 2.14 on a very tough course, and it was at this point that I knew I was on my way. It was a major revelation that I'd finally done what was necessary. After that, I ran Oslo and knocked another minute off of my time on another tough course, and then I went to the European Cup, which was my first representative match, and came fifth.

So, what would you say was your biggest achievement?

Well, it was London. I'm still the only Londoner to have won it, which is quite gratifying. I've lived here all my life really, so you get the feeling of ownership. It's nice for the following few days when you are on the tube and people are coming up and congratulating you.

How long before a marathon did you decide to do it?

I just took what was offered for the first few. I did Oslo, the European Cup, New York, Tokyo and London. In 1981 and 1982, I just took them in my stride, but you can't do that for any length of time. You have to step back and build up again. I was operated on towards the end of the year for a calcaneal bursitis. I then ran in the 1983 World Championships in Stockholm, followed by the Chicago Marathon in fairly quick succession. I got back down to 2.09 in Chicago.

Do you think that the enforced rest did you good?

Yes, it probably did although I think voluntary rest would have been better.

Can you give me an outline of your training after you met up with Alan?

It is difficult to remember what I was doing in the early days, but I certainly got in a long run of around 20 miles instead of what I'd previously being doing, which was nearer 12.

What was your longest run?

Occasionally, I'd do a little over distance - 27/28 miles - and even now I do a really long one from time to time, not that I think I really need to. A long run is 23 miles in training; 20 miles isn't long enough if you are building up for a marathon. You need to get in a few longer than that.

Did you do that every week?

Every, or every other week, depending on the races.

Did you train twice day?

I started training twice a day in around 1978. It took me about six months to get physically used to it. I was probably training up to 90 miles a week when I did the second marathon. In the morning, it would be an easy five.

What about quality?

I never trained on the track. Instead, I might do something like eight by two minutes or alternatively four minutes hard with two minutes easy on a gravel track in the park.

Did you do most of your running on the road?

No, I did most of it on soft ground. If I did an 8-mile run, then a third of it was on the road. If I did an 11-mile run, then a quarter of it was on the road.

Did you ever do hills or fartlek?

I hardly ever did hills, but occasionally I did fartlek. I mostly ran loose type reps by time. Once a week, I also did a paced run of about 10km with a warm-up and warm-down. In fact, I did anything up to 8 miles in the middle, so we are talking about 12 miles in total. I went back on the track more when I returned to London in 1986, but in Liverpool the nearest track was Kirby, which was six miles away. I didn't have any transport as such, and so I did my reps on grass by time. When I got to international standard, I went in for quite complicated sessions, which Alan suggested. This was mainly to avoid falling into the trap of comparing one week to the next even when the weather conditions were different. Apart from when I was living in Hungary, I never trained in a group, which is good and bad. Physically, it's perhaps not so good because you cannot run as fast, but mentally it's not bad. You get used to having to squeeze the effort out when you are not tucked in behind someone.

What races did you do in a build-up to a marathon?

Generally, I used to stay clear of half-marathons. They are just too taxing, and they disturb the training regime too much. Occasionally, I did one, and it would be five or six weeks before a marathon. I'd then have four or five days very easy, followed by a final batch of training before easing off for the marathon itself. Five weeks before the 1987 London Marathon, I ran 62.40 for the Reading Half-Marathon. More typically, I did 10-mile and 10km races. I'd always run them as races, and while I wouldn't train hard the day before, I wouldn't taper down. I don't think I could have run them any quicker unless I'd have trained for them.

What was the highest mileage you ever did?

I did 130 miles a week. In fact, I did 120/130 regularly. I think it was quite productive. I could handle 110/115 quite comfortably. While I probably could have got away with doing less, I think it had an effect. If not a training effect, it had a mental or psychological effect. My normal run was 11 miles, and because I did less specific speed training I occasionally enjoyed going out and hammering it.

How did you taper before a marathon?

Two weeks before, the long run would be 20 miles, and then it would come down to 15 the week before. I'd start easing down from the penultimate Tuesday, and the last two weeks would be frontloaded with effort. So, from 130 miles, I'd drop down to 90 the penultimate week and 50 for the final week. I'd also often do the diet. I'd take Monday and Tuesday very easy, and then on the Thursday I'd do some strides – 15 seconds hard, turn around and 15 seconds hard back. Well, it was a bit more than strides. I was running pretty hard to keep my heart rate up but without taxing myself too much. It's just a consciousness to run fast, as there's obviously no training effect. When you are on the diet, you can lose a lot of confidence. You feel that you are running as fast as you can go when you are just jogging around the park.

Do you think the diet helped?

I don't really know. I've got no grounds to say that it definitely did help, but it didn't ever cause me a problem, which is why I kept on doing it. It also gave me a framework of some sort.

Did you use any form of mental preparation?

I don't think I did in any sort of proper or organised way. I am sure there are certain psychological tricks that you can use to help you relax at appropriate times and to be able to blank out what is not necessary. I don't think I ever mastered any of that. A lot of sports psychology is just about having the appropriate mental approach to the whole thing. Many people who run shorter distances don't take to the marathon simply because they are not mentally attuned. In terms of consistency, it is important to have an approach that is in tune to what is demanded. Some people are up and down in the marathon, and they don't know how to capture the good performances again and again. A lot of that is mental.

Did you use any strategies during the race? Did you ever hit "the wall"?

Personally, I think if you are an elite runner, you shouldn't hit the wall. Your body might feel discomfort, but it should be used to the transition from one energy system to another. You should have done the training that is appropriate to pull yourself together over that transition. I can't say that I ever hit the wall really.

What about the tough stages of the race?

To be honest, I think the whole race is tough. Even at the beginning, there is the uncertainty of it. It is sometimes difficult to keep your confidence together. I was an even-paced runner, and that can be both a strength and a weakness. I very seldom won duels in the last 500m simply because I didn't have the change of pace. However, often those that do have a change of pace aren't there after the first half or even the first quarter.

Did you do any other forms of training?

No, only when I was injured. I did swimming and weight training when I was injured.

Previously, you said that Alan was the only coach you ever had. Is that right?

Yes, I met Alan in the New Year of 1977, and if I ever wanted any advice, he was the only one I would go to.

Did you ever go altitude or warm-weather training?

I went warm-weather training a few times and altitude training a couple of times although it wasn't specifically for that. It just so happened that I was at altitude. Once was before the Chicago Marathon when I was staying for two or three weeks in Park City, Utah, which is at about 6000 feet, and another time was when I went to China for three weeks. I went because Alan was there. It could have had a beneficial effect.

It was a bit short though?

Yes!

Do you think that warm-weather training is necessary for a distance runner?

Yes, I think it is really useful. It depends on the phasing and when the competition is. I went out to Portugal with Dave Long just because there was snow on the ground here, and I thought I might get injured training on the ice. There is also warm-weather training before a summer championships' marathon in order to get used to running in the heat. I think there is great benefit to doing warm-weather training under really hot conditions simply to lose a fear of the heat.

Did you run well in the heat?

Yes, I can handle it. I run better in cooler conditions, but I am convinced most people are afraid of the heat.

251

Did you work?

I was a student for a lot of the time, and I went to Hungary on a British Council Scholarship in 1981/1982. However, I was sidetracked by the athletics, as it was such a great set-up there. I continued to pursue a PhD until 1985, but by then I realised that the athletics was becoming too demanding, and so I decided to concentrate on that. When Athletics Today came out in 1987, I was invited to write a column for them but that was just one thing, and I did it more for interest than anything else. When I dropped out of the London Marathon in 1990, I realised that I ought to beef that up a bit in order to compensate for the tailing off of my career, so I got an introduction and started writing for The Independent. I did athletics features and that went very well for a while. However, I found that I wasn't really cut out for being freelance where you always had to push things and be a salesman. In 1986, I had a family, so there was a lot of time going into that, as well as moving house. I was doing work on the house for five years. I realised from 1994 to 1995 that I wasn't going to earn enough from the writing unless I got a permanent job, and so in 1996 I got a job as the part-time secretary for AIMS, which I really enjoy.

What sponsorship and other financial help did you have?

New Balance were my sponsors from 1981 to 1985 and then Reebok from 1986 to 1998. In the very early days, Eddie Kulukundis was also helpful, and the Sports Aid Foundation sent me warm-weather training. At the beginning, the contract money was pretty good, but the whole market changed in the mid 1980s, and they started paying less and less as prize money became more important. I was running at a time though when it was fairly egalitarian, and you got paid roughly for what you did. You didn't have this centralisation of the market like now where the top guys get paid oodles, but the guy who runs 2.10 and finishes fourth or fifth isn't in it at all.

Did you have a special diet?

I tended to have a lot carbohydrates and little meat. I do eat meat, but I tended not to have a lot of it.

Did you drink alcohol?

Yes, but not very often when I was training hard, and I'd often go three weeks without having a drink at all. When I was training in Hungary, we'd go straight down to the beer factory after our big sessions and have some industrial beer, but it was very weak.

Did you take any supplements?

Occasionally, especially in Hungary because they were very keen on that sort of thing. I took replacement drinks and a fair bit of vitamin C as well.

Did you ever get anaemic?

Just once in 1992. I couldn't understand what it was at all, but I was struggling to run six-minute miles. I took iron tablets every day for a week and then every other day for a week.

Did you take electrolyte drinks at all?

I never took any in competition, as they were just too expensive and new at the time. I mostly took water and juice. However, in championships, where there are feed stations every 5km, I put together a drink with a little bit of vitamin C. I also remember in one competition in Beijing that I made up a drink with a bit of vitamin C and aspirin because I had a slight temperature. I ran OK.

Did you regularly take on liquid in a race?

Yes, always.

How tall are you, and what was your racing weight?

1.77 m and 59 kg.

Did you have a lot of rest or need a lot of sleep?

I slept eight hours most nights.

Did you take a nap during the day?

Very rarely.

Did you get a lot of injuries and illnesses?

I just got the change of season type colds twice a year.
There was a period when I thought I wasn't performing
as well as I should have been in certain races, but I think
it was bound up in my expectations and was a mental
thing.

So, you were constitutionally pretty strong?

Yes.

Did you have regular massage or anything like that?

I used to get a regular massage in Hungary and that
was when I first had it, but when I was in Liverpool
there wasn't really any access. However, when I moved
back to London, I used to have a massage fairly
frequently even when I wasn't injured, as there was a
masseur that lived close to my parents. Now I just go to
him when I have problems. It was never that regular,
but when I was running at my best I probably went
every two to three weeks. It keeps you aware of what is
going on, as not only can he feel the tightness, but you

can too, and it gives you a much better idea of where the stresses lie.

What do you think made you and the others in the 1980s so good?

I think it is a social thing. The whole way society is now organised has changed since the 1960s and 1970s when I was growing up. I didn't do any formal training; my kids do. However, they don't get to run down to the local park as I did when I was four to ten years old. I am convinced that this sort of informal training at a very early stage is beneficial. It's conditioning rather than training. I had the potential to run, and I used to run to school every day. It was only three-quarters of a mile, but it was four times a day. I think that has a lot to do with it. The other thing, of course, is in terms of international comparison, and the way some countries are performing so well. It strikes fear in the hearts of many athletes for various reasons. There were countries doping when I was competing at my peak, but I guess I am more cynical now than I was then.

Veronique Marot

PB: 2.25.56 – London 1989

Highest World Ranking in the 1980s: 3rd

Marathon Achievements:

Winner - Houston Marathon 1986

22nd - Rome World Championships 1986

Stuttgart European Championships 1986

3rd - London Marathon 1987

Winner - Houston Marathon 1989

Winner - London Marathon 1989

Winner - Houston Marathon 1991

Tokyo World Championships 1991

16th - Barcelona Olympics 1992

How did you become involved in athletics?

I came into athletics via my involvement with sport in France. I think I was about 16 years old, and a teacher asked me if I would represent the school in the cross-country championships. I did, and I came sixth, which was really high considering that I did it on no training. In fact, I wasn't that sporty at all really. I didn't take part in any team sports, and the amount of sport I did at school in France was minimal.

So, you obviously had some natural talent?

Yes, a little although I think I had a lot more attitude than natural talent. I was always ready to finish a race. We'd have a weekly run at school for the class, and I'd win it. However, it was more because the others weren't that committed to finishing it and would stop and walk. So there was nothing that special about it. Due to me finishing so high up in the cross-country championships, the girl that won it, who came from the same town, approached me and asked if I would like to join her club. So I joined and started training. Within a week of joining, I was asked whether I wanted to take part in the Northern France Championships, which is basically the same as the North of England Championships. It was quite a big area and included Normandy, Picardy, etc. The race was in Le Touquet by the sea. Because I had only just joined them and hadn't done any training, the team manager advised me to be careful and to start at the back. So I started at the back with a really fat girl, who was going much slower than everyone else. After a while, I thought it was a bit slow and decided to begin moving up a bit. At the end of the first lap, I came across the team manager, and he also told me that I could move up. I really started to go through runners, and eventually I finished two places behind the girl who had won the race at school - the one who had encouraged me to join. I think I finished 30th, and she finished 27th or something like that. In fact, I think she was a bit miffed at me finishing so close to her. From then on, I always did quite well in cross-country races. When it came to the track in the summer, I didn't do so well until they introduced the 3000m. However, as we are talking the early 1970s, nobody was really interested, and so I didn't have much competition. Very few women ran and those women that did, by and large, ran the 400m and 800m, or at a stretch they might run the 1500m. It was unheard of to do the 3000m. Anyway, I took part in the Picardy Championships over 3000m, and I think I came 4th in about 11 minutes. We then had another championships, which was the equivalent to the West Yorkshire Championships. Two of us started the race, and I had already lapped the girl after five laps, so it wasn't really a race. That was the extent of my running in France. I finished school at 18-and-a-half and went to Paris to do a tri-lingual secretarial diploma. I didn't run much there except for occasionally doing two laps of the Jardin du Luxembourg. I then met a man who became my boyfriend, and he had this really weird idea, which a lot of people did in the 1970s, that if I ran, I'd end up with really massive leg muscles. It was a piece of nonsense, but at the time I was only 19/20, and I believed him. I didn't run for the whole time I was going out and living with him. In 1976, I moved to England, partly to be with this boyfriend, who was English, and partly because I wanted to go to university. I applied for university entrance to York and got a place. I started in October 1977 and immediately joined all the sporting things. I joined the cross-country club, the fencing club and the rock-climbing club. I had already done fencing in London when I wasn't running the previous year. The end result was that within two weeks of me starting university and training again, I took part in the Eastern Universities' Championships in Hull. It was an inaugural event, so there were not many competitors. In fact, there were only 10. I won the race not knowing the course. I kept having to stop and ask the women behind me where we were going. It wasn't a very high standard. After that, I took part in a few races and then the British Universities' Championships in 1978. However, I don't remember where I came. At the end of 1978, around November time, we had an annual outing to the Barnsley Marathon. It was very weird because nowadays everybody prepares for a marathon whereas we were just cross-country runners, who would suddenly pile into a minibus and go and run a marathon. The Barnsley Marathon was not that easy either. The course was undulating, and the last six miles were uphill, so it was pretty tough. I ran with a friend of mine, and we decided that if we were going to take part, we would do a bit of training. So, we went out and did a 10-mile run, which was over and above our usual weekly mileage. Our usual training week was something like a three-mile run, a four-mile run and a seven-mile run. So, we did the 10-mile run just to see if we could cope with 26 miles, and it seemed OK. In the race, I did 3.55, and it felt very easy for me. My friend had a tough time though, and at one point a policeman even tried to pull her out. The following year, we ran it again. I stayed with my friend for most of the race, but in the last six miles I decided to go off on my own, and I ran 3.40. In 1980, I took part in an International Avon Race, and as I had never run faster than 3.40, and it was also a very hot day, I decided to take it easy at the start. Because I had taken it easy early on, and people had gone off too fast, I was running through a lot of runners in the latter stages of the race. I can't remember where I finished, but the time was around 3.06 or 3.07, so it was another big improvement on my PB. Later, in November, I ran the Barnsley Marathon again, and this time I won it. Instead of just jogging, I ran it hard, and I did 2.55. A funny little anecdote just to show how little I knew about marathon running at this time was that when I did the London Marathon, which started in Battersea Park back then, I was staying with my mother-in-law in East Sheen. I decided that the easiest way to get to the race would be to cycle there. So, I cycled to the start and put my bicycle on the bus that takes all the clothes to the finish. After I finished the race, I got on my bike at the Guildhall and cycled back to East Sheen. In the evening, the reception was in Knightsbridge, and so I cycled there, enjoyed a few beers and cycled back once again. I didn't think anything of it. It was only later that I realised normal people didn't do that when they are running marathons. It seemed quite normal to me. In 1980, I had spoken to a few other runners at the international event and discovered that my mileage was really low. I was only running 30 miles a week. So, I upped my mileage to about 40 for Barnsley in the last six weeks and that is when I ran the 2.55. I then ran a bit more for the first London Marathon in 1981. I think I was running about 50 miles a week for about two months, and I did 2.46. However, I ran beyond my capacity at that time, as when I crossed the finishing line I collapsed, and I couldn't walk for the next two days.

Did you ever do any other road races before you ran marathons?

I did some road races in 1979. Once I had done that first marathon, I thought it might be a good idea. I discovered that I had some talent.

What distances did you run?

I think I did a 10-mile race, as well as some others.

Did you also do well at that distance?

Yes, I think I won the Rowntree 10 in 1980. I ran 60 minutes, so I could run at 6-minute mile pace. I was doing a lot of fell running races as well. I was quite good at that. I usually finished in the top three, and occasionally I won them. I was the first woman to do the Annandale Fell Race.

How old were you when you did your first marathon?

I was 23.

How many marathons did you do before you set your PB, which was the British Record?

I have no idea – maybe 30. However, I did run a lot of them for fun and as training runs.

How long before marathons did you decide to do them? Did you plan for them?

From 1983 onwards, I used a 12-week build-up. I did about three serious ones a year and two as training runs. So, I did a total of five in a year.

What was a typical training week in a build-up to a marathon?

Monday morning would be a fairly hard 10-mile run, which was hilly and mainly off road, and in the evening I'd do a light jog although not always. Tuesday morning was an easy run.

263

What was your easy?

It was seven to seven-and-a-half-minute mile pace. Tuesday evening was probably fartlek or hill repeats and Wednesday was a hard 15-mile run at sub 6-minute mile pace. Thursday morning was an easy run.

How far were these easy runs?

They were seven miles. On Thursday evening, I would do a track session, which would usually be one of the following: 5 x 1 mile, 8 x 800m, 8 x 1000m or 20 x 400m. They were all with short recoveries. Friday was a 10-mile run at a reasonable pace but not that hard - about six-and-a-half-minute miling or faster.

What sort of pace were the miles or 800m reps?

By and large, the 800m reps would be in 2.30 although some may have gone down to 2.25. The fastest 800m rep I have done is 2.21. The miles would be in 5.05. I think I may have broken five minutes twice, but in general they would be low fives. We didn't hang around. Saturday would depend on how tired I felt and whether there was a race on the Sunday. Usually, it was a fartlek or something on grass. Sunday would be a hard 20 miler at about 6-minute miling.

Martin McCarthy

PB: 2.11.54 – London 1983

Highest World Ranking in the 1980s: 54th

How did you get involved in athletics?

I ran at school and was fairly successful. It was predominantly cross-country, and I was always one of the better ones in the class. I then got to about 13 or 14 and started doing really well. The P.E. teacher suggested that I join the local club, and so I went down to Bedford & County AC and started training with a group of lads there. I became the county schools' champion at cross-country, as well as over the steeplechase on the track. I also made the English Schools' Championships at both although I didn't do so well there. As an intermediate boy, I was just outside the top 100 in the cross-country and fifth in my heat of the steeplechase, so I didn't make the final. Bedfordshire was a reasonably soft county to get into, but it kept me going from there.

Were you training much at this stage?

I don't think I trained very hard at all. In fact, I don't think I began training seriously until I was about 18. I started off in a big group from when I was 15 with lots of other youngsters, but it was all light-hearted. After I

265

was 18, I started to train harder and then the results came. I won the Eastern Counties' Cross-Country Championships, beating Nigel Field, who was a junior international. I thought that was the start of things to come. However, I went downhill a little at 18/19. I think I was burning the candle at both ends quite a bit. The track performances were OK but nothing spectacular. I never had a great deal of speed.

What sort of times were you running?

I ran nine minutes for 3000m as a first year junior and then 8.36 as a 19 year old, so I was a reasonable sort of standard. I then changed jobs and moved from Bedford to Luton and started training with Tony Simmons. It was a great inspiration to run with him on a Monday when he had just won the National Cross-Country on the Saturday. It was brilliant. He was quite sociable, but I struggled to keep up with him. He was stretching me more and more. However, I still wasn't running that well. At 19/20, I started doing a few road races and that gave me a new inspiration. I also started to whack up the mileage.

What distances were you racing on the road?

I was doing 10km and 5 miles, and at 21 I did a 10-mile road race.

Were you quite successful straight away?

Well, I was more successful. As a 21 year old, I ran the Wittlesea Show 10 in Peterborough. I came fifth with 50-and-a-half minutes. It nearly killed me in the process though.

What were you running for 10km at this time?

About 31 minutes or 31-and-a-half – something like that. It was a fairly respectable standard. I then did a half-marathon in about 69 minutes, and I was in the top half a dozen; I was in the prizes. So rather than being predominantly a track and cross-country runner, I was starting to look at the year in terms of what road races I would do.

Did you carry on doing track and cross-country too?

Yes, although I think the track went by the wayside a bit. I didn't worry about it too much because it never treated me that well, and I never ran particularly good times. I still trained on the track though. I also changed coaches from the general sort of club coach to Colin McNeeledge, who was a more specific coach. He had a select group of people, and while he wasn't an experienced coach by any means, he had a rapport, and by trial and error he helped me no end. I did a 15-mile road race, and I was in the top 10. I always had the marathon in mind, and I decided it was so much better

267

than flogging myself around a track. I then moved away to Newbury and got married, so there was a bit of upheaval in my life. However, just before then I ran the Finchley 20. I won it in 1 hour 44 and ran it the only way I know how: I went straight from the front and went out like a madman. A lot of people criticised me at the time for having no respect for the distance and told me that when I did a marathon I'd really come unstuck, but I used to run all my races like that. Be it 5 miles, 10 miles, 15 miles or 20 miles, I'd go out the same way. I pushed myself to the limit the whole way.

What was your first marathon?

My first marathon was Gloucester. I did the Finchley 20 in 1980, got married and then picked up an injury, so I didn't run the intended marathon that autumn. I waited until the following year and did the Gloucester People's Marathon. It was the first one they had ever had. It seemed reasonably flat, and I didn't want to pick a really prestigious one. I lead from start to finish. I predicted 2.16 on my application form and that caused a bit of a sensation. I was actually on for 2.12 at 15 miles, but I fell apart between there and 20 miles. A lot of people watching thought I'd had it, but I picked it up again over the last five or six miles and ran 2.18.31. I was in all sorts of trouble, but I was able to run through the pain. I did learn to pace them a bit better after that, but every race I ran I always went out hard. My attitude to racing was to go out hard and make it tough for everyone else. I always felt more comfortable and relaxed as a front runner. I also often used a tactic of kicking a mile after the start in a 10-mile road race when everyone was just settling into the pace. Sometimes I took people with me, sometimes I didn't. It quite often broke up the race, and people hated me for it. After I moved to Newbury, I changed clubs to Oxford City. It was the nearest decent club, and I knew Pete Flavel, Ron Harris and some other internationals there. Plus, they had some of the university lads like Nick Brawn. We had a really good group. We never did any reps, but we used to do a 10 miler, and it was almost like a race. It was a 10-mile burn up. I think that Nick, myself and one or two others could handle it, but there were quite a few casualties who never made it to the Saturday race. It worked because I was doing that plus three quality sessions a week and a good 20 miler on a Sunday. I rarely topped 90 to 100 miles a week. It was all good and quite intense stuff. I also kept the track and cross-country going. In fact, I was winning the Chiltern League Cross-Country races because I had this added confidence.

How old were you when you did the Gloucester Marathon?

I was 24. At this time, I also set a PB at 5000m, and I did it without even going on the track. I was living in

269

Newbury and doing a hard 10 miler on the Tuesday, a run with the Newbury lads on occasions on the Thursday, and then running on my own around a grass field on the Monday, Wednesday and Friday. I was running some fairly intensive rep sessions, and I ran 14.14 for 5000m. I took a minute off of my PB, so I knocked a big chunk off of it.

How many marathons did you run before you set your PB?

I know I did 15 in five years in total. I did Gloucester, and then I went to Jersey. I won it as a training run in 2.27 or something. Following that, I was ninth in the AAA's at Gateshead in 2.18, and then I went to Berlin and Italy. So, it was probably six although I did some as training runs. When I did the AAA's, I was third Britain or third Englishman, and technically speaking, I should have gone to the Commonwealth Games. However, Mike Gratton went instead and won a medal. I accepted that at the time. I never expected to get in the team, but having done it on the day and made the criteria, it was quite hard. It was always an outside chance, but it didn't happen. I was new to it then, and I didn't fight for it. I got a trip to Berlin out of it though; I got my first Great Britain vest and so that was alright. Mike knew the ropes. He ran very well in London and was third, but then he dropped out of the AAA's trials. He could rest on the laurels of London, and he got the Commonwealth Games slot.

What was your biggest achievement?

It would be that 2.11.54 and placing seventh in the London Marathon. There were some other good races but that was the highlight.

How long before a marathon did you decide to do it?

I had a very definite plan, and I did the same for the Finchley 20. I had seen other people go wrong, especially track runners, who thought that by just adding in a few long runs they could do a marathon in the autumn. I kept hearing that you have to respect the distance and that you've got to make sure you've prepared. My coach, Colin, and I sat down and worked out a three-month build-up. Through listening to other people and trying a few things with shorter races, we also found out that I needed a fairly gentle reduction in mileage at the end. If I came down too quickly from the high mileage, I suffered, as I got some withdrawal symptoms, and my legs seized up. Therefore, we always worked back from the marathon with a three-week taper. So, it was probably three-and-a-half months for the build-up. Everything was geared towards recoveries, and there were certain sessions I did. In the first month, I'd have a minute-and-a-half recovery. It would then go down to a minute in the second and half a minute in the third. It was normally a half-minute reduction on all recoveries over the period. The second month in the build-up was also predominantly on hills. I would do short reps up hills and a hilly circuit of fartlek. I'd run them all hard.

So, what was a typical training week in the build-up to a marathon?

It was very focused. If I didn't have a marathon in mind, I was still doing sessions, but it wasn't as focused because there was nothing in mind at the end of the road. However, the mileage wasn't too high; I'd try to hold back on the mileage and get the quality in. I would alternate and do a 20 miler one Sunday and then a 15 the next. I didn't do a 20 every week and occasionally I would do a longer one, such as a 25. In fact, I did a 30 once but that was mentally just to say I had done it; that I had gone over distance. I was a great believer in quality and the 15 and 20 were still hard runs. We are talking sub two hours for the 20 milers. Before I did my first marathon, I did a training marathon. It wasn't entirely accurate, but it was certainly sub 2.50. So, I had the confidence I could do it. Nothing was easy with me. I very rarely went out that easy. Maybe that was my downfall sometimes. I never went over six-minute miling.

Did you train twice a day?

Yes, I normally trained twice a day. I was able to work it with my job as I had flexi-time. I'd usually run at lunchtimes and evenings; I'd do an eight at lunchtime and an eight in the evening. On Tuesday, I generally went over to Oxford for my second run and did the hard 10 miler with a few miles before and a few miles after. I'd do 54 minutes in a full tracksuit. On Wednesday, I would do two runs, and on Friday there would be a rep session. Occasionally, the second session on the Monday would also be a speed session.

So, what were the sessions?

Colin built up a series of sessions to suit me. I never ran particularly well on the track, so we used to do fartlek. It would be something like three minutes, four minutes, five minutes, four minutes, three minutes with 10 x 30 seconds at the end. There were some variations on that. I also used to do things like five by five minutes instead of five by a mile. They were on grass or road, and the recoveries came down as I outlined earlier. So, in the third month it was five by five minutes off of a minute recovery. The third session was usually going out for 40 minutes where I'd run 10 minutes easy, the next 10 minutes flat out or at a medium pace and then repeat it with no recovery. I built that up until I could do it for an hour-and-a-half. It would be at six-minute miling for the first half hour, five-and-a-half for the second and the third would be flat-out, aiming for five-minute miling. Whether it was or not, I don't know, but I would be on my knees. That was the ultimate session. We did a lot of that sort of thing. Occasionally, I'd also do a more structured 20-minute fartlek with a definite kick in the middle to bring it down by half a minute more. The shorter rep session would be something like 20 x 45 seconds with a minute or minute-and-a-half recovery. It was the equivalent to running 200m or 300m reps. If I were racing, I wouldn't do reps on the Friday; I'd just do an easy run.

Did you ever have a rest day?

No, I never did. In fact, I think I went six years without missing a day. I was going for the "Ron Hill approach." If I were racing at the weekend, I would front load the week. This would help me psychologically, and I'd feel really good if I had done 60 miles by Wednesday. I rarely ran twice on a Friday, and it was normally only a six or seven mile-run if I were racing on the Saturday.

So, there was not much rest, and it was all quite hard?

Yes, it was all pretty intense; it was really hard. There were times when I went out for a session and my legs were so sore that they seized up. It would take me five miles to get going.

When you had your period of doing predominantly hills, was that instead of the other sessions?

It would be that three, four, five-minute pyramid on a hilly circuit. I'd just run up and down, and round and round the circuit. I would be legging it up the hills, down the other side, and round and round. I'd stop for recoveries but that was it. I did straightforward hill reps as well. However, I'd never stop at the top. I'd always make sure that the rep went over the brow, and I'd sprint off the top to really kick it in. I did four weeks of that in the middle of the build-up.

And then the next phase would be back to as it was before the hills, followed by the taper?

I was cutting the recoveries but running fewer reps, so instead of doing five by five minutes, I'd do four and get the quality in. I was racing over that period as well, but they were carefully selected races.

What races did you do in a build-up to a marathon?

I always tried to get in a 20-mile race about six to eight weeks before. However, it wasn't always easy as there weren't that many around. If I couldn't find a 20, I'd do a half-marathon. I'd then do a 10km or 5-mile race about two weeks prior. I might also do a half-marathon or 10 miler earlier on just to get me into the swing of things. The only race that I'd do in the final week would be a road relay, as it normally coincided with the area road relays. In fact, the week before I did the 2.11, I ran really well at the Southern. I did a short stage, which was a three-mile leg, and I was quicker than I'd ever been before. I also did a PB at the Worthing 20. The idea was to sit in for the first 15 miles and then kick the last 5, but I got a bit eager and kicked in the last 7. I think I took two minutes out of them in those last 7 miles. Occasionally, I might throw in a cross-country race, but generally speaking I would rather train at the weekend than run cross-country. I only liked to race every two weeks and sometimes I went three or four weeks without a race.

Did you ease down a lot for these races?

No, I didn't ease down a lot for the 20 miles. I think I ran it off of 90 miles.

Was 90 miles a week your regular mileage?

Between 90 and 100. Occasionally, I did 110, but I don't ever recall going over 110.

How did you taper?

I did a three-week taper. I came down from 100 miles a week to 80, followed by 60 and then 40. The last week was just ticking over, and the week before that I concentrated on speed. I kept the long runs going but two weeks before, instead of doing a 20, I did a 15 in order to keep a bit in reserve. I also did the glycogen bleed-out diet in the final week. I'd do the 15 miler hard on the Sunday, and then I'd start the depletion phase until the Wednesday when I'd start to load.

Did you always do the diet?

I did it strictly for the good ones, but I didn't bother for some of the training marathons. I just did the loading phase.

Do you think that it worked?

I think it did. A lot of it is psychological though, and once you've tried it and it works, you don't want to take a chance. The first time I did the depletion phase before the 20 miler, I felt awful. I felt very weak and like I had the flu. So I adjusted it and didn't deplete completely. I only partially depleted and then loaded up. I think I got used to it. I would try to run a rep session on the Wednesday. It would only be something like four or five by three-minute reps, but it just felt awful. I would only be cruising round, but my arms and legs would feel terrible. Straight after that, I would start the loading phase. After having done it a few times, I think the body fights back though, and I certainly didn't gain the benefits so much later on. Marathon running is a discipline, and I found the important thing for me was to have the end in mind and then to train specifically towards it with a number of different benchmarks along the way.

Did you have a special diet or take any supplements?

I took iron and multi-vitamin supplements but not all the time. I ate anything and everything. When you are doing that sort of mileage, you don't realise until later how awful you look with your bones sticking out of your cheeks.

Did you generally drink a lot? What did you drink in marathons?

I took some of the drinks that were around at that time, such as Accolade and Gatorade, but I didn't use them in races. I just drank water in marathons. Actually, I tried to drink as little as possible. When I ran the first marathon in 2.18, I didn't drink a thing. That may have been why I cramped up near the end though. However, in the good one I ran, I also drank very little, as the weather was cool enough. I just drank a little water at every other feeding station. I rarely drank in training. I used to do 20 milers and not drink a thing.

How about in general?

I think I kept myself hydrated although I didn't consciously drink water. I drank tea, coffee and other things, and I just topped up before a run. I think your body gets used to it, and it goes back to the discipline thing. If I could do a 20-mile run on a summer's day without a drink, then when it came to a race, I could do it. I drank a little alcohol but not to excess. I was careful, and I wouldn't go out on a bender if I had a race coming up. I found it relaxed me, and we'd always go to the pub after training for a pint or two – that was normal.

Were you also one of the top 10km runners?

Not at all. I was always a good club standard 10km runner. I ran 29.05 on the road, but my track times were awful. I didn't break 30 minutes on the track. The PB came during my marathon build-up. I was running Houston, which was after the 2.11, and I did a race in Battersea Park. Charlie Spedding outsprinted me, but I was quite pleased with that. Charlie was also building up for the same marathon. It was his first one, and I went out there with him. He won it, and I was 10th in 2.13.24, which was my second best marathon. I was a bit disappointed with the time. I didn't think it was that special really. I was also disappointed to be in the group and only finish 10th but that was the way it was. My 10km race times definitely got better with the marathon training.

Did you use any form of mental techniques before or during a race?

I've always had a philosophy with running and that is if you feel bad, speed up. I tell the youngsters I coach the same thing. I'm not sure that it worked, but it was something I always tried to do. If I was going through a bad patch for whatever reason, I'd try to speed up and change the pace, and sometimes it would relax me. It wouldn't be a massive surge, but I'd just pick up the pace and see what happened. I'd then occasionally drop back again. The other thing was I would never drop out of a race. You have got to be there at the end. I'd never ever think of dropping out, and I'd finish under whatever circumstances. I would often hear people say that they were going to run the first mile in such and such and the second mile in so and so time. My view was you just went out and ran as hard as possible. You ran until your legs dropped off. There is nothing scientific about that. Well, not that I could see anyway. You just went out there and ran as hard as you could - in my case that was five-minute miling - and you just kept that going. If you made it through the 26 miles in that, then you got a good time. I never worried about the stopwatch. If you go through 10 miles in 50 minutes like I did in my first marathon, you don't panic. It doesn't matter; it is fine. I think I went through PBs on route during my 2.11; I certainly did for 20 miles.

Did you do any other forms of training like weights?

I did some circuit training early on, and I used to try to do a bit of work at home like sit-ups and press-ups. I also tried to do some stretching although I didn't do as much stretching as I should have done. The circuit training was once a week either in a gym or at home, and I experimented with weights. I think they have a benefit, but it is a question of time. I thought that any time that I had was better spent running. I was fairly strong physically; I was light but strong. I was fortunate in that respect. When I was injured, I used to cycle or swim. I didn't particularly like swimming and preferred cycling, but if I had to swim, I would. When I had a stress fracture, I swam. All these years on, I've now resorted to cycling to keep fit because I cannot run as much as I would like to.

How tall are you, and what was your racing weight?

I am five-foot nine, and I was nine stone six.

Did you do most of your training on your own or with a group?

Quite honestly, when I was doing marathons, I had trouble finding anyone to train with. I could do the hard 10 miler with people, but I couldn't find anyone that would do the rep sessions with me. They were also so special to me that I couldn't take the risk of doing them with just anybody, so most of them were done on my own. I think that was why I could front run because I was used to it.

What about the long runs?

I mostly did them on my own although sometimes I would go out with others. However, as for the rep sessions, I wanted to do my own thing, and unless I met with another good standard runner, it was difficult. There were very few people that could actually push me that hard. I used to get bored on the long runs, there's no question of it, but I just used to get out there and get them over and done with.

Did you ever use altitude or warm-weather training?

I used warm-weather training on a limited basis in order to get more training done in a warmer environment. However, I never had the luxury of being able to go that much. I think it was something that I wrote about in the Road Runner's magazine at the time. Following my 2.11, I got picked to run in the European Cup team. We went out on the Friday and then ran in 80 odd degrees on the Sunday. We had no preparation at all, and all the other foreigners had been out in Portugal for two weeks acclimatising. We were completely drained. Try as you might, running at home in three layers of clothing is not the same. I ran in Rio, and I knew it was going to be hot, so to build up for it I ran in the sauna on the spot. I didn't do it for that long, but if nothing else, it was a bit of mental preparation for it. I never had the chance to go to altitude to train.

Did you work full-time?

Yes, I worked full-time right from leaving school. I had the benefit of flexi-time, but earlier in my career I had to work evenings. I worked in local government as a committee administrator, and so I had to do agendas and minutes for council meetings. I used to train at lunchtime and then as the meetings didn't start until half past six, I'd go down to the sports centre to do a second run. I squeezed it all in. The only time I got off was on a Friday or Monday if I had a race abroad, and I used to either make up the time or take it as holiday.

Did you have any forms of financial assistance or sponsorship?

I had a trust fund with a limited amount of prize money in it from the various marathons I ran. I earned a reasonable amount, but I couldn't live on it. In the early success years, I was pretty naïve. I tried to do things myself and struggled. It was only when I picked up an agent in the States that I started to get more races and could negotiate some start money. I never won the big time though and was always back in fifth or sixth place picking up the lower end of the money. I tried really hard to get sponsorship, but I didn't get a penny. I used to get my physiotherapy reimbursed via the IAC [International Athletes' Club] but that was stopped after a while. I needed it a lot as I suffered from a fair amount of knee problems right the way through my career. As far as kit was concerned, I kept changing companies because they kept dropping me.

Did you suffer from a lot of injuries and illnesses?

I wasn't often ill, but I sometimes used to pick up throat infections in the autumn at the change of season. However, it was probably no more than is normal. I'm pretty strong and robust in that way. I did pick up a few knee injuries though, as well as a stress fracture, which I developed in the London Marathon one year. I'd had an arch problem and then ended up with a stress fracture. I still ran 2.17, but after that I was out of action for six weeks. I'd have a lot of easy weeks due to knee problems. I'd have swollen knees and niggles all the time, and I'd have to run on grass. In fact, the knee problems finally got the better of me and stopped me from competing. I've still got the problem now; my knees are fine until I run.

Did you get a lot of sleep and rest?

Just the normal amount. I'd go to bed at eleven o'clock and be up at seven o'clock. I was always tired and never had any problems sleeping.

Did you have regular massage or any other therapies?

I tried it later on and found it very beneficial. There was a member at the Newbury club who trained up to be a remedial therapist, and he was very good. He'd massage knots out of my calf muscles and do some preventative work. I generally went to him when I had a bit of a niggle in order to stop it from becoming a full-blown injury. I also sometimes went as a precautionary measure, especially if I had a marathon coming up. It was fairly ad hoc and normally reactionary. It certainly wasn't weekly.

Do you have any ideas as to why you and the others in the 1980s were so good?

I think there were just so many good people around at the time. Wherever you went to race, you had to run hard. You had to run sub 49 minutes for 10 miles or 66 minutes for a half-marathon, otherwise you'd be nowhere. There were fewer races and people tended to pick the better ones. I don't ever recall thinking I am not going to a race because so and so is there. In fact, it probably attracted me to go there, so that even if I didn't win, I'd get a fast time out of it. I ran good times and didn't make major games because there were always other people around at the time who were running that much faster. I also think we were 100% focused and intense. If we went to a cross-country league race, it would be eyeballs out. I don't think we worried about things quite so much though. We tried to play down the scientific. I don't recall reading a great deal about diet and other things, and we weren't obsessed with it in that way. It was more a case of not worrying about it and just going out there and doing it. Preparation was important though, and you have to gear the training up to it. If you haven't got all the preparation in, then you've really got to question if you are going to do it. It was a great period of time, and there were lots of good people.

Sarah Rowell

PB: 2.28.06 – London 1985

Highest World Ranking in the 1980s: 6th

Marathon Achievements:

Gold - Edmonton World Student Games 1983

3rd - London Marathon 1984

14th - Los Angeles Olympics 1984

2nd - London Marathon 1985

I know you were a hockey player originally, so how did you become involved in running marathons?

I guess I had always been reasonably good at running at school, particularly distance running, but I think it was the combination of only getting to be reserve for an England under 18 hockey team and doing my A-Levels at the same time that prompted me. I just started doing a bit more running, partly to get fit and partly just to take a break from studying. I then went to university as a hockey player but suddenly found myself right down the bottom of the pile after having been at the top. I was also finding that I was enjoying the running more and more, which naturally led me to do a lot more of it. I then saw the first London Marathon advertised and thought it would be a nice, fun thing to do. So, it all just went from there really.

So, you did some athletics at school and were obviously quite sporty?

Yes, but I never trained for it. I just ran. I was very active at school and did a lot of sport. I did cross-country when everything else was rained off. It was probably only in my last summer at school that I started running purely for running's sake rather than just turning up and doing races.

Did you do much running as part of your hockey training?

Not intentionally. What happened, of course, was once I started getting more and more into the running, I was probably doing too much to the detriment of my hockey. Certainly, during my first and second year, the running probably wasn't helping my hockey training.

So, you had no major successes at a junior level in running?

No. I was Suffolk Schools' 100m Champion once, but I wouldn't say I had any real success. I also did the English Schools' Cross-Country once; I think I finished about 250th.

So, the marathon was purely because you liked the idea of it?

I had always found running distances easy, and the marathon was something that was there, so I just thought that I wanted to have a go.

How old were you when you did your first marathon?

It was the first London Marathon in 1981, so I would have been 19.

How many marathons did you do before you ran your PB?

On the road – it was my eighth.

Did you have a meticulous build-up to your marathons?

Once I started being coached by Cliff Temple, then yes, I did. Before then, I had help from a colleague at college, but I wouldn't say it was a meticulous build-up. It was just a build-up; it was simply working with him to follow a training programme. Once Cliff started coaching me, we worked towards each race. As soon as

I'd finished a race, we'd put the next one in the diary and then ultimately everything was geared towards that marathon. However, my training didn't vary that much throughout the year, and I had a fairly set pattern as to what I would do each week. We didn't have periods where I just ran steadily apart from rest periods. We followed a fairly standard pattern to the week and just worked on that.

Can you outline a typical training week in a build-up to a marathon?

A typical training week would have been 20 to 22 miles on a Sunday morning, and if it were a hard week, there would have been another run in the afternoon.

How fast was the long run?

About 6 to 6.15-minute mile pace.

Would that be on your own or with other people?

It was mostly on my own, but I had a couple of people who I would try to train with. We usually worked on the basis of a hard week, followed by an easy week. On a hard week, I would probably run again in the afternoon for four or five miles. On Monday, it would be two steady runs of five miles or a five and a seven and on Tuesday, a steady run in the morning and a track session in the evening.

What was your idea of steady at this time? Was it still quite quick?

Yes, my steady pace would not be much slower than 6.30 per mile.

Was the Tuesday track session long or short reps?

It was from 200m up to 1000m reps or a mixture.

Did you have long or short recoveries?

Typically, we used to work on at least the same recovery time, so probably a lot of people would say that they were quite long recoveries. If you look at my running profile, I didn't operate in a very large range; I didn't have a change of pace. One of the things that Cliff was trying to work on was my speed, so if we were doing 400m reps, then there would be a 200m jog recovery. In fact, Cliff would often encourage me to take a longer recovery in order that I could try to push the speed. On Wednesday, it would be anything between 10 and 15 miles in the morning and then maybe nothing to 4 or 5 miles in the afternoon.

At a decent pace once again?

Yes, the long runs were all around six-minute miling. On Thursday, it was a steady run in the morning and then a run incorporating a minute or 45-second surges in the afternoon. I'd set the watch to beep every minute and then stride out for a minute and ease off for a minute. On Friday, it would be an easy day of just 5 or 6 miles and on Saturday, a hard 10 miler with maybe something in the afternoon if it were a hard week.

Did you do any hills?

Living in Kent and Eastbourne, a lot of the runs were hilly and every now and again Cliff would hold sessions down at his place on a Sunday, which would include some hill running.

What about tempo runs or time trials?

Well, the nearest would be the 10-mile run on the Saturday.

How fast would that be?

It would certainly be sub-six-minute miling. You would probably be looking at 57/58 minutes for 10 miles.

Were you also a top 10k runner at this time?

I don't know if I would say I was a top 10km runner. I was certainly a top 10-mile and half-marathon runner. Unfortunately, I never really ran a decent 10km. I am sure I probably could have run faster than I did, but yes, maybe 10km and certainly 10-mile and half-marathon.

So, what was your best 10km time?

It was about thirty-three-and-a-half, but I have not been far off that going through in a marathon.

How did you taper for a marathon?

I'd have two to three weeks of slowly coming down. My last long run would be two weeks before.

Did you do the carbohydrate depletion/loading diet?

I tried it a couple of times and didn't like it. I don't think there is a need, and if you are travelling abroad, it becomes very difficult. I probably used it to a semi degree before London in 1985, and it seemed to work, but I don't know how. The strictest I used it was before Columbus, and I didn't have a very good run there.

Did you do any sessions in the last week?

Yes, I would do a session. The last week would usually be a 16 miler on the Sunday, one run on the Monday, a session on the Tuesday and just a reduced, reasonably paced run on the Wednesday. After that, it was just easy, steady runs on the Thursday, Friday and Saturday.

So, you didn't rest at all?

No, I didn't have a day off.

What races did you usually do in a build-up to a marathon?

I would do set races because they were the ones that were local. Cliff would have an idea of when he wanted me to do them. Usually, we'd look to do something a couple of weeks before, but it was generally building them in as training races.

Did you use any form of mental techniques before or during the marathon?

I don't know. I just tried to keep going, I guess. I tended to become very introverted and quiet before a race, so I suppose I was mentally preparing for it in a way. However, it was just one of those things that happened naturally rather than consciously doing it. During the race, it would be a mixture. Sometimes I'd be thinking outside of myself, but usually I'd be trying to think inside of myself. It would be things like how I was feeling, who else was around me, how far I had gone, etc. When I got to twenty miles, I'd start thinking that it wasn't so far to go and that it was just a six-mile training run type thing but not before then though.

Did you do any other forms of training like weights?

Exercises at home would be the nearest thing. I'd do sit-ups and press-ups incorporated into a stretching routine.

So, you didn't go to the gym or anything like that?

Personally, I think it is probably worth it. However, in the first two or three years that Cliff worked with me, there were other things that he felt were more important than spending time down at the gym. I had a reasonably good background of that from playing hockey anyway, as at that point, I was in the gym two or three times a week. So on that side of things, I probably still had some upper body strength. I don't think that you have to get big, but I do think some light weights and some work around the middle body can help.

Were you coached throughout your career?

Yes. When I started running, one of the guys who I was sharing a house with at college was a 1500m runner. He had gone down with glandular fever and wasn't training. So after sort of using books and articles to devise my own training plan, he started helping me. By the time I ran London in 1983, I had joined a club. When I went down to the club, one of the fathers, whose daughter was coached by Cliff, suggested that I get in touch with him, and it went from there.

Did you mostly train on your own or with other people?

Mostly on my own.

Do you think that was that good or bad for you?

I don't think it did me any harm. I tended to train quite hard and intensely although because I ran on my own, maybe I ran too hard at times. However, if you run with other people, you tend to run fast as well. Certainly, I think it was beneficial for me to work with people on the track because that way I worked on my speed a bit more, but I was just as happy running on my own; I was just as happy to go out the door and run.

Did you ever use altitude or warm-weather training?

No.

Did you work at all during your running career?

To begin with, I was a student in my final year of doing a degree. Then in 1985, I was in effect running full-time. However, I found that as much as anything else it was way too boring. Therefore, I went back to do a masters degree. So while running was having the priority, there was something else keeping my brain occupied. I was a full-time athlete as much as any full-time student is. The year I went to the Olympics, I was doing my finals.

Did you have any forms of financial assistance or sponsorship?

I had a couple of little things. One of the running magazines helped me to go to the World Student Games, and then I got minor help from a local businessman. In 1983, I picked up a contract with Adidas, which started out as just kit and then after I broke the British record in 1985, it was renegotiated with some financial bits as well.

Was that salary and bonuses?

Yes, it was an annual retainer plus bonuses.

Did you win much prize money? Did you get any appearance money?

Yes, I got both for the London Marathon. It was a mixture. Prize money tended to come out of the marathons but also some of the half-marathons. Later, we could start negotiating appearance money, especially if I was racing abroad.

So, you had enough to live on?

Yes, for the time at that stage, I could very easily. If I finished second in London, it was enough. Obviously, in that era it was going into a trust fund, but you could draw from that.

Did you follow a special diet or take any supplements?

I was conscious of making sure I ate enough carbohydrates, but I wouldn't say I was on a special diet. I tended to take iron tablets because I didn't eat much meat, and I also took a general multi-vitamin. However, that was more for protection than anything else.

So, you didn't actually suffer from anaemia?

No, it was more of a case that because I didn't eat much meat, I used Ferograd C as an insurance policy. I would take a packet or sachet on a week on, week off basis.

What did you drink in a marathon?

I took water probably as much as anything else because that was what the literature said at that stage. There wasn't the same understanding of electrolyte drinks as there is now.

Did you generally drink a lot during the day as well?

Yes.

What is your height, and what was your racing weight?

I always thought my height was around five-foot four, but someone measured it at five-foot six the other day. I guess seven stone nine to seven stone twelve for weight.

What factors do you think made you and the others in the 1980s so good?

I know this sounds awful, but personally, I think it was because we trained bloody hard. At the end of the day, every Sunday I was running the equivalent of a 2.36 marathon. All my training was done at six-minute mile pace; it was all hard. My VO2 max isn't particularly high, but I've obviously got a lot of endurance. I honestly believe that a lot of it was down to the fact that there was a group of us who trained very hard and who were dedicated to what we were looking to do, and that was to run fast marathons.

Joyce Smith

PB: 2.29.43 - London 1982

Highest World Ranking in the 1980s: 3rd

Marathon Achievements:

Winner - Tokyo Marathon 1979

Winner - Tokyo Marathon 1980

Winner - London Marathon 1981

Winner - London Marathon 1982

9th - Helsinki World Championships 1983

11th - Los Angeles Olympics 1984

How did you become involved in athletics?

I did athletics at school although the furthest we were allowed to run in those days was 150 yards. I got to county level, but I didn't continue after leaving school. Later, at a holiday camp when I was 17, I won all the sports' races. There was this girl with her tracksuit covered in badges, and I beat her. No one would believe that I wasn't an athlete. So after that, I decided to join my local athletic club. At first I thought I was a sprinter, but I soon found out that I wasn't because they asked me to run the 880 yards, and I broke the club record by about nine seconds. I had never even done the event before!

How old were you at this time?

I was seventeen-and-a-half.

Can you remember the time you ran?

I think I ran 2.41. So, I became the club's middle-distance runner, and I also started doing cross-country.

What club was that?

Hampstead Harriers. I gradually did more cross-country and track at club level, and I won the National Cross–Country in 1959 and 1960.

Were you a senior by then?

Yes, I was a senior then. I just missed the Olympics in 1960 over 800m. It was going into the Olympics for the first time. I didn't like 800m running, but it was the furthest you were allowed to run at that time.

What was your time at this point?

I ran 2.10.2 in 1960, which was the third fastest in the country. However, I finished fourth in the trials. I didn't really like track running and preferred cross-country at that stage. The International Cross-Country

Championships came about in 1967, but I had already been running for 13 years by then!

Was it very frustrating for you at the time?

Well, it wasn't there, so it was just something you accepted. In the winter of 1970/1971, I started training twice a day because my first daughter was at playschool. That was the first winter I started training seriously, and I won the International Cross-Country Championships in 1972. I then converted my form to the track and made the Olympics over 1500m, which was going into the Games for the first time. I look back and think that was still my most outstanding performance. I was 34 and ran 4.11 in the heats, which was a PB and British record. I got through to the semi-finals and came sixth with another British record, but I didn't make the final. I ran 4.09.37. I never dreamed that I would go to an Olympic Games. I then moved up to 3000m in 1974 because that was in the European Championships for the first time. In 1975, I was injured a lot and in 1976 I moved back down to the 1500m because it was an Olympic year again. However, I became pregnant and so that put pay to that. After having Leah, I found track difficult. I was also 38/39 by this time, and I wanted to do a marathon purely to see what it was like.

Why do you think track became more difficult? Was it a mental or physical thing?

Leah never slept through the night until she was three years old, and it was the first winter I got up early to train before Brian, my husband, went to work. I coped with it all winter, but by the time the track season came round it had taken its toll on me, and I ended up with a stress fracture of the foot in my last track international. So I thought I'd try the marathon. It was starting to be talked about for women, and there had already been a British Championship on the Isle of Wight in 1978, which Margaret Lockley had won. In 1979, it was held in Sandbach. Avon had come into the sport by then, and they did a whole circuit. Also, through Katherine Switzer, they wanted to get a women's marathon into the Olympics. So in 1979, every country in which Avon sold products had to send someone to their Avon International, and I got sent to Germany with two others. Brian ended up becoming race director for their full circuit, and we had some 10km and 10 mile races that year.

So, 1979 was the year of your first marathon?

Yes, Sandbach. I won it in 2.41 and knocked nine minutes off of the British best. I then went to the Avon International in Germany and won that in 2.36.

How much gap was there between them?

Not a lot. Looking back on my marathon career, I probably did too many marathons too close together. The Japanese were at the Avon International, and they were keen to promote women's races, so they invited me to Japan in November 1979, which was only two months later. I went, and I won it in 2.37. It was from there that marathon running really took off for me. I started travelling the world when I'd thought I might just do one and retire.

Did you do any road races before the marathon?

Yes, I did 10 miles. We didn't have many 10km or other races to choose from at this time. Half-marathons came in later, and I started doing them then.

What about road relays?

I would still turn out in the Southern and National Road Relays and try to run the fastest lap.

Did you know before doing the marathon that you had the ability to run the distance?

In the winter of 1971/1972, I was training with the boys down at the track, and we used to go out for a 10-mile run. They were good sessions, and they used to say to me that if I could run road races, I'd be very good. However, there just weren't any to do. I actually did an inter-club five-mile road race at Alperton at one point, but somebody saw me, and I got told off for running in a men's race.

So, after you did the three marathons in quick succession, did you stop and think how you could run them even better?

No, I was just so overawed with all the invites coming in. I went to Miami in January 1980 and blacked out in that one, which scared me. I was dehydrated because it was very hot. So as I knew I was going to return to Tokyo in November 1980, I did Sandbach again in June to get my confidence back, and to make sure that I was OK. I got down to 2.33 and then to 2.30 in November.

How many marathons did you do before your PB?

My best was in London in 1981, which was my seventh. However, although my two London Marathons were my best times, I still think my second Tokyo Marathon in 1980 was my best race. It was a women's only race run under very strict championship-like conditions, and it was a race from the word go. We actually went through 10 miles in 54 minutes. However, it was very windy, and as we turned and hit the wind, we slowed. I still ended up with 2.30.27 though, which stood as the course record until Rosa Mota ran it.

How long before a marathon did you decide to do it?

Well, the first one came off of the back of the track. I said I wasn't looking to do track any more and that I wanted to run a marathon. We looked to do one the following year, so I had the whole of the winter through to the following June to build up for it.

So, it was about nine months then?

Yes. I then took them as the invites came along. After London in 1982, the European Marathon came in, but I got injured and had to pull out of the team. Then in 1983, we found out that the marathon was going to be in the World Championship's programme, so we knew I was going to do that. However, because I came out of 1982 injured, I went to Osaka in 1983 to run. I wouldn't do London again because the physio had said that my 1982 injury had been caused by the cobbles on the course. Following this, I did the Avon International in LA in 1983, which was on the 1984 Olympic course, and then I ran both the World Championships and Olympic Games.

In hindsight, do you think you should have done fewer marathons and turned some of them down?

I don't know because my age was always against me at this point. I was looking back the other day. In 1984, I did one before the Olympics, followed by the Olympics itself, and then Paris and New York all within three months, and I came out injured. However, by that time, I knew if I didn't do New York, then I'd never do it because I was going to be retiring from top-class marathon running. We always had a 13-week build-up before a serious marathon, and I would start that after having had a bit of a rest although being that I was always at a reasonably high level of fitness, I never went into that build-up totally unprepared.

What was a typical training week in a build-up to a marathon?

My average was between 70 to 90 miles a week. I'd do a couple of 70 plus weeks and then go up to a 90. I never went over 100 miles a week.

How long was your long run?

At the beginning of my build-up, I'd do 12 miles on a Wednesday morning, gradually increasing that to 15 to 18 miles, and on a Saturday I started with a 12 miler and increased that to 25. I went over distance once before the Olympics in 1984 when I did 30 miles. We brought that in as Ian Thompson had done it once. I did it on a hot day, so I thought if I could do that, then I could run 26 miles on a hot day at the Olympics. Personally, I think doing 25 milers gives you the confidence that you can do the distance. On a Wednesday, I would do 15 miles, get back to my front door, and then immediately turn round and do another hard three.

How fast was the long run before those three miles?

About 6 to 6.15 minute miling. I ran as I felt, but I did check my watch because I was running on my own and had check marks. On my 20-mile runs, I would try, if I was running well, to do it in under two hours but not every week though. I'd also have a day's rest before that run.

What quality work would you fit in around those long runs?

I'd do a track session on a Tuesday. It would be reps of miles or 800m and things like that.

Were they fast?

In the winter of 1983/1984, I was looking to do the mile reps on the track in five minutes.

How many?

Five. For the 800m reps, I would get down to 2.22 to 2.24 and do about six of them.

What was the recovery between them?

I'd do a lap jog in about three minutes between the miles and 800m reps, and it would be a 200m jog or a minute for the 400m reps. The mile was the longest rep we did on the track.

Did you do any sessions on the road?

We used to do another stride session on a path where the last 100m goes up over the M1 motorway. We'd do 600m and 1000m reps there instead of on the track.

So, you only did one quality session a week?

Yes.

Did you do any hills or fartlek?

I did hills specifically in 1983 because we knew that there were 36 hills in the World Championships marathon in Helsinki.

Were your other days easy?

Monday was eight miles, Tuesday was a run in the morning and track in the evening, and Wednesday was the slow build-up to a long run with occasionally another short run in the evening. Thursday was two runs although before the Olympic year, we brought in three runs: eight miles in the morning, five miles at lunchtime and three miles in the evening - all hopefully getting faster. Friday was a rest day, Saturday was a long run with occasionally another shorter run in the evening and Sunday was one run of around 15 miles or something like that.

Did you do absolutely nothing on your rest day?

Yes, I did nothing. I liked a rest day, and I caught up with all the housework and shopping.

Did you do any other forms of training like weights?

No, I just did some sits-ups and press-ups in the evenings before I went to bed. I'm not a good swimmer.

What races did you do in a build-up?

I definitely did a half-marathon where it would fit in, and I did the Belgrave 20 one year. There weren't many to choose from to fit in at the right time. I'd also do a 10 miler in there somewhere.

Did you treat them all as races?

I would treat them as races, and generally my mileage would be down that week. It would go down to around 60 or 70 miles.

How did you taper for a marathon?

I would taper down the last two weeks. However, before the 1984 Olympics, I went out and did a 20-mile run on the Sunday before the race. I did the diet, so I was depleting as well. I then did practically nothing for the rest of the week.

Do you think that the diet worked?

I think it did when I ran Tokyo in 1980 because I was stronger towards the end. I didn't do it for my best two times in London though. It never gave me any ill effects. I did it six days before: three days of just protein and three days of carbohydrate loading.

Did you do any more track races while you were doing marathons?

Brian put on a 10,000m track race at Barnet Copthall when the distance came in for women. It was on a cold Wednesday night a couple of nights after the National Cross-Country Championships. There were about 20 starters, and we made it into a team race to get clubs to turn up. Kathryn Binns won it and went on to run the European Championships. It was the only 10,000m I did on the track.

What time did you run?

Thirty-four minutes-something. It was cold and windy, but the times were very good considering. Kathryn did thirty-three-something, which was a British record at the time.

What are your PBs for the track distances?

My PBs are 2.08.08 for 800m, 4.09.37 for 1500m - set at the Olympics - and 8.55.6 for 3000m, which I did just before going to the European Championships.

Did you ever do a 5000m?

No, there weren't any really. I don't even consider that I reached my potential at 3000m because I did that in 1974 and then moved back down to 1500m to try to make the Olympics again. After that, I had a baby and didn't get back for a year. In 1978, I returned to the 3000m, but by then it was too late. I think I could have run 8.40ish. I ran the 8.55 on my own and slowed in the second half.

What times did you run for 10 miles and half-marathon?

My best for 10 miles was 53.17 and for half-marathon, 71.45. I think if I was in my 30s now with what is around, I would have been even better. I didn't train very hard at the beginning of my athletics career – only later on. In my second London Marathon, I thought I could run 2.27 going on how my training had gone. However, at the last minute on the Wednesday, Chris Brasher threw Lorraine Moller into the race. She had run eight marathons and had never been beaten, so whereas I was going to go for a time, I decided to go for the win. Lorraine put herself on my shoulder straight away, but after two-and-a-half miles I decided that she wasn't going to stay there for 26, and I took off. I didn't want to lose *and* end up with a slow time! I did it a bit too fast though, and at 25 miles my legs just absolutely went. I hate seeing myself coming across Westminster Bridge. I still did a slight PB, but I was on for 2.27 at 25 miles.

Did you use any form of mental preparation?

Well, before the Olympics in 1984, I cried my eyes out in the morning and was asking myself what I was doing there. I was so nervous. I also remember being very nervous in 1974 before the European Championships because I was second or third fastest in the world and felt under pressure. However, I did nothing specifically for the marathons.

What about during races?

When I was running well, I always found that a marathon went very quickly. You have your feed stations every 5km, and you are watching what other people are doing and that sort of thing. I used to tell myself to keep relaxed. It is surprising how quickly they can go. I remember before the Olympics in 1984 that everyone was saying how hot and smoggy it was going to be, and that it would get worse as the race went on. It was that year that Brian brought in the hard three to five-mile runs after longer runs in order to get used to it being harder at the end. I recall in the actual race coming up to where we went over the freeway, and the pace was beginning to pick up. I decided that I would have to let them go. I knew I would come back stronger

311

later. I just didn't dare go with them at that time. I was conscious of my age, being 46, and that I couldn't finish looking bad. I was also aware that I had been picked over Veronique, who had run 30 seconds quicker than I had in Helsinki. I was picked over her because they said the course was harder and that I had more experience. So, I did have those two pressures on me in 1984. It turned out that I did feel strong at the end, and in the last six miles I passed a lot of people who had gone with the pace at the time I had decided not to. I did the right thing, but I will never know if I would have been able to cope had I gone with them.

Did you ever have any really bad marathons?

Yes, the one in Miami in 1980 where I collapsed due to dehydration. I started to weave, and two men took me over the line. I was later disqualified. I didn't know that had happened to me and woke up in bed. I just saw it on film afterwards. There was also my very last race in Twin Cities, which was a personal worst. It started at seven thirty in the morning, and it was absolutely freezing. I took over 42 minutes to do the last six miles. I was in a bad way.

Was Brian always your coach?

When I started with Hampstead Harriers, I had the club coach there, and then Harry Hicks started coaching me

312

for a little while. Later, when I began going out with Brian, he started coaching me.

Did you do most of your training on your own or in a group?

Tuesday night track training was always with a group. It included some women, but it was mostly men, and it was usually so big and the standard so wide that you could run as hard or as easy as you wanted. You just slotted in where you wanted to be within the group. However, a lot of my marathon training, like the long runs, was done on my own although Brian would come out on the bike for some of them. When I did women only races, being on my own probably helped. However, fast times come from mixed races.

Did you use altitude or warm-weather training?

The only time I used altitude training was in early March before the 1972 Olympics. They took a group of us, who were doing from 800m upwards, out to St Moritz for a week to see how we coped with it. Originally, I hadn't been invited because I hadn't shown any form on the track, but when I won the International Cross-Country that year, they suddenly helped me.

Did you find it beneficial?

I don't know. I think it was just having three weeks of good training and recovery in a relaxed environment. In

April 1984, we went to La Santa for warm-weather training. However, we also had a good summer in the UK that year, so I went from warm-weather training early on and just kept it going. The whole Evian Marathon squad went to Athens and Spain in 1982.

Did you work full-time?

I worked full-time right up until I had my first daughter in 1968, and then I went part-time doing two days a week. I did office work; I was a wages clerk. I stayed there until Lisa was five and about to start school, and then I realised that I wouldn't be able to take her to school on those two days. So I got a local part-time job in Watford. I worked 20 hours a week from 11.00 A.M. to 3.00 P.M. every day. I used to take her to school and train, and then pick her up from school and train again in the evening. It was perfect actually.

Were you ever a full-time athlete?

No, I always had a job. As a teacher, Brian had school holidays, so he was around quite a lot. I don't think it has worked for those who have given up their jobs to become full-time athletes. People like Jack Holden had manual jobs, and he used to run to work and back. He was on a 100 miles way back then.

Did you have any sponsorship or financial assistance?

I was sponsored by Puma for shoes before the 1972 Olympics, in fact, from around 1965. That was purely because Derek Ibbotson was the Puma rep in the UK, and his first wife, Madeline Wooller, who was another Middlesex runner, raced against me quite a lot. He gave me stuff right the way through until 1981. So all my first marathons were in Puma. I then started to get injured, and while I was in Japan for the first time, Asics took a lot of photographs and researched the pressures on athletes' feet, as they were looking to bring in better shoes and get into the market. When they heard about my injuries, they sent me two pairs of shoes to try because they said that the problems might have been due to my current shoes. So I tried them, and I liked them. I then went back to Derek and explained what had happened. He told me to go to them because Puma didn't have marathon shoes. At first, it was purely shoes and kit, but when I found out in 1983 that some people who I was beating were being paid to wear Asics kit, and I wasn't, I decided to look elsewhere. At that time, I was friendly with Mel Batty of Brooks. He asked me if I'd like to come over to them and offered me something. I said no, but I was then able to go back to Asics and tell them what I'd been offered. They immediately responded and gave me a contract. However, if I didn't make the Olympic Games or a big race, they could come and ask me to do a race that they wanted me to do. After 1984, I retired from internationals, but I carried on running marathons for another two years, as there were promoters who still wanted me in a race. I'd tell them I'd only run 2.42/2.43, but they still wanted me to run. I didn't get any money from Asics for that, but I still got gear.

Did you ever get appearance money?

That began in those two years, and that was the only time I earned any money from starting.

As well as prize money?

I didn't get any prize money in Tokyo or London. I won a watch for both of my London's. The first money came in the third year although I have since found out that they did pay money from 1982. Lorraine got money, but I didn't, and that is one of the reasons I never did London any more. I didn't do London in 1983 and 1984 because everyone thought that I had got money, and I hadn't. Mike Gratton was third that year, and both he and Hugh Jones got money. They were surprised I didn't. It was unfair.

Did you have any other forms of financial assistance?

Only from the Evian Marathon squad. We didn't get any money personally, but they supported us. We had trips abroad and regular weekends together for training throughout the year. I think that was one of the reasons why the depth was more outstanding then. To get into the Evian marathon squad was the first step for a female runner. In Japan, I probably picked up $3000 for a couple of my races and that was a lot to me. However, the first years I went there, I used to pick up presents. It was nearly always jewellery, such as pearls, gold, etc. I guess they were probably worth quite a bit though.

Was there anything special about your diet?

Not really. I just ate a normal, balanced diet with meat, fish, vegetables, etc.

Did you suffer from anaemia?

No, but I took iron tablets. It was just something I always did. However, when I was up in St Moritz in 1972, they tested us and said I was a bit anaemic, so they put me on extra iron. They caught it before it got too bad. I still take iron tablets now although not all the time. I might take three in one week, or something like that, just to keep my iron levels up. I also used to have a friend in Robinsons Barley, so I got free drinks.

What did you drink in the marathon?

When I was serious, I would have Robinsons Lemon Barley, but it was very diluted. It was mostly just water. I used to have my own personal bottles. They were those little hairspray bottles you can get from Boots.

They would take a whole glass of water and you could squeeze them, so you didn't choke. Also, because they were so small, you could to carry them for quite a way. I would always have bright purple ones to make them easy to pick out.

Did you always have a high fluid intake?

After I collapsed in Miami through dehydration, I did. Every marathon after that, even if it were cool, I would drink. I don't drink much water at home though, just when I am training.

What was your racing weight, and what is your height?

My best races were when I was 7 stone 10. I am five-foot six-and-a-half. In the winter, I used to be around 8 stone 3, but when I was racing well, I'd go under 8 stone. I didn't think that I had to get down to 7 stone 10, but it just sort of happened naturally as I peaked.

What were your sleep patterns and rest like?

I am not a good sleeper. I think that comes from having children. You become a light sleeper because you have to get up in the night when you hear any movements and to feed. Leah didn't sleep through the night until she was three years old. I also cannot sleep when I go away and am in a strange bed. In fact, in 1972, I had to take sleeping tablets in St Moritz because my sleep was so poor and whenever I went to a Games or Tokyo I would take them.

So, you were never an eight hours a night person?

Never!

Did you have regular massage or anything like that?

Only when injured.

Did you get many illnesses or injuries throughout your career?

I was injured after the London Marathon in 1981, and I was injured in 1982 with a stress fracture of the pelvis for something like 14 weeks. I've had quite a few stress fractures at different times. I never got that many colds and have probably been quite a healthy person most of my life.

Do you have any thoughts and opinions as to why marathon standards haven't gone up?

This is a question I get asked a lot, and I honestly don't know. I don't know if people aren't training as hard. I think I did train harder than some are now, but I think my ability allowed me to. Priscilla and Veronique both trained harder than me. They were doing 120 miles a week. It seems that right the way through, from the track distances to the marathon, times are static. The only thing I can think of is the Evian squad. Perhaps there are also too many road races now, and people are doing too many other bits and pieces.

[Brian enters the room, and so I ask him the same question.]

Basically, people aren't doing the right training, and they haven't got the right background. The other point is that you now only have to break 2.50 to get an international vest, but in those days you had to break 2.35. It's the same with British 400m running - peer pressure. People don't set their standards high enough. They think that because they are the best in Britain, it will take them to a championship, but it's not good enough. They seem to forget that in those days there was a standard to get in. Now they are dropping behind world standards and moan when they don't get in. I think there was a different attitude as well. When we had the Evian squad, people used to train and work together. That has disappeared; now there are just individuals.

Charlie Spedding

PB: 2.08.33 – London 1985

Highest World Ranking in the 1980s: 6th

Marathon Achievements:

Winner - Houston Marathon 1984

Winner - London Marathon 1984

Bronze - Los Angeles Olympics 1984

2nd - London Marathon 1985

3rd - Chicago Marathon 1986

6th - Seoul Olympics 1988

How did you become involved in athletics?

My very first recollection of any type of race was at junior school. I would have been six or something like that. It was a handicap race in the school sports' and as it was based on height, and I was the shortest, I got the most start. As we lined up, I thought I could win it, but I finished dead last. It was a 100 yards race, and I couldn't sprint at all. I was devastated. So that was my first introduction to athletics, and it wasn't a very good one. Despite that early sporting setback, I was always interested in lots of sports, especially football, and I spent loads of time kicking a ball against a wall. I always wanted to be outside. Later, when I was about 11, we had compulsory cross-country runs and probably due to that earlier experience I decided that I was going to try really hard. Most of them didn't want to do it; they would only run until they were out of sight of the teacher and then walk or take short cuts. However, I wanted to try hard because I didn't want to be humiliated again. I did really well, and it was the first success I had in any sports. So, I went from hating it to liking it straight away. I also learnt the very important lesson of being immediately rewarded for the effort I put in. I had a very positive experience, and it went from there. I was still involved in a lot of other sport, and I wasn't serious about running but because of that first success I tried hard every time we had those races, and I even won some of them. There were one or two guys that were quite good at school, in fact, they possibly had a lot of talent, and there was one guy in particular who could always beat me if he bothered, but they didn't try as hard. When I was 13 or 14, I started to run a bit better, and I got involved in some track races at school. I also continued with the cross-country and was doing well in inter-school competitions. However, I was still enjoying other sports like rugby and cricket. It wasn't until I was 16 that I really concentrated on running. A new teacher came to our school fresh from Loughborough University. His name was Nick Willings, and he broke new ground by really encouraging athletics. He personally encouraged me, and eventually I joined Gateshead Harriers. From then on, I was a runner.

Were you doing any road at this point?

We ran quite a lot of road races in the winter, for in the North East at that point we not only had a senior men's race but also races for youths and boys. There were shorter races for different age groups, and I used to run over three or four miles. A 10km is too far when you are 16 or 17. They don't have these types of races so much now.

How did you progress from there?

I was running road races, and 1500m and 3000m on the track. I ran 3.45.03 for 1500m and 4.03.05 for the mile. It wasn't bad, but it wasn't good enough. I had to work at it, as I didn't have the basic speed. After a while, I felt I had fulfilled my potential, and so I moved up to 5000m where I finished third in the AAA's in 1976.

Had you had any successes at English Schools' Championships?

Yes, I was second in the 1500m. However, this was only because I had made a mess of my A-Levels and was back at school for another year. I was quite old and right at the end of the age group. That was one of the first big races where I ran really well, and I started to think that I liked the big events and championships. I noticed fairly quickly that a lot of guys who had been beating me in that age group disappeared.

So, at what age did you move up to 5000m and 10,000m?

Well, I had quite a lot of injuries and operations on my Achilles' tendons, so I had a few years that were messed up. It took quite a while. It was in 1980 or 1981 at the

323

age of 28 that I ran my first 10,000m. I had a spell from 1980 to 1985 where I didn't have any injuries and that was the period of my greatest success. I won the AAA's 10,000m in 1983, finished fourth in the Commonwealth Games 10,000m in 1982 and was eighth in the European Championships. I was pretty good, but I just didn't have enough basic speed to run on the track. If there were anyone with me with a lap to go, I would often be beaten.

So, is that why you decided to move up to the marathon?

I had thought about it for a few years, but after talking it over with Lindsay Dunn, who whilst not my coach I had a close relationship with, I decided not to at that point. Lindsay persuaded me to wait a bit longer and until I had fulfilled my potential over 10,000m. I ran the AAA's in my last year at 10,000m and won it. However, it wasn't the trial for the World Championships, and I missed the qualifying time by three seconds. After that, I thought it was time to move up to the marathon. I had always wanted to run at the Olympics and so as it was the Olympic Games the following year I decided to go for it and started searching for a marathon to test the event. I chose Houston, which was in January, on account of the fact that it would give me plenty of time to prepare for the 10,000m trial if I should find that the event wasn't for me. It had also been won in 2.11/2.12,

324

which was a decent time but not too fast. I didn't want to be in a race that was won in 2.08 for my first one, as I wanted to be competitive. I was pretty sure that I could run around 2.11, and if I couldn't, then the marathon wasn't for me. Anyway, it went really well, and I won it, bizarrely with a sprint finish. It was a flat-out sprint, and I had spent my whole life being outsprinted. I won by about a foot in 2.11.54 and made up my mind straight away that this was the event for me.

How old were you by this time?

I was 31.

How many marathons did you run before you set your PB?

It was my fourth.

How long before marathons did you decide to do them? Did you have a meticulous plan?

I had a specific plan, and it was 12 weeks. I wanted to be in reasonable shape when I started it, and it was designed to really build me up to a peak for the race. I found having a specific 12-week period helped me mentally as well. It concentrated my mind and focused me on the event.

How many marathons did you do a year?

I averaged two marathons a year.

What was a typical training week in a build-up to a marathon?

I would run about 90 miles a week, which I know is less than most. I would do 75 to 80 on average and one long run on a Sunday. I would do that just about all year round even when I was running 3000m and 5000m on the track. The long run would usually be two hours or at least an hour-and-a-half. A typical week would be easier days on Monday, Wednesday and Friday where I would run twice but not particularly hard and not particularly far either. I'd maybe do a five and a seven or a five and an eight. They were recovery days.

What was easy to you?

It wasn't jogging, but it wasn't running hard. It would be between 6 and 6.15-minute mile pace or something like that. I was flowing along without it being hard. It wasn't intense at all. It was still training, but I thought of these as my recovery days. On Sunday, I would typically do two hours at probably 6.30-minute mile pace. It would be around 18 to 19 miles. On Thursday, I would usually just run once. I'd do 15 miles at maybe 5.40-minute mile pace. It would be deliberately brisk but not hammering myself at all; it wouldn't be really hard. On Tuesday, there would be a track session of some sort. One of the harder ones I did was 5 x 1 mile at about 4.40 pace - 70 seconds a lap - with one lap recovery in 90 seconds, so you'd end up running a 10km in 31 or 32 minutes. It was hard, and it was a session that was an important gauge for me. If I handled that well, then I thought everything was going well. On Saturday, there would be some other sort of session. Occasionally, it would be on the track, but more often or not it would be on the grass or a railway line. I would try to go somewhere else for variety, and it would usually be something shorter and sharper. I might do hills, fartlek or short recovery stuff. Closer to the race, when I was trying to peak, I would do some shorter reps quite quickly. I wouldn't go for pure speed, but they would be fast with short recovery in order to really work on heart rate and coping with lactate.

What was the longest run you did in a build-up to a marathon?

Three or four weeks before the marathon, I would run about 28 miles. I used to do it once and thought it was very important both psychologically and physiologically. I think you need to know all the systems on an enzyme energy producing level that you get down to in the last stages of a marathon. You've never asked your body to do that sort of thing unless you have been for a long-distance run. The rest of the time though, 20 miles was enough.

Was most of your training done on your own or in a group?

Being in Gateshead, I was brought on a great deal by the group. However, once I started training for the marathon, it was very specific to me. I would train with people when I could, but the bulk of my training was on my own. The 15-mile run was done on my own because it had to be done at my pace, but the long runs were often done with a group. Sometimes I did them by myself, and I think you should always be capable of doing them alone. I much preferred to do speed sessions with other people, but it depended on what the other guys were doing. If I was doing more general stuff on the track, and the guys were doing something similar, then I'd happily do that because it wasn't that important. However, when it got to my specific marathon training, they had to either fit in with me, or I would do it by myself. I usually did the 5 x 1 mile session on my own though because it was not easy to find someone to do it with me.

Were you also a top 10km runner at the same time as you were doing marathons?

Before London in 1984, I ran my best 10km and won the AAA's in 1983. After marathons, I used to try to get back to my 10km running, but I never ran particularly well on the track again. I did the training, but I think it was a mental thing. My heart wasn't in it any more because by then I knew I was a marathon runner. I was still one of the main guys over 10km, but as the years went on, and I started to run more marathons and started getting injuries again, the speed went. I was getting older as well; it got harder to recreate that speed.

How did you usually taper for a marathon?

I used to keep training quite hard until eight or nine days before. The Sunday prior to the race, I'd just do 15 miles and on the Monday, a five and a seven. On Tuesday, I might do six fast quarters with a good recovery. I just used to go to the track and run fast with plenty of recovery purely to turn my legs over quickly. On Wednesday, I would do a couple of five-mile runs and on Thursday and Friday, one five miles. Saturday was a total rest day. So, in the last three days before the race, I would only do a total of 10 miles, and I'd do the diet. I wouldn't do the depletion phase; I would just do the loading.

Did you ever try it?

No, I just made sure that I had a wholesome, balanced diet with plenty of fresh fruit and vegetables, and ample carbohydrate. It would just be a typical diet. I think it becomes negative if you become too wound up with that kind of stuff. I would eat whatever I liked. However, in my mind I knew what was a good diet and

329

what I should be eating. The last three days, I would eat more than usual and greatly increase the carbohydrate.

Did you take any supplements?

I would take them occasionally but not religiously.

What was your fluid intake like?

It wasn't drummed into you at all, but I was aware of it, and I was certainly very careful with it during the last week or two. Maybe I wasn't as careful with it during the training. If I were thirsty, I would drink.

What did you drink during marathons?

I just drank water. I thought water was the most important thing I needed. I also didn't want the worry of having to find *my* drink because it is actually quite difficult to find your own bottle on a table full of bottles when you are running at 12 miles an hour. You don't even want to slow down to get it. So I just used to have plenty of cups of water. I preferred not to think about it. I drank at most feed stations.

Did you have set races in your build-up to a marathon?

Yes. I used to get a large piece of paper, draw a line on it and put in the date of the race. I would start by filling in the specific sessions I wanted to do, such as the extra long run and some other ones that I did in order that I had the right recovery between them, and then I would fit in the races. I would have that plan all on one piece of paper. I'd have specific sessions and specific races, and then I'd build in the rest of the training. Obviously, it could change, but it was very important for me mentally to have that plan laid out. It said to me that all I had to do to run a great marathon was laid out on that chart. As each day went by, I would cross the day off. It became like a self-fulfilling prophecy. It was important because it didn't actually matter how well I ran in the races.

What was your attitude to these races?

Well, I would slightly taper for all of them, but the more I developed the system, the worse I ran in all my build-up races. It got to the point where I was running atrociously. Before the Olympics in 1984, and even more so in 1988, I ran some competitively bad races. It was a mental thing; I couldn't dig deep. I would run as hard as I could within my frame of mind, and my mind was saying that there were bigger things to come. Because I believed so much in the programme I was doing, my mind was fixed on that day at the end when I was going to give everything. Subconsciously, it was saying that I didn't want to empty the tanks on that day for that race, as I was saving myself for something bigger. As long as I had a go, it didn't bother me at all though, and I just used to dismiss it. However, sometimes I surprised myself how badly I ran.

So, were there set distances that you liked to run?

I used to like to run a 5-mile or a 10km race as my last one a week or two weeks beforehand. I would also run a couple of 10 milers or half-marathons. I wouldn't bother about whether it was one or the other. I didn't have anything cast in stone about running a half-marathon the way other people seem to. It is only three miles further than a 10 miler, and in any case, a half-marathon doesn't tell you anything about how you are going to run over a marathon. It is a different event altogether. So, I would probably race once every three weeks and a couple of short ones as well.

Did you use any mental techniques before or during a marathon?

I used to do it a lot when I was out on easier runs. I would think about the race and visualise it. As the marathon got closer, I'd also sit down by myself, close my eyes and specifically think through the stages of the race. I'd try to visualise myself running really well at various points, especially in the latter stages around 20 miles or after. I would feel myself there; I would feel myself going through the 20-mile mark tired but striding out really strongly. I used to get a really good picture of that. I didn't visualise the finish though because then you are making a prediction about what is going to happen. I am sure a lot of people visualise when they are out running, but I used to sit down and do it as well. I also had some sort of plan as to how I was going to run the race and what was likely to happen although you have to be flexible. If there were African guys in there who always tended to go off at 2.05 pace for the first 10 miles, I would decide that I was only going to go at such and such a pace and no quicker. I would plan like that. However, you can only have a very rough plan for the first half of a marathon. I would never plan anything beyond halfway because it is a race, and you have to respond in a race.

What about during the race?

Just before the race started, or even during the last couple of days, I used to avoid thinking about how far it was to the finish and how far there was to go. I just used to imagine that I was going running and there wasn't an end; that I'd have to run as efficiently and smoothly as possible because I was going to have to keep doing it. I didn't divide it up, as otherwise I'd go through 5 miles and think there were 21 miles to go. I didn't even think how far there was to go until I got beyond halfway. I would then change at some point after this, depending on how I was going, and go into race mode. You don't want to do that too soon. I used to be mentally, as well as physically, exhausted after marathons because I had concentrated so hard on putting one foot in front of the other as efficiently as possible. It was a big strain.

Did you do any other forms of training like weights?

I did some sit-ups and press-ups, and a little bit of upper body exercise, but that was as far as it got. If I was starting out again, I would probably do more, simply due to the fact that while your arms are not carrying any weight, they are moving backwards and forwards as many times as your legs. To run efficiently, you've also got to hold your body up straight, as when you slump you don't stride out as far. Therefore, maybe some stomach and torso work is useful too.

Were you coached during your career?

Early on, yes. The schoolteacher I previously mentioned gave me a bit of coaching, and then I joined Gateshead Harriers and had some coaching there. It was just a club coach and wasn't particularly personal. It gave me direction though. I then went to live in London for a year with my work and coached myself. When I went back to the North East, I continued to coach myself, but I also used to chat to Lindsay [Dunn]. He was part of the running group there and was coaching a lot of people. I would talk things over with him, and then later on I would sit down with him and discuss my goals. He would help me come up with a plan. I would also sometimes go to him for specific sessions. One of the things he was great at, both when I was running 10,000m and the marathon, was turning up to the track for a session and not telling me what I'd be doing. I would turn up, do a warm-up, jog to the start line and only then would he tell me. Sometimes, it would be to run at 72 seconds pace until he told me to stop. You had no idea for how long, and you didn't even know when the session was going to finish. He would have me exhausted, jog a bit and then back to the line again before saying the session was over. The sessions were really good and helped me to race because all his sessions would have surges in them. They were great for race simulation. He was very good at that. Obviously, those were sessions you couldn't coach yourself to do. You cannot do a session where you don't know what you are doing if you are the one setting it. I also picked up bits talking and listening to other people, which is something I don't think runners do so much now. I don't understand that.

Did you ever use warm-weather or altitude training?

When I was on the track, I tried altitude training in Kenya. I found it useful, as it helps you cope with oxygen debt. However, I didn't see any point for the marathon. It is harder to run at the same intensity when you are at altitude, and personally I would prefer to run the sessions at the quality I wanted to run. Warm-weather training is important; especially as a lot of the championship marathons are held in ridiculous conditions. Before the Los Angeles Olympics, which was 85 degrees or something like that, I went to Boston for six weeks. It was actually hotter and more humid in Boston than it was in Los Angeles, and so when I got there I felt fine and had acclimatised. I generally used it when I needed to acclimatise. I also used to go to Portugal quite often in November just for a change and to be able to do some sessions in shorts rather than two tracksuits and a hat.

Did you work full-time throughout your running career?

I went to college to study pharmacy and qualified as a pharmacist. I then went to work at a hospital in London for a year before going back to the North East. My father was also a pharmacist and had his own business, so I worked there full-time. When I got to about 27 or 28, I'd been running alright but felt that I hadn't fulfilled what I really wanted to do. I was also finding it very difficult to work all day and then go out for a second run when I was tired. You do it, but you don't really get the benefit. I therefore made a big decision to totally commit myself to running. My dad was ready for retiring, and I realised that he was only really hanging on for me, so I told him that I didn't want to take over the business and that I wanted to go off and concentrate on my running. He had his business sold within three months. I knew some people in Boston, and I went there for a year. I don't know if it was Boston, making the commitment to running or the fact that I changed my training slightly when I got there, or perhaps it was all three of those things combined, but it transformed my running career. When I came back, Nike were starting up business in Britain. Brendan Foster was in charge, and so I got a job with them. It was a full-time job, but the hours were more flexible. Therefore, if I wanted to go for a 15-mile or two hour-run at lunchtime, I could. As long as I got my work done, it didn't matter. Later on, I became more part-time and was the kit man. I signed up runners and supplied them with kit. I actually travelled around quite a lot and went to all the race meetings. However, it was a problem at times because I would go to races where I was running myself, and while I was warming up everyone was nagging me for kit. That didn't particularly work although the being more flexible for training did.

Did you have any sponsorship or financial assistance?

Looking back, I was probably foolish to work for Nike. They were paying me to do a job when they probably would have paid me the same amount of money to wear the kit. However, I started working for them at a time when I hadn't really achieved anything. I was getting free kit, but I didn't get a contract and bonuses until later. What I did get from them though was a year off. After the Olympics in 1984, I went back to America for a year, and they continued to pay my salary. It was like a sabbatical.

So, did you also get bonuses, appearance and prize money?

Yes.

Did you ever get to the point where you thought you could live on this and retire?

No, it never got that good. This was the early 1980s, and there still wasn't much money around. It was fine when I went from earning nothing to winning money; it was great, but when I look at what today's athletes earn it was nothing really. I started my career in the early 1970s and that just wasn't an option at all. I always thought of my running as a sport and not a profession. I always wanted to do it, and I was always motivated by trying to see what I could achieve. Championships were what I was interested in. They motivated me. I don't think athletes today achieve in championships because they are trying to make a living, and they have to compromise their plans. For instance, the plan that I mentioned earlier would not be possible, as most guys would have to fit in a certain number of races to pay them a certain amount of money. The really good guys now make huge amounts of money. I could have certainly made more money than I did, but I was not that way inclined. I wanted to do championships.

How tall are you, and what was your racing weight?

I am just under five-foot nine or five-foot eight-and-a-half, and I think I was about 10 stone. I would be a shade under for a marathon.

Why do you think you and the others in the 1980s were so good?

For me, it was always trying to banish the horrible feeling of coming last in that handicap race as a kid. I had an inner drive, and I wanted to find out how good I could be. When I reached one level, I was always trying to reach the next. It was to do with personal satisfaction. It wasn't the money that was a driving force at all. It was nice when I got it, but it wasn't my motivation, which is why, as I said previously, I probably didn't make more. It was about trying to achieve and fulfil a dream. I was 32 when I went to the Olympic Games. I had been running for 16 years, which was half my life, and I had always wanted to go to the Olympics. It was a dream; it is what drove me. I was also lucky that I was in Gateshead Harriers from an early age. When I first joined, we had international runners there like John Caine and Brendan Foster, who were going to the Commonwealth Games. These were the people I was training with, and I think it was important because straight away I had this influence and mind-set that you become a good runner and go off to major championships. It was the peer group thing. I think the big problem we have now is that the standard of distance running is so low, and there is none of that. You can be a big star running relatively poorly. I think that is the reason the Kenyans do so well because to be any good in Kenya, you have to be world class. When they see the guys down the road, who they went to school with, running 2.08 for a marathon, they think they can do it too, and they go and run it. I am sure that they train hard and all the rest of it, but I believe very strongly that the most important thing in achieving performance is really wanting to do it. To really perform well, you have to believe you can do it. It took me a long time to believe that I could do it; a long time to reach the level where I had done enough in races and training to believe that I could run really well. Another important point to make is that I think a lot of people nowadays want to prove that they can produce the performance before they go and run it in the race, and for me that is completely wrong. In my opinion, the race is the place that gives you the opportunity to do better than you have ever done before. When I went to the Olympics, it was only my third marathon, but I was absolutely convinced that I would run one of the greatest races of my life because it was the Olympic Games. I thought that if I couldn't run my greatest race at the Olympics, when I had dreamed about it all my life, then there was something badly wrong. It just seemed obvious to me that I would run great whereas so many people succumbed to the pressure of it being the Olympics, and it had a really negative effect on them. My approach was that this was the day I had been waiting for, and I wanted to get on with it.

Susan Wightman (Tooby)

PB: 2.31.33 – Seoul 1988

Highest World Ranking in the 1980s: 44th

Marathon Achievements:

12th - Seoul Olympics 1988

20th - Split European Championships 1990

How did you get into athletics?

I started running at school, but it was very limited and was mostly cross-country. We [referring also to her twin sister, Angela] were also members of the nearest athletics club. However, because we lived in a rural environment and were quite a way from the town, we never trained there. It just wasn't convenient. So, as youngsters we were never fanatical runners. All we did were the bits you did at school. I always ran the county championship though, which I won most years from when I was 13 years old, and I ran three or four English Schools'. I think the best I ever finished was 21st.

341

Did you do any track?

Yes, I ran the 800m and 1500m, which is all we did at school. I also ran one English Schools' on the track and that was in my last year. I don't think I made the final though. We were guided a little bit at school, and we would do a bit of training outside of lessons, but we didn't really do any more other than that. Later, Angela and I went to different universities and being that we were identical twins it was a good test as to the effects of the environment, in terms of how much they play or don't play in a person's development.

Which university did you attend?

I went to Bangor. Although it didn't have a very strong athletics club, I helped run it and started to train regularly. I was slightly weighty then. Well, not trim for a distance runner in any case. You certainly wouldn't have looked at me and thought that I was someone who was going to make it to international level. I wouldn't have! So, I ran BUSA and things like that and did reasonably well. I then went on to Loughborough University to do a PGCE and joined George Gandy's group. I started doing interval work there. I suppose that was the first time I did any really controlled training. I lost weight and coincidentally so had my sister where she was studying. I think it was because we were training harder and had more of an idea of what we wanted to do. Before then, we were hockey players come basketball players or whatever.

So, what happened after you left university?

I moved to Chepstow and became a P.E. teacher in a school in Bristol. I also started running with Ann Hill's group and began training really hard. I was 23 by this time, and up until this point I hadn't really trained properly, which in some respects I don't think was such a bad thing because my body was able to grow and establish itself without any growing hiccups or anything like that. I was also old enough to cope with the pressure. It was tough though because I went from a point of small dosage to over dosage.

Was Angela also with Ann?

Yes, she was also with Ann by this stage and because we were twins we produced a bit of competitiveness. We both wanted to train as hard as anybody, if not harder, and we were known for being very tough trainers. God knows how we survived! Ann had a group of girls that included people like Kirsty Wade and Kim Lock, and the trouble was that everyone just bred off each other; it was very competitive. It was also at the time when Zola Budd was around, and she raised the standard, particularly in the middle and long-distance events. It was during 1984 that Angela and I started coming to the forefront. We won the Mike Sully and the Avon 10 miler, but we were still relatively unknown. I think it was a bit twee because we were both identical twins. From there, we went on: Angela won the Nationals and we both ran the trial for the 1984 Olympics. Angela came second to Zola Budd, but they had to have a re-match because Wendy Sly hadn't run.

Was that over 3000m?

Yes, we'd moved up to the 3000m, and I always had to compete for a place with Angela. At 800m and 1500m, I had been slightly faster, but at 3000m, 5000m and 10,000m I was the slight underdog, which was a bit of a problem. Well, it wasn't a problem, but there was usually only one place and basically I never got it. So, they had the re-run, and Angela only had to come second, but she ended up dropping out. Angela was the weaker of us two psychologically. I came second, but they didn't take either of us, which was a big shame really. However, we had come onto the scene very quickly, and if six months later we had gone to the Olympics, then maybe the goal would have been too obtainable. It made both of us realise the significance of an Olympic place. I suppose my best year was 1988. We had both changed coaches to Harry Wilson. He was extremely good, but if there was one criticism I have, it is that the training was geared more towards Angela's needs than mine. I suppose it was the same with Ann Hill a little bit too because Angela was slightly better than me. Although we were identical twins, we worked differently. I was faster, but she was gutsier. I didn't cope with that very well, and Angela was getting further away from me. We then moved up to the 10,000m, and Angela got a place in the European Championships, followed by the World Championships. Once again, I was the one left at home because there was also Liz McColgan and Jill Hunter by this time. I was always fourth, and when I was third, they never took the third place. However, my chance came in 1988 before the Olympics. This was the year that they had a combined GB team for the World Cross-Country Championships. We did the trial in Gateshead and Angela won it, Jill was second, and I came third. So I knew at that time that we were running quite well. In January, we went to New Zealand for the World Cross-Country where Angela got the silver, and I came ninth, which was probably my best place in the World Cross-Country. However, coming towards the Olympic trials, I realised that I wouldn't get a place because Angela, Liz McColgan and Jill Hunter's times were all a bit faster than mine over 10,000m. My only option was to move up to the marathon. It was also getting too competitive with Angela. It got to the stage where I had tried to beat her for so long and thought that she was always going to beat me that rather than try, I'd let her go past me. I accepted second place, which wasn't the right attitude.

So I moved away from her, and I moved up to the marathon, which was probably the best thing I did. It was a bit like the blind leading the blind though. Harry had no idea of coaching for the marathon, and I had no idea of the training. I also had to safeguard myself and still train as a 10,000m runner because I had a chance to run the trial if I didn't do very well at the marathon distance. Consequently, I became very fast over half-marathon and before the London Marathon I broke the British record for the distance. In fact, I was the first British woman to break 70 minutes on the road; I ran 69.56. So, I knew I was in good shape. In the actual marathon, I came fourth overall and was second British woman. You had to come in the top two British women to go to the Olympics, and so I made the team.

Was that your first ever marathon?

My second. However, my first one was a bit of a jolly when I was twenty-one and weighed nine-and-a-half stone.

Where was that?

That was in Hereford.

What time did you run in London?

I ran 2.32, and then I went to the Seoul Olympics and ran 2.31.33. I was very pleased with that but felt that had I given myself more time to settle into the distance,

I would have perhaps broken 2.30. Unfortunately, the opportunity never came. My sister and I were very hard trainers and probably bordering on anorexic. However, nobody could tell us that then. We weren't naturally skinny, and I had amenorrhoea for 10 years, which means your bones are not as strong. Something had to give. In the late 1980s and 1990s, I was injured. It was one thing after another. I went to Split and ran the Europeans, and I ran disastrously. I ran about two more after that, and they were in the 2.40s. The problem was that I didn't have the continuity. I tried to change my training and do the distances instead of the speedwork, as I was only on 70 miles a week when I ran 2.32, but I couldn't cope with it, and I started getting injured. The fast stuff suited me, but the bigger mileage didn't. So, I came to a point in the early 1990s when I wanted a family. I had suffered with amenorrhea for so long, and I wondered what I was doing to myself. After a month, I'd get injured with stress fractures. My body was knackered.

How old were you when you did your first "real" marathon?

I was 28.

So, what was your biggest achievement?

I suppose it has to be the Seoul Olympics where I came 12th. London was also special, as it was unknown as to

347

what I would do, and I came 4th. My World Cross-Country Championship performance was another big achievement. I think I came 9th or 11th. Maybe Jill came 9th, and I came 11th. I can't quite remember.

How long before a marathon did you decide to do it?

It was probably six months. I was training as a 10,000m runner, so all I really did was add in a long run. Harry and I were very fortunate there, for as I realised later on, I wasn't the type of marathon runner to do well over long distances. I was the type that needed to do qualitative runs with a few long runs thrown in. It was just what happened coincidentally, and it suited me.

Can you outline your training in the build-up to a marathon?

I never used to do more than 75 miles a week. The only time I ever did over 75 miles was a week of 80 when I went to Açoteias. I promptly got injured. All my runs were qualitative, and so 10 milers were very hard. I'd do a long run on a Sunday, but it was not more than 15 although I did do a time trial over 24 miles during the build-up. I would probably do a 10 miler in the middle of the week, and I had one rest day a week.

Did you do absolutely nothing?

I might swim, or I might do nothing. I would usually do four days of twice a day during the week. The first run would be a five miler, and the second session would be a three-mile hard, a fartlek session or a track session.

Were your morning runs easy?

Yes. Well, they were with my sister – I thought they were easy!

How fast were your 10-mile runs?

They were definitely under six-minute miling. I never used to time them though, so I didn't realise at the time. When I was coming up to the marathon and running 15 miles, I was running under six-minute miling. They were never slow but that's what suited me. It was qualitative.

Did you do your sessions on the road or track?

A bit of both really. Harry was a great believer in getting off the track if we could. We'd do things like three-minute efforts with only a minute recovery. We'd do five or six of those. We also did 1000m reps on the track with short recoveries and things like 10 x 400m or 4 x 800m. So although the reps were long, the recoveries were very short.

How fast would you do the 1000s?

We'd do them in around three minutes. The 400s would be under 70 - 68s/69s.

How many 1000s would you do on the track?

We'd do four at the least and six at the most. I was always very consistent. I would never falter. If I had to do six reps, my last would be the same as my first, but we never did mega amounts. I was still training with my sister and doing the same training as she was doing. It was only the mileage that was greater and that was it. Most weeks we were on the track, but some weeks we would meet Harry at Crystal Palace and that would be instead of a track session. In the winter, there would be a fartlek session in there and hills, and we used to do those rigorously. We didn't do so much fartlek in the summer and definitely not any hills.

Did you do any other forms of training?

I would swim a mile on my rest day in 30 minutes, and I did circuit training once a week although that wasn't routine. It would depend on the circumstances. I probably did a gym session at school in 1988. There would be more emphasis on circuit training in the winter and not so much in the summer. We would also do some light weights, but we weren't fanatical about it. I think that perhaps we should have done more. It would have been beneficial to have more upper body strength because I had a tendency to lean forwards. I probably do more now. However, in those days if you did it, then you took something away from the running, and at that time the running training was more important.

Did you stretch regularly?

Only after running. I would always do some stretching but not religiously.

What were your PBs for the various distances? Were you one of the top 10k runners at the time?

Yes, I was a top 10km runner. I ran 32.41 on the road and 32.20 on the track. I ran 15.32 for 5000m, 8.57 for 3000m, 4.16 for 1500m and 2.13 for 800m.

How did you taper? What races did you do in a build-up to a marathon?

I did a half-marathon but not any closer than six weeks before and a 10 miler or 10km - a 10km probably - closer to the time. There was a drastic reduction in mileage in the final two weeks but especially in the last the week. The maximum I would be doing is four miles in a day. My last long run would be a 10 miler on the Sunday two weeks before, and then I'd probably do six or seven miles the Sunday before the marathon. The mileage would come right down to 30 or perhaps even less than 30. When I ran a marathon and didn't taper so much, I didn't run as well. Three days before, I would do strides, and a week before I'd do some mediocre efforts of 200s or something. Everything else was at a mediocre pace. I didn't lose momentum to be able to run at a reasonable pace, but at the same time I didn't do any hard sessions at all. The day before, I wouldn't do anything at all and probably only two or three miles the day before that.

How did you treat the races before the marathon?

I have never treated a race as a training run. A race was always a yardstick as to how I was running.

Did you use any form of mental preparation?

All the way through my life, I never had any problems with exams and gearing myself up for them. I was never a stressed-out person or highly strung, so I'd always take things as they were. I am probably a bit of an optimist really, and the same would be for races. Like everyone else, I was a bit anxious and nervous, but I would never feel completely bottled out in my head. In that respect, I never felt the need for relaxation tapes. Geoff, my husband, gave me some tapes for the last couple of marathons, but I don't think I ever used them because I didn't want to start something I wasn't used to or to do something that I didn't think I needed.

What about during the marathon?

At the time, it came naturally; it was natural for me to concentrate. I focused on my running, but it wasn't 100% focus all the way so that my head hurt! I used to work in five-mile blocks. So, I had to run the first five miles in under 30 minutes, and then I had to run the second block and so on. There were other runners at the same time as me who used to do nothing else but marathons; they did nothing on the track and were pure marathon runners. The reason they were so good was because they could switch off. They weren't fast runners, and I could name a few that had awful styles, especially if you put them on the track, but the fact was that for 26 miles they could just switch off and be almost robot-like. You'd have to say that over the marathon distance that is an asset.

Did you do most of your training for the marathon on your own or with a group?

On the Sunday, it was with two or three chaps. On the track, it used to be with a group. However, as time went on, especially during the peak time, it just used to be with Angela. When I was training with Ann Hill, it was with a group but with Harry it was mostly just with Angela, or we used to meet up with a few other people he coached – mostly chaps.

What track did you use?

Woking or Bracknell. We used to travel.

Did you use altitude or warm-weather training?

I didn't do any altitude training. However, I used warm-weather training for the fact that you could get some early quality sessions done. We used to go Easter time because it becomes long, boring and tedious in the winter. I didn't use it for acclimatisation for Seoul or anything.

Was Ann Hill your first coach?

No. When I was at university, there was a chap there called Sid Hope, who now coaches Sarah Bentley. He coached me for a while. It was really only because I was in South Wales and because Angela was there that it seemed more appropriate for me to go to Ann.

I expect Geoff [her husband] has thrown in a few ideas from time to time as well?

Well, he hasn't been very useful to me. His way of training obviously contradicted mine. I took it on board once and then said – right, thank you!

Did you run for Cardiff at this time?

Yes, I've always run for Cardiff.

Have you always worked?

Yes, I taught P.E., and so I have always been on my feet. I left university and taught full-time for two years and that is the only time I have taught full-time. After that, I went part-time. During the 1988 Olympics, I was teaching part-time.

Was that purely so you could do more training?

Yes, exactly. I was getting too tired. When I was working full-time in the summer, I was just leaning against the tennis courts. Working part-time was also more flexible, which meant I could take time off. Later, I left teaching altogether and worked for the health authority in a sports science aspect. We were promoting health and fitness in industry. I then studied for an MSc in order to do that further. However, when I finished, I couldn't get a job, and so I went back to teaching. I still teach a bit now. I always felt like I needed the extra stimulus; I needed an extra life.

You didn't want to be a full-time athlete?

No! There were times when I struggled and was constantly tired, but I didn't want to be a full-time athlete.

What sponsorship or financial assistance did you have?

I was with Nike for 10 years. However, it was just kit and some incentives, such as if I broke the British record or something. I didn't receive that much money or assistance.

So, you didn't get a contract with them for regular money?

Well, if I did, it was minimal. I had a Sports Aid Foundation grant one year and Eddie Kulukundis helped us a little bit on trips and things. I got prize money, and I used to go to the States to earn money on the roads there. I got $14,000 for coming fourth in London. I also used to get appearance money for track races. We did a lot of 3000m track races, and I used to get invited to the IAAF fixtures and Grand Prix events.

What was your diet like? Did you do the carbohydrate depletion/loading diet?

No, I just tapered. I put a lot of thought into this, and Harry had his own views. I also listened to other people's experiences. I just felt that because I was mainly a track runner, I didn't want to faff around with carbohydrate depletion/loading, and so I really just tapered. My diet was very basic. A typical day was a grapefruit in the morning, a scone for lunch, and then quiche, salad and a yogurt in the evening.

It is amazing that you managed to train on that!

Absolutely amazing! Both my sister and I had a problem. Well, not a problem, but we weren't perhaps born to be a weight for running. I went down from nine stone to just under eight stone. I never went over eight stone. That was hardened discipline. I wouldn't let myself go.

What was the lowest weight you got down to?

Just under seven-and-a-half stone – seven stone five/six.

How tall are you?

I am five-foot four, so it was quite light, but I was running at my best at that weight; I ran my best at my lightest. My sister is slightly taller than me and was slightly lighter. That was probably why she fell to pieces before I did!

What was your fluid intake like?

Just water.

What about at the feeding stations?

Just water. I don't believe in taking a lot of electrolytes. I'd maybe take them after the race but not during. I always used to drink at every station. Water was important, and unlike my diet, I didn't neglect it. I didn't overdo it, but I didn't neglect it.

How much rest and sleep did you get?

I never burnt the candle at both ends, so I nearly always got eight hours sleep. I was always good at getting up early and used to train at seven o'clock. I was never one

357

to be on the town at weekends, and I hardly ever drank alcohol even at university.

Was that a conscious decision because of your training?

Yes, but I never really drank anyway. There were no temptations.

Did you sleep in the afternoons when you were part-time?

I never slept in the afternoon. I was brought up in an environment where you never sat on your bottom and did nothing; you always did something.

Did you have regular massage or anything like that?

Yes. The more I ran longer distances, the more I needed the massage. I'd have it twice in every three weeks.

Do you think it helped?

Yes, because I was such a hard trainer. The training coupled with the races meant I used to be crippled. It relaxes your mind too.

Did you suffer a lot with colds and injuries?

I hardly ever got colds. We were brought up in the countryside and were hardly ever inside. When I taught, I was also always outside and never came down with colds. However, when I did get them, I was nearly dead! It was that extreme. Luckily, I hardly ever got them.

What about injuries? Were they mostly later on in your career?

Yes, it was more niggles; it was never anything major. I think it all accumulated though and took its toll at a later time when I was more vulnerable.

Do you have any thoughts as to why you and the others were so good at this time?

I think the training was quite different, and I believe in those days we did actually listen to our bodies a little bit more. We were less informed, and so we did things as we felt we should do them. Now, there is so much scientific input, and a lot of people feel compelled to do certain types of training. I know I am contradicting myself because I was a hard trainer, but I think people do overtrain, especially for the marathon. I hear of phenomenal distances that even the women are doing in training. They are mind-boggling. I'd die in a week, and I don't think it has been to the advantage of the distance runner. I worked through the distances, and I think that my background of speed helped me a lot. People like Zola Budd helped too. Unless you are going to train with those people and running the times, you are not going to improve, are you? I can't put my finger on it. There is no surge of women coming through, and there are so many more options of things to do nowadays.

Children also specialise too early in the clubs now, and the intensity is too great.

Pilot Study Interviews

As part of my MSc thesis work, I was required to carry out a pilot study, and so I interviewed three marathon runners from a previous era. They are included here for further reading interest.

Bill Adcocks

PB: 2.10.48 – Fukuoka 1968

Marathon Achievements:

2nd - Kingston Commonwealth Games 1966

Winner - Karl Marx Stadt Marathon 1968

5th - Mexico City Olympics 1968

Winner - Fukuoka Marathon 1968

Winner - Marathon to Athens Marathon 1969

Athens European Championships 1969

Winner - Otus Marathon 1970

How did you start running?

I actually started running cross-country when I was 12.

How did you fare?

In the first year of the secondary school I went to, you were not allowed to run cross-country, so I didn't run. However, the following year we moved to a new building and joined up with a school called Templars. They were very successful at cross-country in the Coventry area, and so I became a part of that. They had an inter-schools' league on a Wednesday afternoon. I did the first one in early October and finished 14th, which from nothing was quite good.

And then you joined Coventry Godiva AC?

Yes. My father was very interested, and so I was encouraged. It was something I enjoyed doing, particularly as I was quite small and not that good at football or other ball games. It wasn't even really a conscious decision. It was just something that happened and the natural thing to do.

What events did you do?

In those days, the furthest distance you were allowed to run at 14 was 200 metres. It was painfully obvious that I wasn't any good at that. I think I was 15 before I could run a mile on the track. I always ran as far as I could run at the age I was at because it was clear that my speed wasn't particularly good. I did cross-country in the winter and track in the summer. Even after I left school,

I was doing a lot of track training, and some of the sessions were quite demanding, as well as enlightening. I could just go on and on. I remember one of our club members asking me which were the fast ones when I was doing a session of 400m reps. People nowadays don't seem to run their intervals; they have a rest. I never did that. Perhaps that's indicative as to why I was a marathon runner. There's no rest in a marathon.

Did you have any successes as a junior?

I was seventh in the AAA's Mile and second in the National Cross-Country in my last year as a junior. In my first year as a youth, I finished 48th in the National, but in the second year, when I was expecting to do pretty well, I finished 72nd. I finished 106th in my first year as a junior and in the low 30s in the second year before achieving that second place in my third and final year.

What made that big improvement?

I think it was a number of things, but perhaps a significant thing was finishing 12th in the Midland Championships. There was a lad around at the time called John Farrington. He was a very good cross-country runner and steeplechaser, and he was winning everything by miles. The day I had to face him at the Midland Championships, a combination of nerves and over-expectation caused me to finish only 12th. I was well down on what I expected and for me that was the end of the season. The National was still to come, but I'd had run such a bad race there that I almost didn't go. However, I did go, and it turned out to be a watershed moment. The important thing was my whole attitude, and I remember being quite blasé about it. The race started off, and it just unfolded, and the next thing I knew I was a minute behind the winner, John Farrington. I'd let him get on and do his thing, and I, in turn, had done mine. I hadn't worried about him or anyone else and that's how it happened. It is one of the philosophies I then carried into everything I did.

How old were you?

I was 20.

Were you doing any road at this time?

Yes, around this time I was. The first road race I did, other than road relays, was the Horsham Blue Star 10 Miles in 1962. I think Mel Batty won it. As I recollect, I did 53-and-a-half minutes and was about 10th. I would have been 21 going on 22 and that was my first excursion into road racing.

And you carried on with the track too?

Yes, the whole lot from 800m to 10,000m/6 miles.

What times were you running?

At this stage, I was running around mid 28 minutes for six miles. The British record was 27.49 at the time, so I was reasonable. I was doing just under 14 minutes for three miles and 14-and-a-half for 5000m. My bests transpired to be 13.45 for three miles, 27.51 for six miles, 14.15 for 5000m and 29.01 for 10,000m. It was nothing inspirational, but it was solid. I was training very hard and doing a lot of speedwork, but the results really weren't there. It didn't stop the effort I was putting in though, and all the time the volume was increasing slightly.

When did you run your first marathon?

It was in 1964 in South Wales. I was 22, and I did 2.19.

Did Brian Kilby and Juan Taylor inspire you at Coventry?

I don't know if it is a matter of inspired, but it was just the kind of environment I was in. I was being carried along in an environment where I was doing something I really wanted to do with others who really wanted to do it and who were successful. It obviously had an effect.

How was your first marathon?

I'd experienced people coming back from their first marathon saying that they'd never do one again, but I just knew it was something I wasn't going to do. I knew there would be pain involved. It was a matter of not being turned off by it because you knew that was what it was all about. If it hadn't hurt, you hadn't tried.

How many did you run before you set your PB?

Eleven.

Quite a few then?

People don't develop into it nowadays; they come into it having done good track times. I could have spent a lot of time trying to improve my 5km and 10km, but I wouldn't have got very far. One has to make a conscious decision to go for what you are going to be best at.

You all seemed to be quite young when you started at the marathon compared to nowadays, don't you think?

Perhaps we were more perceptive. I also had role models close at hand. I'd see them week in week out, in fact, day in day out on some occasions. So, it wasn't something that came across as special whereas today there is so much written and so much blurb given that you'd never get out of bed if you read half of it or were tempted to take notice of it. We discovered things instinctively and obviously enjoyed what we were doing.

Did you consciously build up to your first marathon?

The year before, I had run two laps of the course at Port Talbot, and I had also run a 15 and 20 miler by that time, so I was moving that way. However, the idea of a specific period of training didn't occur in those days; you just kept running. You didn't think that in three weeks time you had a race. We raced every week.

You seemed to do quite a lot of marathons in a year what with trials and everything?

There was nothing you could do about it. Between May 1968 and September 1969, I did seven. Even after having broken the European record twice, I still had to run the trial to get into the European Championships. These days there is pre-selection. We are not comparing like with like at all.

Do you think if you'd had today's benefits like pre-selection, you would have run faster?

Possibly. We did our running as a bolt-on to the rest of our lives though. The whole idea of saving yourself for one marathon a year would be quite abhorrent to most people of my age because we just ran. Saturday was race day whether you raced to your ultimate or not, and there was the social aspect too. It was an end in itself and not just a means to an end.

367

Do you think there are perhaps too many egos involved today?

I think that is definitely the case, but you tend to operate in the environment and conditions that are there at the time. We tended to think that if we'd stopped at home, we'd have gone training anyway. I don't think we whinged as much. We ran with colds and didn't think about it.

How did you prepare for marathons when you were more established?

My best year was 1968/1969. I got married in September 1967, and then after my honeymoon I started the really big push. [Flicking through his diary] In the first week, I did 55 miles, training twice a day. I then did 76, 82, 77, 70 and 60. It was in November that I got up to 90 miles. By December, I was on over 100 miles a week all the way through to 126 in February. I then ran the International Cross-Country Championships. I actually made the team for that. So, there was a lot of volume of training, and I was probably at my fittest there. The interesting thing is [flicking through his diary] even at that time I wasn't really doing what I'd call a long run. On the 27th of January 1968, I did 15 miles in the morning and then 5 miles in the afternoon, which makes 20, but it was over two runs.

368

Did you often do two runs on a Sunday?

Yes. You can see here again [looking at diary] that on the 17th of February I did 20 miles over two sessions. In fact, the first run I did over 20 miles on a Sunday morning was on the 20th of April. Up until then, it was all two runs totalling 18, 19, 17, 15 and 15. I even did one day here of three sessions: a seven, a four-and-a-half and a seven-and-a-half. Most of the time my runs were quite fast, even the morning ones. I'd do seven miles in 42 minutes; that was the order of the day. [Looking back at his diary] Yes, so you see, 20 miles on the 20th of April - I was only about six weeks away from running a marathon – and then there's one of 22 miles and a 27 miler on the 4th of May with 132 miles for the week. A couple of weeks after that, I broke the European record. I did 2.12.16.

So, you were doing quite big mileage? You were quite strong then?

Well, I was working physically all day as well. I was a self-employed plumber. What you can do from a physical point of view is quite unbelievable, but the major stumbling block is the thinking; it is the psychological. While you are out working and thinking about the job you are doing, you really haven't got too much time to be thinking about the running. You have to get up in the morning and be at a place at a certain time. The whole structure is much tighter. In 1969, I went into teaching, and my worst time for training was in the summer holidays when I had six or seven weeks off. All of a sudden, I was like a full-time athlete. I had all this time, and therefore I'd end up going out later and not being as structured.

Did you have any medical back up or massages?

We used to go to a local physio, who would rub your legs and whatever for five shillings a time. Most people did get injuries and have problems but that was just par for the course.

Did you get a lot of injuries?

I got a lot of back problems. It first went in 1966, and then I was plagued with it on and off for the rest of my career really.

What type of quality training did you do?

By 1968, I had been running for something like 15 years. I'd been through all this kind of rigmarole of heavy track sessions, and it hadn't done me much good. Well, it had done me good in terms of the discipline. Anyhow, if you look at this [pointing to his diary], it was simply running. I was running and running and running, mostly at a good lick. Take this week here in March 1968 - Monday was three sessions: six miles in the morning, four miles at lunchtime and seven miles at night, all

370

covered at a brisk pace. I did the seven miles in 39 minutes. We had road relays at the weekend where you did some of your fast work, and there were also times when I did two miles of striding the straights. It wasn't speedwork in itself, but you were just going that bit faster. There is one here [back to diary] of 4 x 400m with 4 x 200m, so there were little bits of that, but I had been that way and done that, and it hadn't done me any good. I just did the thing back then that I thought I should be doing.

Did you do most of this on your own?

Leading up to the Olympic Trials in 1968, there was myself, Colin Kirkham, who went on to the 1972 Olympics, and Brian Kilby running the Sunday morning long runs together. So I was running with people like that. You tend to get people who are followers or leaders. Throughout my career, I always went down to the track as a meeting point and ran out from there. If people wanted to come, then they'd come.

Did you do any hill training?

Not at that moment in time. There was quite a lot of variance though. I used to run on the grass in the parks, and if I took a profile of a 10-mile run, it would almost be like a fartlek. It would be ebbing and flowing. If there were a hill in the run, then I'd make an effort up it as opposed to doing a hill session as such.

371

Did you do most of your running off-road?

No, it was mostly on the road, including my long run. My running was just out and out effort.

What were your biggest successes?

Every marathon I ran was special in some way, even those where I didn't run particularly well. Be it my first one or the Olympics, every one had a special place. I suppose some of my biggest achievements were things like winning the AAA's in 1965 in my best time at that point; winning the Karl Marx Stadt in 1968 in a European record, which was a big breakthrough; finishing fifth in the Olympics, which was at altitude; and going to Fukuoka in 1968 and winning in my best time there. After all these years, Fukuoka is special, as I am the only British man to have gone to Japan and won. Obviously, my Athens one too because of where it was, and naturally your fastest marathon is always going to be special. They've all got special memories for slightly different reasons.

How did you taper for marathons? Did you do the carbohydrate depletion/loading diet?

No, Ron Hill was the one who started that off just after 1968. In 1966, the AAA's was held on a really hot June day, and it was a really competitive race. I blew up from about 17 miles on, and I finished absolutely flat to the ground. When I got home that night at about ten o'clock, I was eight stone two, and my normal peak racing weight was eight-and-a-half stone.

How tall are you?

Five-foot five. I reckon that I was well under eight stone when I actually finished the race. I thought about it and realised it was a bit silly. If we say that the race doesn't really begin until around 18 miles, then you don't want to be at your best racing weight until that stage. You want to be a bit heavier at the start. That is very basic but pragmatic. So the week leading up to a marathon, I obviously used to reduce my training. [Looks at training diary] Here, when I ran 2.12, I did my last really long run a fortnight before, and I might have done a 15 on the Sunday in the last week. My mileage would also come down from 100 to 70 miles. In that time, I would expect my weight to go up to about nine stone. The other thing is because you have been doing all your training fast, you tend to be locked into a mode where when the gun goes there is a good chance you will go off too quickly. If you are a little overweight, it will slow you down. It is very simplistic really. As the weight falls off, you will naturally get back into your faster mode. The scientists would probably blow that out of the water. When I did all my best times, I was the slowest starting, but I was able to run the best way possible for me as an individual. There was one race in Japan where

I let them go off, and I could just see their heads at 10,000m about a minute in front. I decided to catch them before halfway and about 200m before, I did. I then proceeded to run away from them and won. The most important thing is to run as best you can for yourself and not land up being scrapped off the ground. That was my philosophy.

Did you have a special diet?

No, but in 1968 I did take a lot of vitamins and things like that. I took vitamin C and iron before going to Mexico because that was the advice.

Did it make any difference?

Not really. I ran pretty much as I expected.

Had you been altitude training before Mexico?

No. In the winter/spring of 1967/1968, quite a few groups of people went to Font Romeu. I was asked if I wanted to go, but it was at the same time as the Karl Marx Stadt Marathon. Having not run a marathon since the 1966 Commonwealth Games, I felt it was more important for me to run a marathon, which I did and got a good result. Psychologically, it gave me more of a boost than going to altitude would have done.

Did you ever go warm-weather training?

We used to have warm-weather training once a year at the end of season, and we called it a holiday! I say this a little bit tongue in cheek because a lot of these people who are going so-called warm-weather training are basically having their holiday before they've done the business. Many of them come back with a number of problems and injuries. It is another one of those fads of the day really. We also paid for ourselves, and we'd only get a fortnight's holiday from work.

Did you use any form of mental techniques?

Yes. I've already alluded to the Junior National Cross-Country Championship's example and the attitude of not getting uptight, keeping it all in perspective and having the confidence in what you've done. There is nothing more you can do. One other thing is that very early on we used to have the London to Brighton Road Relays, and on the Friday night we'd stop in a hotel, which was quite a big deal in those days. The hotel was just over the road from Kensington Gardens, and each year I just used to walk in there and talk to myself. It is one of my earliest recollections of doing something of that nature. I didn't want anyone around me. I just wanted to be left alone to calm myself and to focus. I also used to employ a little gamesmanship at times. Once was in Fukuoka in 1968. There was a big group

375

containing a lot of people that I didn't know and who didn't know me, other than I was the Brit or whatever. During the race, I kept peeling off to the side, so that they'd wonder what I was up to. It gave them something to think about and put the onus back on them to worry. I'd then suddenly rejoin the group. I used to do that quite regularly although, of course, you can only do that when you are in control. It might backfire if it wasn't your day.

What did you think about during the race?

Survival! At the end of the day, as long I could say that I had done the best that I could have done, that was it. I might have done things differently given 30 years and how things have changed, but given the conditions that were there at the time, I did my best.

Were you coached at all?

In the early days, I was coached by Lionel Pugh, who was one of the national coaches. However, I wasn't coached later on as no one touched the marathon back then. I did it by trial and error and with the help and influence of those around me. In that way, I developed my own strategy. I don't understand it nowadays. You see all these people into endurance running, but I am not sure where they've got their information from because very few of the good exponents have been interviewed to the extent whereby their philosophies and their methods have actually been dissected. There is a lot of information on the science and theory but not the practical day-to-day stuff. One of the things that perhaps we didn't have back then were constraints, and the barriers weren't defined. People were at the forefront pushing barriers. This is something that isn't written about in books because the people writing them haven't experienced it. All they have found out is from other books. Given the level of scientific knowledge and back up, there is a good reason for looking at the two and getting the best of both. It is fundamentally something quite simple.

Did you do any other forms of training like weights?

I used to do weights and circuits early on but not when I was training for marathons, except for a few press-ups and sit-ups. I also had a set of dumbbells at home. I was working full-time, so I didn't have the time. I just put on my kit and went out the door. I didn't have to go anywhere to do it. If I'd had to take half an hour to go down to somewhere else to do weights, it would have been time wasted when I could have been doing another five miles of running.

Did you have any financial assistance or any forms of sponsorship?

No. When I won the AAA's, I wrote to Robbie Brightwell at Adidas, and I was told that all the

377

allocation for marathon shoes had already been given out for that year. So, the AAA's Champion couldn't get a pair of shoes. I subsequently wrote to Derek Ibbotson, who was at Puma at the time, and they came up with some stuff. I ran in Puma from 1966 through to 1970, but it was just shoes and tracksuits. I then went to Japan in 1970 and Asics, or Tiger as it was then, came down to the hotel. I was the only foreigner in the race, and they did a few sketches and asked me what I would like. Two days later, they had made me a shoe. I didn't know if I could wear them having got them only two days before the race, but I wore them the night before and then in the race, and I won. I then ran in Tiger for the remainder of my career. That was the only kind of support I had. When I went away to the Olympics in Mexico, I didn't have any money for six weeks, as I was self-employed.

Did you win any prizes?

The maximum prize in those days was meant to be £12, which was something like three-quarters of a week's wages. The last race I ran abroad was in 1972 in Catania, Sicily. It was a four-mile road race, and I finished fourth. I won £34, but I felt cheated, as I didn't come back with a trophy or anything. It was a hobby; you went to work to earn money. It was the travelling, vests and meeting people that were more important. You made the most of it. It is the memories and the people and places that you remember more than the running.

Did you drink a lot generally? How about during races?

In general, I never had drinks in races, and I certainly didn't have drinks in training or anything. I also never purposefully hydrated before races; I just drank normally. The first time I attempted to take drinks was in the 1966 Commonwealth Games. When we finished, it was 90°F and 90% humidity. We used babies' bottles, but we cut a big piece out of the teat, so there wasn't such a small hole. However, just like a baby, you'd take in air as well as liquid and get wind, so it wasn't too successful. Before the Olympics, Mike Down at Loughborough came up with a formula. It was some powder that Boots made up for me, and it supposedly had trace elements in it. I drank this in my bottles. In the actual race, Jimmy Alder and I purposefully started slow. When we got to the first feed station at 10km, it was like a battlefield, and our drinks weren't there. We literally stood in the middle of the road cursing and that was the end of Jim. He went to pieces. However, that really got me going, and I carried on and didn't take any more drinks. I went through the field and finished fifth.

So, you never took on much fluid in any of your marathons then?

No. I don't know from a scientific point of view, but I do know that if you take on a lot of liquid, it can make your stomach feel uncomfortable and that's the last thing you want if you are going to be running at a really high level. I know they have done a lot of work on this, but I am not so sure about the assimilation of it in your body. If you are training the kind of volumes we were, I don't know if it is possible to train the system not to be as dependent, or maybe it is a function of how good you are. Perhaps it is one of the peculiarities of the people that are good, that is, the ability to maintain high levels of output despite fluid loss. Whether it is something that is purely physical or whether it can be trained for, I don't know. It might also be part psychological or a combination of factors. It is another viewpoint anyway.

Did you drink alcohol?

I've never been a big drinker. Before Fukuoka, I had a few beers, and I still did 2.10.48. Similarly, the night before the Athens Marathon, I went to an embassy reception with the people I was staying with and had a few drinks there. It is like a lot of these things - if you think it's going to do you some harm, it probably will. It's all things to all people, and it's finding what is right for you.

What races did you do leading up to a marathon?

I liked to do a 20 miler some time before a marathon. [Looking in his diary] Here, I did the Hereford 20 on the 21st of April. I ran 1.41.33. I won it by nearly four minutes, and this would have been about a month before. This is interesting [looking at diary] – following my 2.12.6, I did a PB for two miles in the week immediately after, and I did a six-mile PB two weeks later. I am the only person to have won a Japanese Championships and a AAA's Championship in the same week: I ran a marathon in Japan and a long stage in the 12-Stage Road Relay on the following Saturday. People say that they cannot run a race because they've run a marathon a week before, but I think within certain barriers you can do what you like. Here you are [looking at diary] – on the 15th of June, I ran 1.12 for 15 miles, and a fortnight after that I ran the Preston 10 in 46.24, which would hold up pretty well today. The next day I did 22 miles.

Is there anything else you'd like to add?

One of the main things is that the period from starting in athletics to reaching a peak represented something like 15/16 years for the vast majority. It was much more short-term than it is today; the line on the graph was much steeper. When you've had your time, there is very little you can do. I don't mean pack up, but an acceptance that you've had your time. I think even if I could go back, and I could run one marathon a year for the next 10 years, I probably wouldn't choose that route. I remember in the last 18 months I had set my goal to retire following the 1972 Munich Olympics. After that, I would have to get on and think about my career. In actual fact, I think I got it about right. I didn't run a marathon in 1971 because I was having foot problems, and I didn't run a marathon in 1967 because of my back. In 1972, my training was going well. I had a good winter and broke the course record for the Finchley 20, which still stands. Ten days later, I got an injury and didn't recover from it. I got in touch with the selectors, and they said if I didn't run the trial, I wouldn't be picked. I'd done 2.10/2.11 and placed fifth in the Olympics, I'd comparatively recently run 2.13 for a marathon, and I had broken the record for the Finchley 20, but I still had to run the trial to get picked. Perhaps one other regret I have is the year that I was in my best form – 1968 - I did the two fastest times in the world by two minutes, but the Olympics happened to be in Mexico at altitude. A few months later, I beat all the people that had finished in front of me. I know other people might equally say that if it hadn't have been there, they might have done things differently, but I know, and the records show, that I was at my best. That is a regret. Perhaps I would have been laughing all the way to the bank, even now, if that had been the case. However, that's life, isn't it? There is nothing you can do about it, so it's not worth dwelling on.

Jim Alder

PB: 2.12.04 – Edinburgh 1970

Marathon Achievements:

Winner - Kingston Commonwealth Games 1966

Mexico City Olympics 1968

Bronze - Athens European Championships 1969

Silver - Edinburgh Commonwealth Games 1970

How did you come into running?

I was born in Glasgow and was a war orphan. Later, I was fostered down in England. I had a huge chip on my shoulder and was a shy, nervous lad and a bit out on a limb. One New Year's Day, I was taken down to watch the Morpeth to Newcastle race, and I saw this little man there called Jack Holden. He meant nothing to me at the time, but he had a Union Jack on his chest. I decided then and there that I wanted to win the race and that is how it all started. I was always good at running at school. I didn't win every race, as there were one or two lads who were more talented than me, and I couldn't make the Northumberland team, but I was always prepared to hurt myself. When I was 16, I joined Morpeth Harriers and ran well on the cross-country. However, I hated the track, and I wasn't that good on the roads either. I had no speed; I just had lots of staying power.

Did you carry on doing track though?

Yes, I always ran it, but I didn't like it. When I was 17, I could run a mile on ash – remember it was all ash in those days - in 4.43, so I wasn't too bad but nothing fantastic.

Did you win any titles or place highly in area and national championships?

I was second in the North-Eastern Youths Cross-Country Championships, but I didn't run the Northern's as I packed up running for four months to go and play local football. Later, I started back running again and placed eighth in my first area championships as a first year junior. I also made the Northumberland/Durham senior team, which was fourth in the Inter-Counties Championships. There was no junior race in those days and juniors had to run as seniors. I was 33rd in that race.

So, when did you decide to make the transition to the marathon?

Well, as I previously mentioned, I always wanted to win the Morpeth to Newcastle race, especially as I lived in Morpeth.

How far is it?

It is 14.1 miles. All the big names used to come and run it, and there were many of them that never won it. Class runners like Ron Hill, Bill Adcocks and Basil Heatley ran it and none of them won it. I was the first Morpeth man to win it. It meant an awful lot to me to live in the town and win it, and you'd think I'd been crowned king. There were celebrations in the town.

How old were you then?

I was 25. You had to be 21 to run it. The first time I ran it, I was second. After that, I just had a hankering to run marathons. I knew I would be a reasonable distance runner. You couldn't run more than 10 miles until you were 21. I remember getting banned from one race because I ran it when I was still a junior. It was the Billingham 10, although it was actually 11 miles. I won it. However, when I went the next year, they said I couldn't run it as I was a junior and that I had to start behind the field.

So, how old were you when you ran your first marathon?

I was 23. It was the Scottish Championships. I'd won the English Inter-Counties 20 miles, and I'd run a good half-marathon in about 67 minutes, so I thought that it would be easy. Everyone told me I'd win it easily. It was an out and back course, and I was three-and-a-half minutes clear at 20 miles. However, I got beaten by seven minutes. A man called Gordon Harris from the parachute regiment passed me at 23 miles and beat me by seven minutes. I died horribly. I came back into Glasgow, my birthplace, and I was aware that people were looking. I was walking two lampposts and running two. I ended up in the first aid tent. It was horrible; I did 2.31.

But it didn't put you off then?

No. I was still the Inter-Counties 20 miles Champion, and at that time I had been ninth in the English Cross-Country Championships. I had also won the Scottish Cross-Country title, so I knew I was a distance runner. I'd just broken 60 seconds for 400m; I remember that. I was close to international standard before I broke 60 for 400m. Even when I was running for Great Britain on the track, my best for 400m was only about 57 seconds. I was all strength-orientated. I remember reading about Brian Kilby's long runs and his 150 miles a week. I decided then to get stronger. I also read Arthur Lydiard's books like LSD (Long Slow Distance). It appealed to me, and I liked what it had done to Snell.

Did you have a coach at the time?

No. I just read lots of books. I also read Emil Zatopek's book and the things he would do. I seem to recall that he worked at a factory that made Wellington's and rubber boots. He used to do things like walk down a tree-lined drive and practise holding his breath to see how far he could go. He eventually blacked out. Things like that appealed to me. It showed how hard the man was and that he was prepared to experiment. When I was working in the building trade, I used my work as training too. I used to run with a barrel to see how strong I was, and I would push myself while hacking off stone. When I was tired, I used to say to myself that it was just one more minute, and I'd drive myself on and on. I could take punishment.

Do you think it had a bearing on your running?

Yes, it did. You see, I know myself. I used to use the physical work and get into it. I'd close my mind down. I would just get into the boring, unskilled, repetitive work and apply myself. I was also running 100 miles a week and twice a day. I was running up to work, working as a bricklayer and running back.

Did you always train twice a day?

Yes. Well, from 1963 I did, and I averaged 100 miles a week from then until I was 41 or 42. I averaged over 100 miles a week for 20 years.

How many marathons did you do a year?

I did four or five. We think today's marathon runners don't race enough. We did four or five a year, a couple of 20 milers, four or five half-marathons or 10 milers and track racing. We used to mix it all in. I've done five races in an afternoon. I've also run the first leg of a road relay in Edinburgh at 11.30 in the morning and then got into my van and driven 140 odd miles back to Tyneside to race at three o'clock.

Did you plan your marathons in advance?

No. I just went in for mega miles. It was structured, but it was basically just heavy mileage. I raced prodigiously. We stumbled across it. We were reading schedules in Athletics Weekly and modifying them, but the philosophy was the same. It was just mega miles and work. I used to get excited about it. I remember flying down to run at White City and getting a shiver down my spine. I also remember in 1966 that I ran four miles to work, wheeled concrete all morning, had a three course dinner and then caught the bus back to Morpeth to meet my father who took me to the airport. I couldn't drive and had no car in those days. I flew to London and ran the seventh fastest time in the world for 10,000m. I told Steve Ovett that tale when we were at a training camp and asked him if he would like to try it. I didn't know any different. I am horrified at what I did. I was permanently tired. When I went to the championships and the camps, and all I had to do was train, I was only sleeping five hours a night within a couple of weeks. It was the only time I caught up on my sleep. It was so much easier. However, my job while stressing me physically, didn't stress me mentally. When some of the national coaches asked me in Athens if I did any weight training, I told them that I was as strong as a bloody horse. I told them to try running to work, brick laying for eight hours and then running back again. If I had been a shopkeeper, which I was for the next 26 years, I might have considered it a bit although I think I'd still rather run than do weights.

So, you never did any formal weight training?

No, I have never needed to. I am 58 now, and I can lift a 100-weight bag of sand over my head. I'm still strong.

And there was no system of planning and peaking?

Not early on. However, I must admit that in the later years, when I was a bit more experienced and had won a few medals, I learnt when it was time to ease off and back off.

How many marathons did you run before you set your PB?

Well, the first one was 2.31, the second 2.23 – Ron Hill won that – and my third was 2.17 in the 1964 Poly Marathon when Basil Heatley broke the world record. I finished fifth in the race, and it ranked me seventh in the world. There I was, at 24 years of age, ranked in the world listings. That was a wonderful feeling. Little Jimmy Alder in the world rankings - in the top 10 - and only in my third marathon. I then did a steeplechase in a league match and hit my knee on the water jump barrier. I missed two weeks of training. I went to the trial, but I dropped out. However, I then broke the world record for 30km during the 1964 Olympics. I'd hit world-class form but just a bit too late. I had to wait another two years for the Commonwealth Games and European Championships.

You ran your marathon PB at the Edinburgh Commonwealth Games, right?

Yes, I did 2.12.04. I'd say that even now, in 1998, you could run 2.12 in a major championship, and you'd be in with a shout of a medal. You can forget the 2.07s. There are the men and women who run big city races, and there are the others who run championships. The two don't necessarily go together. It is the only event on the athletics' calendar where the world's fastest runners are not necessarily the medallists. The big city marathons are usually run in cooler weather. Towards the end of my career, I would love to have run a New York, a Chicago or a London. We usually ran our marathons in this sort of weather [the day was very humid and warm].

How old were you when you ran your PB?

I was 30. I ran my 13th marathon when I was 26 and that was the Commonwealth Games marathon, which I won. I also got a bronze medal in the six miles just six days before, and I ran in the European 10,000m only 12 days after and was leading at halfway.

What was your PB for 10km or 6 miles?

I did 27.27 on ash. The world record was 27.11, so I was close to the world record even as a marathon man. All the marathon men like Ron Hill, Jim Hogan, etc. were good 10,000m runners. Bill [Adcocks] wasn't the fastest 10,000m man, but he was still class.

So, you were a top 10km runner as well at this time?

I was *the* top 10km runner. I missed the British 10,000m record while running for Great Britain against Hungary at the White City. I was leading the field and won by 140 yards. I was on my own for 10 laps. I had no picture, no scoreboard and no people telling me, so I missed the British record by six-tenths of a second. I just finished, and they announced it. They said I'd missed it by four feet, and then they wondered why the trade language came out!

It is quite amazing really, as you said earlier you don't have any speed?

I've got pace, but I haven't got any speed. I'll quantify that. My best 400m was 57 seconds, my best 800m was 1.59, and my best mile was 4.13. I could run 8.45 for two miles - the world record was 8.32 - and for my 30km I ran at 69 seconds for 75 laps. It was like the cruising speed of a car, and the ability to operate near to my optimum. However, if it came to a sprint finish, I was done for. It came over to me loud and clear in the Cross-Country International: the Martini in Belgium. I came through, passed Gammoudi, and got up to Mel Batty and Derek Graham. I had about a mile to go and thought I could win, so I cruised past. However, after you came off the cross-country, you had to do about 250 yards around part of a track. Derek Graham and Mohammed Gammoudi beat me by about 70 yards. I couldn't believe what they did to me in that sprint finish, and I learnt in that one race that at that level - at a world-class level - I was a carthorse. Following that performance, I then trained to run a fast 800m in the middle of a race. I ran 2.05 in the middle of the Inter-Counties 10,000m, which was the trial for Mexico, and I broke the field. I told Roy Fowler before the race that all

392

being well I would go five laps out. I was 100 yards clear and won by 20. They all come at you in the last lap. I developed that ability to change pace. In a long run for home, strength beats speed.

So, you managed to get the optimum out of yourself?

I genuinely think that I got the best out of myself. When I was 25, I improved my 5km by over half a minute. After bricklaying all day, I went down to the track in South Shields and ran the fastest time in Britain to win the Northumberland/Durham title. It was an ash track with five laps to the mile. I just flew. At that time, I was going to the track and doing lots of long reps with short intervals and really pushing it. I was also doing fartlek through woods and hills.

What was a typical week in a marathon build-up?

Well, as we lived in a little town where there was no track, we used to go to Gateshead or Newcastle once a week to train. I think marathon runners need to go to the track once a week from February onwards. I also think you need a 12 to 14-week build-up to a marathon. I used the cross-country and did mega miles of up to 140 before Christmas, as well as doing fartlek on the roads three times a week. I'd drop down to 100 miles in October though to have a bit of a rest. I'd run very easily and slowly, and I'd do a couple of races for the club where I'd just finish seventh or eighth. It would be very

393

simple in the winter with lots of miles, fartlek and a few club races. After Christmas, there were the Championships, and I'd start to sharpen off. I'd go to the track, and I'd also do some intervals on the road. I used to like a 10-minute burn up. If you are running anything over 800m/1500m, then a 10-minute burn up in the middle of a six or eight-mile run once a week or once a fortnight is good. Sometimes it would go well; sometimes there would be nothing there. I used to have one bad session a week every week at some point. I never worried about one bad run. I'd worry about two or three bad runs. It's a numbers game. Marathon runners only have a handful of good marathons in them, maybe a dozen, so why waste them on some little championship or something. There is no point. In a year, if you race say 30 times, you'll have five or six blinders, four or five good or reasonable ones, a dozen or so average ones, and the rest will be poor or stinkers. I don't care who you are or what you do. No one performs at the absolute zenith for 12 months. It's the same for football teams, but footballers can't come to terms with that. I warned Mark Hudspith [who Jim coached] that he'd get no written schedules and have some bad runs, as well as good ones, in front of him. I told him he'd have to accept the bad ones and try to get the good ones out on the big days. That was the secret. And when he could come to terms with the bad ones, then he'd be laughing. I see people crucify themselves, and I tell them to forget it. If it's on a big day, then OK. Mark dropped out of the World Championships, and I felt for him because I'd dropped out of Mexico. I knew to leave him because you feel like you've let everyone down, and it is in your memory for a long time.

Did you do a weekly long run? If so, how far was it?

In the early days of training, I was doing a minimum of two hours. It was a standing joke in Morpeth Harriers that if you trained with Jimmy, you'd run up to a village called Middleton, which is 10 miles from Morpeth, have a slash in an outside urinal and run back again. "You'd go to Middleton for a slash." Alan Storey could probably quote you that. It was at a reasonable pace of around six-minute miling. We didn't hang about.

Were all your runs done at a quick pace?

I ran as I felt, but by and large they were. During the second half of my career, when I was 27/28 up until I was 30/31, I was doing a second long run a week. I've now got Mark Hudspith doing that - a 15 miler midweek. Once a month, I'd do three hours, and the longest run I ever did was 33 miles. I can remember it now. There are times in my life when I pushed myself to complete exhaustion. I'd experiment with pushing myself. Today's runners don't do that. I used to see how far I could go; I'd push and push. I would be so tired, and my blood sugar would be so low that I'd come in spinning and ravenous. I met a building trade friend out once one Sunday morning while he was walking. There was snow on the ground, and it was really cold. He was eating chocolate, and I asked him to give me a bit because I had pushed myself that far. However, you don't want to do that too often. I also recall getting down to nine stone three once.

How tall are you?

Five-foot seven. It was liquid loss. If you miss a day's training, you can gain nearly five pounds, but it's merely liquid retention that you haven't sweated out.

Did you drink much in a race?

I used to get a sponge early on. I love one-liners. I've got a retentive memory for those sorts of things, such as Ron Hill's "Be the hunter; don't be the hunted." I used to identify with that and things like "Take no prisoners" from Lawrence of Arabia, and Shakespeare's "Know thy self." I'm not a well-read man, but I read that. I used to be very self-critical, but I would to say to myself a bit later on that a number of people had said I had done well. I tried to believe it, and then as I got older and a bit more sensible and experienced, I'd look around and see that I had a lot going for me; that I'd done alright. I am not a bright lad; I'm a bricklayer, and I don't have any academic qualifications, but I've achieved all my life's ambitions. I wanted to win Morpeth, I wanted to run for my country, and I wanted to build my own house and start my own business. However, I didn't think at 55 I'd end up going bankrupt, lose my house and everything, and bring my wife to abject poverty. I didn't think it would get to that. People talk about stress, but I don't think you know what stress is until you lose your business and read about it in the papers. It hurt me deeply, but I've kept going, and I'm building again.

You are obviously quite a tenacious person then?

Well, I learnt that you get out of life what you put in. I also get a lot of pleasure from Morpeth Harriers and coaching, especially when I see Mark and Ian [Hudspith] do well and also Terry Wall.

Coming back to drinking – did you drink much during a marathon? How about generally in training?

I didn't take drinks in training, and I used to try to get used to it. In the second half of my career, I would put on a full tracksuit in the summertime and train. After a while, I found I could run in the heat. I used to be terrible in the heat as a youngster, but I trained for it.

Did you do the carbohydrate depletion/loading diet?

That came later in the 1970s and towards the end of my career. I followed it and, in hindsight, I should have been kicked from here to the other side of the track [the interview was being conducted at a track meeting]. Our club treasurer, who was a man of few words, told me that I'd had a great career and asked me why I was clutching at straws by going in for this new fad. I followed the diet, but I'm the sort of person that has trouble remembering what I've had for breakfast, and so what I gained, I lost in worrying about it because I am a free spirit. Basically, I didn't eat much fatty food. We didn't have a frying pan, and I never ate chips. I ate lots of carbohydrates, lots of salads, bread, jam, sugar and tea; I drank lots of sweet tea. I drank cup after cup from a big pot. What I noticed about the diet was when it went wrong people would say that their bodies felt good but that their legs just went like lead. I'd followed the diet slavishly. I did the two-hour run and bled myself out. I should have gone to Rome, but I finished ninth and died. I was really angry. It went wrong for Ronny [Hill] in Munich. He thought he was going to win Munich. Anyway, I think the consensus is a water-downed version is better.

Did you take any vitamins or supplements?

I took vitamins, and I think they helped me a little bit. I've no medical proof, but I am sure that they did. I also got iron injections for anaemia once, as my levels were so low. One of the homespun philosophies that I've always had is to run a short-distance track race a few

398

days before a marathon. Your legs are stiff, but it gets the lactic acid out. Anyway, I ran a 1500m, and I did an 80-second last lap. I knew something was wrong because I should have been running a 60/62, and so I went to the doctor. He gave me iron injections and put me on a high protein diet of red meat with tomato and no carbohydrate. It worked. I then took iron tablets right up until the time I was a veteran although not the same ones. I used to mix them, as you build up a resistance to them. I also had periods off of them when I was having a rest.

What sort of sessions did you do when you went on the track?

I used to kick off early season, well in February, with 600m, 800m and 1200m reps, and that type of thing. The philosophy I developed over two years was that as the season wore on, the distances got shorter and faster. I'd start with 1200m reps and then work my way down to 800m, 600m and 400m. I'd also mix them up a bit and do 400m and 200m reps. One of the sessions I used to do at the finish, after a warm-up, stretching and strides, was a 400m at three-quarter pace. So, if 57 was my fastest flat out, I'd do it in 61/62 to get my pulse rate up, and then I'd do 10 x 100m flat out with a 15-second interval. I used to love it, but if you are not fit, you will pull a hamstring. With a session like that and the distance I had done in the winter, it was no wonder I was Britain's top 10,000m runner. If I had done the English National Cross-Country in the summer time, I don't think anyone would have lived with me. When I ran it in the winter, I was always in build-up training. I also did fartlek in the woods. It is lovely around Morpeth. We could do a 20-mile run from the centre and only ever be three miles away, but it would nearly be all off-road and through woods. Only two miles of it was on the road.

Did you do most of your running off-road?

Yes, particularly when I was working from eight until four thirty or five o'clock during March to October. Half of it was off-road; it was through woods and on grass fields and footpaths.

Did you do hills?

Yes, in October/November time. I'd do 100/120 yards and some were very steep. Morpeth is in a valley, so you had to climb out of it wherever you went.

What about the long runs?

If it was very windy on a Sunday morning, then we used to go out on the roads. We'd do figures of eight and cut about, so we were doing the miles but with only very short spells in the wind, or alternatively, with a tailwind. There is nothing worse than running with a headwind. You'd turn round, and your sweat would go cold. I also used to go in the woods because then I'd be sheltered.

Did you do most of your training on your own or with a group?

I did a lot on my own, but the track sessions were with a group of club lads. Some of the lads would also come and meet me at night and do half my session. We'd meet on unlit roads. They were awesome sessions, and in the darkness you'd get a sense of running fast.

What was your biggest achievement?

The Commonwealth Games gold medal has to be because I was sent the wrong way. I entered the stadium, and Billy [Adcocks] was 50 yards ahead of me. The royal family then landed unannounced, and so all the officials followed them. I ran the full distance the wrong way. Bill ran 200 yards short, but it was not his fault. I thought Bill had gifted me, but he told me that he gifted no one. He ran faster times than me and was a better marathon runner. He was called the Little General. His 2.10 in Athens is an awesome record. However, in championships he only beat me once. Ronny [Hill] was head and shoulders above me; Jim Hogan, Ronny, Billy were all better marathon runners than me. Ronny was also a superior cross-country runner, but I valued the track racing, and I was a better 10,000m runner than most of them. Mind you, Billy won

401

the Inter-Counties 10,000m once, and in those days everyone ran the 10,000m. He was also fifth in the English National Cross-Country, so he wasn't that bad. He wasn't the fastest man and nor was Jim, and I was faster at a sprint finish, but he could run at pace, and when he went he took no prisoners.

What races did you do leading up to a marathon?

I liked to do a 1500m or 3000m within two to three weeks of a marathon. I knew I had the miles in, so if I could run a good short-distance race like a 3000m, I knew the speed was there too. It was strength first, speed second. After that, it was just a question of keeping the mind and body together. Before I went to Jamaica, I was fourth in the North East Mile Championships. At the beginning of the track season, I always did one 400m, two or three 800m and four or five 1500m races. It was a culture shock, and every snotty-nosed kid in the North East would beat me, but it got my mind attuned to track racing.

What about longer races leading up to the marathon, such as half-marathons or 10 miles?

The point is they weren't exactly 10 miles. They'd be 10 miles and so many yards. But so what? You'd get a good race. People nowadays are too preoccupied with the correct distance. I'd do the Morpeth to Newcastle in 64-and-a-half minutes. Today's runners are hiding their light under a bushel, and they don't race enough. We probably raced too much. I don't know what Bill and the other lads think. I think if we met halfway with what today's runners do, it would be ideal.

You had to do all the trials too, right?

The trials were in May, and the race would be in July/August. At the end of the day, you had to do them, and they made you hard. None of them go head to head today. There were five or six of us. There was Billy Adcocks, the tail end of Brian Kilby, Juan Taylor, Ronny Hill and Jim Hogan. These were all world-class men. Then there was myself, Don Faircloth and other lads like Alastair Wood. If you were just a bit off and had a bad run, you'd come sixth and were down the swanny. That was the name of the game: to make the first three. I ran the 10,000m trials as well.

Did you use any form of mental preparation?

Very early on, I realised the point in not being too fit too early and that was my philosophy for getting sharper towards the end of the season. This is why I am against distance runners running indoors. Flowers don't bloom twice a year. I sometimes used to run 20 miles in the morning before a race in the afternoon. I stopped drinking alcohol during the good years, except after big races.

What did you think about during races?

I would just run hard and see how it went. The highs and lows, that is. The early part of my life, I had doubts, but once I won medals and broke a couple of world records, I thought that was it. I knew it wasn't easy, and I'd still look to Ronny and Jim Hogan.

Did you ever go altitude training?

Yes, I went to Font Romeu; I had a fortnight at the French altitude training camp twice in the mid 1960s. I remember doing a mile race up at 7000 feet, and my heart rate was 205. The British Board took us to try it out, but what might suit one person might not suit another, and you've got to find what is best for you.

Do you think it made any difference?

When I came back, I was running well, but I failed at the Olympics. What I have learnt is that when it goes wrong at altitude, it goes horribly wrong. Ronny Hill and I were the fastest Britons over 5000m; he ran 14.17, and I ran 14.19. We were faster than the actual 5000m runners. I was going bloody well. I ran a time that would have got me 10th place in the Olympic final at 10,000m at altitude. However, on the day I ran like a drain. It was my only big failure.

Did you have any forms of sponsorship or financial assistance?

As I mentioned earlier, I hurt my knee on the water jump barrier in a league steeplechase, and so I ended up only being reserve for the Tokyo Olympics. However, I knew I was getting near world class, and I proved it by breaking the 30km world record during the Games. I did the equivalent of a 2.13 marathon when the world record was 2.14. I was wearing red, flat sand shoes at the time, and so I wrote to Robbie Brightwell at Adidas to ask for some stuff. I got Adidas gear from then on. I didn't get any money though. During the good years, I got a set of gold cufflinks, vases, cut crystal and things like that. I picked up £100 a couple of times on the continent in the 1960s. You are probably talking £1500/2000 in value nowadays. Running actually cost me a lot of money. But at the end of the day, I've been to nearly 50 countries, and I've dined with the Belgium royal family. I've been to Buckingham Palace six times, and I've been to Downing Street. You can't take that away. I was a working-class lad working as a bricklayer. I didn't have any O-Levels or A-Levels; I never passed a single exam in my life. Academically, I am not bright, but I am not stupid either, and I've got the best out of myself. I've had a wonderful life.

Are there any other factors that you'd like to add?

Several things. Rightly or wrongly, most of us were very patriotic. I know it's an old fashioned word, and queen and country and all that, but it meant a lot to me to wear my Scottish vest, my county vest, my club vest and my Great Britain vest. In Britain now, you've got Richard Nerurkar, Paul Evans and John Brown, but Paul won't run championships. There is also Mark Hudspith running 2.14/2.15. We are talking five men under 2.20. I could run 2.20 nearly every bloody weekend. Today's runners have lost their way. They are putting money first. They are running races for the wrong reasons, such as to pay the mortgage and buy food. They are also full-time runners, and if their running is going wrong, they have 24 hours to worry about it. Part-time work is the way to go. You must get away from running. We were all into football as well, and we liked to socialise. Running is very important, but it has to have its place, and I still think of it as a relationship. One of the best bits of advice I was ever given was from Mike Rawson. I was at the Windsor Hotel in Lancaster Gate where the British team used to go, and I was getting uptight before an international. Mike asked me if I had trained hard, if I was in good racing form, whether I was sleeping well and whether I had any financial or emotional worries. When I replied with a negative to all of his questions, he then asked me what the hell I was worrying about, and he betted that one of my rivals had at least one of those problems. I never forgot that. It was a throwaway remark from Mike at the time, but I don't think he realised how important it was. I've cited that to him time and time again. Today's runners want the money and to be full-time. They want the goodies before they've earned them. I know the older generation always criticise the younger ones but that want to win has to burn. There has to be an attitude of playing to win. Are you remembered for how much money you've won or for how many medals and championships you've won? In my opinion, you are remembered for the big days. I told Mark [Hudspith] to forget the money and go for the championships. He is the only British medallist in the 1990s. I've got four, Billy Adcocks has one, Ronny has three, Don Faircloth has one and Basil Heatley has one.

And you all seem to have been self-coached?

I started my distance running based on Brian Kilby's stuff. Brian ran 150 miles a week, and I thought I'd try it. I then added in some of Arthur Lydiard's training ideas. So, I used a bit of Brian's, a bit of Lydiard's and some other sessions that I picked up along the way. We stumbled along and did make a lot of mistakes. I was impetuous by nature, and I had to learn to control myself. Again, it's that Shakespeare thing of first of all know thy self. You have to look at yourself and try to get the best out of yourself. I got the best out of myself and very few people do. They are all old men in Britain now. Richard [Nerukar] is 34, and Paul Evans is 38.

You were all quite young. It seems that people now move up through the distances more. Do you think that is wrong?

I think it is wrong, and you should mix the two. If you look at the world's best, you will see that they are younger people. We all had a good range. I've got a Commonwealth 10,000m medal. We all did a bit of this and a bit of that, and we were all coming from the same direction. We all ran track, and we all ran cross-country. We all raced more, and we did all the meetings. We were all much more rounded athletes. We had a greater armoury. Track races give you pace judgement. We would blow people away winning the Southern and Northern now. People are too frightened of getting beaten now. I only won seven marathons, but I ran 57. I was second and third in about 16 or 17, and I was well placed or highly placed in several others. They are running races for the wrong reasons now because most of them are professional. They don't race enough, and they are not round enough. They don't do enough track, and they don't experiment enough. I once did 213 miles in a week and three times a day. In fact, I did three times a day for a year, and the week I did 213, I won a 10-mile race at the end of it in 47 odd minutes even though my legs were continually aching. I just wanted to go over 200. I averaged 160 for over six months. The top Kenyans do three times a day. They just don't train hard enough now. I was doing three times a day back in 1970. Two fives are better than one ten. I can't explain why. About 10 to 13 of us did that in the 1960s, and we can't all be wrong. So, why don't they follow it? It is now 1998, and what have they learnt? They don't have to take everything we say on board, but they could take on most of it. To sum up, I think you get out what you put in, and you've got to be doing 100 miles a week or something of that ilk if you want to get anywhere. You also need to be a well-rounded athlete and do road, track and cross-country.

Don Faircloth

PB: 2.12.19 – Edinburgh 1970

Marathon Achievements:

Bronze - Edinburgh Commonwealth Games 1970

How did you become involved in athletics?

I started doing athletics in my first year at senior school. They had a cross-country trial around the local park, and everyone was supposed to turn up and do it. I hadn't done more than a 100m or 100 yards at junior school, where I was pretty average, but I actually finished second. I just ran it on the basic fitness I had from playing football and rugby. Two weeks later, they had another race, and I won that one too. From then on in my age group, I was unbeaten at school. That was the impetus to start running. My school, Selhurst Grammar, had a very good background in cross-country, and two of the teachers were members of Blackheath Harriers, so I really got sucked into it. However, I found the track very difficult because I didn't have a lot of basic speed. I was very average at 800m and 1500m – well, 800m and the mile as it was then. I joined Croydon Harriers, which was the local athletic club, at around the age of 12 and it was really just a gradual progression from then until my third year at senior school. I finished around seventh or eighth in the Surrey Cross-Country Championships and 33rd in the English Schools' in Coventry. It was quite an incredible increase in performance really. I was absolutely taken by athletics and at this point gave up football and anything else that I was doing. At the beginning, I didn't particularly train, other than at school, but once I joined Croydon Harriers I would train on Tuesday and Thursday nights, as well as on Sunday mornings. A year after this, I progressed to finishing fifth in the English Schools' a year below my age group. There was a good crowd of senior athletes at Croydon Harriers, and there was a coach that used to train them, so I just used to hang in on some of their sessions or do part of the sessions. I often did the Sunday run of up to 15 miles as well, even when I was only 15/16 years of age. They were a good, friendly bunch of people, and it was better than running on my own.

So, you laid down a good base at a young age?

Yes, but I never had any aspirations to do marathons at all. In the National Youth's Cross-Country, I was fourth and fifth. I was fifth in the year below and fourth in my age group. In the National Junior's Cross-Country, I was fifth and sixth and went to Tunisia for the International Cross-Country where I actually finished fourth. I rose to the occasion. It was on an equestrian racecourse with sandy tracks and absolutely flat. Despite the cross-country successes, I was still thinking very much in terms of the track. However, my basic speed continued to be lacking. I had run about 4.14 for the mile whereas those around me in the same age group like Ian Stewart and Tony Simmons were running nearer four minutes. I ran 10,000m on the track for Great Britain in 1969, but my fastest was only 29.01 on all-weather and 29.02 on cinder.

Were you one of the top 10km runners though?

Well, Ron Hill was still running seriously and so was Mike Freary. There were also people like Dick Taylor, Alan Rushmere and Dave Bedford coming through at

411

the same time. I had every intention of carrying on trying to improve my 10,000m time, and certainly no intentions of doing anything longer, but I picked up a couple of stress fractures in the cross-country season of 1969/1970 and had to stop doing any speedwork. I carried on running but only steady and just kept increasing the distance slightly. It wasn't for any real reason other than the lads in the club were doing that. I was then persuaded to run the Kent 20 in April 1970 and won it in about 1.44. It was a quite unbelievable really. However, I carried on trying to get my track times down until a good friend, Ted Chapel, who was the Great Britain team physiotherapist, persuaded me to run the Inter-Counties 20 in Leicester. It was a very hot day, but being that I was a horticulturist by trade and used to working outside all day with the sun on my back, it was kind of my forte. In fact, my job determined my training to a large degree. I wasn't coached by anyone, and I would adapt my training depending on how I was feeling after pushing wheelbarrows of manure around all day.

How many hours a day did you work?

I worked about eight or nine. I would always try to get a run in at lunchtime and then again in the evening. Actually, I used to get some really good fartlek sessions done in the park at lunchtime. I think that is why I didn't have too many injuries over the years as I tried to keep off-road as much as possible. Anyway, I was persuaded to do the Inter-Counties 20 and won it by about three minutes in very hot conditions. In fact, it was so hot that the tar was coming off the roads. I had a guy with me until 17 miles, but the heat must have got to him, and he went back. After that, Ted persuaded me to run the Poly Marathon, which was the trial for the Commonwealth Games. Although there was no pre-selection policy, we all knew that Bill Adcocks and Ron Hill, who had both run very fast times in Japan and Boston respectively, would be selected, and we didn't expect them to turn up for the trial. I was a bit naïve really, I suppose, and I didn't go into it with any real aspirations of winning it or making the Commonwealth Games team. However, once more I was lucky, as it was a very hot day, and I won it in 2.18. That was my debut for the marathon, and I was selected to go to the Commonwealth Games. At the Commonwealth Games, the field was very strong. There was Jerome Drayton, who had the world best at that time, Derek Clayton, the world record holder and a number of other pretty good runners. It was reasonably warm again, and they went off at the most kamikaze pace you could ever imagine. I went through ten miles in 48.40, and my best was only about 48.30 at that time for the distance. I remember making the turn and seeing Derek Clayton sitting on the side of the road with his head in his hands. Ron Hill had

413

already well passed me going back the opposite way with Jerome Drayton. Two or three others were in front of me: Bill Adcocks, Jim Alder and a guy from Tanzania. I just ran on really. I ran with Bill Adcocks for a time and then the Tanzanian guy.

So, you ran at your own pace?

I guess it was naivety again because you don't really know what you are doing when you find yourself going through 20 miles in 1.39, and you have never run that fast. As it turned out, I managed to burn the guy off and got the bronze behind Jim Alder and Ron Hill. That was that really and I was hooked on marathon running.

Was that your best time?

Yes, it was my best time: 2.12.19. I must say I couldn't believe it and probably said all sorts of things at the press interview about what I expected to do in the future. I went to Kyoto in Japan in February the year after and ran 2.14 odd. I finished second or third and thought it was just a stepping-stone. There isn't really anything I could pinpoint as to why it didn't progress from there really.

Was that your biggest achievement?

Yes, I think so. It's got to be really. A medal at a major games is a high point in anyone's career and for so

414

many years that time still ranked me in the top 10 in Great Britain - for over 10 years, in fact.

How old were you when you ran that?

I was 21. It was the ninth fastest time in the world ever at that time, and it was certainly the fourth fastest time in the world that year. In 1971, I consolidated with the intention of bidding for a place in the following year's Olympic team for Munich. Things were going really well right up until a week-and-a-half before the trial when I picked up a virus of some kind and a dreadful throat infection. I had to go on antibiotics and ended up finishing fourth in the trial with a lacklustre run in about 2.15 odd. I was just 50 yards short of third place. However, fourth is nowhere if they only take three. About three weeks after that, I ran the Poly Marathon again and that was the infamous year when they sent everyone off course. We ran 29 miles, and I ended up winning by about seven or eight minutes from the guy that was only 30 seconds behind me at the trial. Arthur Gold, the Great Britain team manager, was very kind, and he wrote me a nice letter. He said I was reserve, even though they didn't have reserves for the Olympics, and told me not to do any more long races before the Games in case anyone got injured. Nobody did get injured and drop out albeit I know that Colin Kirkham was badly laid up with sciatica problems just before. However, I would have done exactly the same in his

415

shoes. You always hope the physios can sort you out. So, that was that. It was a big disappointment.

Did you plan much for these marathons or were you just doing 10,000m training?

In hindsight, I should have gone back to concentrating on the track because track speed is really the answer to getting faster at the marathon. Most good marathoners are also good track men. In our day, people like Ron Hill were quality 10,000m runners although there were others who were more road and cross-country orientated with just some track background. Nowadays, it seems elite track runners move up to the marathon. They've certainly got faster at the very top with people dropping in 4.30 miles and the like. You can't compete with that unless you have been a top 10,000m track runner.

So, what was your training like?

I really didn't vary my training that much. My average throughout the year was somewhere between 70 to 80 miles a week. When I was training for a marathon, I would go into a 10-week build-up, which would consist of 8 weeks of very hard work and a couple of weeks of easing down. I would also push it up to somewhere between 90 to 100 miles. However, in the early part of the 1970s, I was still working manually, and I didn't increase it a lot further until I became more office based.

In fact, it may be that moving to office-based work had an effect as to why the improvement didn't come. I experimented with twice a day and even three times a day. I'd run to work one of those times and run again in the evenings. When you are trying to hold down a job and set up a home, as we were at the time, it is physically and mentally quite tiring. Because of what Dave Bedford was doing, people were trying out heavy mileage. Personally, I have always been a slight runner, and I didn't see the point from a body weight perspective. I really didn't need to pound out those sorts of miles. The most I ever did was 138 miles in a week, and it probably took my legs about three weeks to recover, so it was completely pointless.

So, can you outline a typical week?

My week started on a Sunday, so I always got in a long run on that day, which would vary between 16 to 23 miles. The most I ever ran in training run was 23. It was on hilly roads and was about the only time I did heavy work on the road. The great majority of my training, and certainly at lunchtime, was done on parkland. I was lucky, as where I lived and worked in Croydon, I had Lloyd Park and Addington Hills. You'd only have to come a mile out of Croydon and be on parkland. I would then rely more on fartlek, hill work and grass repetitions than actually going to the track. When I was using the track, I would do a maximum of two sessions a week, which would be on a Tuesday and Thursday I'd run at Croydon Arena, which was a cinder track in those days, and we'd just do typical pyramid type stuff like 200m, 300m, 400m and so on up to 800m or maybe 12 x 300m with a 100m jog. Sometimes, I'd go back to the type of sessions that the Croydon Harriers' senior coach had brought me up on, such as 52 x 200m off of a 100m jog with a flat out quarter mile at the end. It would total 10 miles exactly, and was based on the Zatopek type regimes. It was a mental thing. I don't think it is a lot different to the way most of the Australians seem to train. I know Rob de Castella used to train like that. As I understand it, they used to do quite lengthy repetition sessions. Whilst they weren't intense from the absolute speed point of view, the interval was quite fast. I think, albeit naively, that is what we were also doing. If you can go on a track and do a session like that, which is 10 miles long, it toughens you up mentally, especially for when you get into a difficult situation in a race.

Did you mostly do these sessions on your own or with a group?

I always did them with a group. I was very lucky in that respect. My philosophy was that if I was doing long runs, and I could get company, I would actually run at the pace that the person wanted because I always felt that company was the best thing. If you did the long run and thought that you hadn't worked hard enough, then there was always the option of going out for another session in the evening although you hardly ever did. The company was good, and it helped them as much as it helped me, which I felt was also something worthwhile. On the track sessions, I was probably the person taking the lead by the end. I'd have people with me for the first two-thirds, who may have been faster than me, but they hadn't got the pace judgement quite right and would run themselves out. It worked very well for us; it worked well to help each other. We had a hard-core group of three or four that used to meet and do the sessions.

Did you have a coach when you were doing marathons?

No, I never had a coach as such although I did discuss my training with a local guy who had an international cross-country background. He just had some spare time to sit and listen to what I was suggesting, and then he would then come up with some alternative ideas. Some of what he said made sense, and so I would go along with a few of his sessions. It was bouncing off ideas really.

Did you do anything that you might call mental preparation?

I would like to say that I did because it would make me appear to have been a thinking runner, but I did

419

nothing other than the fact that I trained hard for a particular race, as you needed to, and then I turned out and did it.

Did you use the carbohydrate depletion/loading diet?

In 1970 at the Commonwealth Games village, I remember there was all the talk about carbohydrate loading and bleeding out, but it seemed to be the first year that people were doing it. From 1970 through to 1975, I was competing all over the world in marathons for Great Britain, but I had no idea what they were talking about.

So, you never tried it?

I tried carbohydrate loading on a number of occasions, but I am not sure that it did me any good; I'm not convinced that it necessarily helped. In fact, doing the full the diet might harm you more mentally than help you physically. Large numbers of people I spoke to said it had an adverse effect.

So, you just ate a balanced diet?

Yes, that was all I did.

Did you take any supplements?

I took iron and that was all. I took it because of the workload I was doing and because occasionally I got anaemic. That was all really.

Did you use any mental techniques during the race?

No, and to be absolutely honest with you, if I had realised in 1970 that we were going so fast for the first five miles, I would probably have psyched myself out. I was in a pack of people, half of whom I didn't know from Adam, and that was that. I was set up. In all my races, I had pretty good pace judgement, and I knew my state of fitness. I knew whether I could go with the main pack or a particular group or not. If I couldn't, then I'd hold off with the hope that some would come back. I never instilled that into myself mentally or anything though. I also never went into a race thinking I was going to have a bad one. I always thought that I had prepared well enough for it.

Did you use altitude or warm-weather training?

I went to altitude pre-Munich in 1972. I found it no problem at all albeit that I wasn't doing any intense track work. However, I was doing long runs and hills.

Where did you go?

We went to St Moritz. They were warning us that we should only walk for the first couple of days, but we ignored that. I think they were a bit worried that we might die or something.

Was it an organised trip?

Yes, by the British board. It was the first time they had decided to go to altitude because of the supposed difference of the Africans.

Do you think it had any beneficial effects?

When we came down, we had a bit of a mad run while we were waiting to go to the airport because Brendan Foster was the only one of the group doing any heavy work on the track at the time – well, from a distance point of view.

And warm-weather training?

No, warm-weather training wasn't available at all in those days. I happen to believe in mad dogs and Englishmen, so I did most of my training in the middle of the day even in the heat in the summer. I certainly wouldn't avoid hot weather because I always felt that if I could train in hot weather, then it would prepare me to race in those conditions. I also tried running in quite heavy tracksuits although I didn't do it for very long, as I found my body was losing extra energy. In the winter, I mostly trained in track trousers because of the resistance, not so much due to the cold. It was pure and simply because I felt that if you trained in track trousers, except for sessions, when you came to race and wore

422

shorts, you would feel faster and your knees would come up just that little bit further.

Did you have specific races in your build-up for a marathon?

I would probably do track races rather than road, as there weren't that many 10km road races in those days. All you could find were 10 milers unless you wanted to do a 20. So, I'd concentrate on 3000m, 5000m and 10,000m although 10,000m races were often a bit harder to find. In addition, as I found those races so hard from a speed point of view, they'd mentally prepare me for the more relaxed pace of road running.

How did you taper?

I'd do a long run on the Sunday two weeks prior to the race and then only a 15 the week before. The mileage would also come down from between 90 and 100 to 70 miles for the penultimate week and then 35 to 40 miles for the last week. People get carried away with wanting to do that extra session. If you're not fit two weeks before the race, you aren't going to get any fitter. In fact, you could do yourself a lot of harm by trying to force yourself on.

Did you do any other forms of training like weights?

No, I didn't. I always felt that I'd rather be out running than doing weights. Physically, I never felt that my arms weren't capable of carrying what I needed to carry. Even after moving from manual to office-based work, I still did - and still do - a lot of physical work a weekends. I still run a little business on the side, which keeps me physically able and that would be the equivalent of doing weights. I probably regret not doing warm-up stretching though.

How tall are you, and what was your racing weight?

I am five-foot eight, and I weighed eight-and-a-quarter stone at my best. I am now nine-and-a-half plus.

In general, did you drink a lot? What about during a marathon?

There weren't any electrolyte drinks as such in those days, but I experimented with glucose and salt drinks However, your body metabolism reacts differently in a race. So, you could get used to something in training and then find that the solution is too strong in a race to the point where it makes you wretch. In a marathon, used to take on drinks as early as I could and then jus little and often really. Also, naively or otherwise, I used to think that if you could get through all your training without drinking, then you were getting your body used to any eventuality. So, if you found you couldn' take on any water in a race, it wasn't such a huge problem. I probably still don't drink as much water as should.

Did you always work full-time?

I never packed in work for my running. I worked in local government, which you might think would have made it easier for me to get time off with pay, but actually it didn't. They did give me a week-and-a-half off for the Commonwealth Games and a short time off to go to Japan, and I think there was one other time, but everything else had to be taken as holiday. My wife suffered more than anyone else because I couldn't be with her.

Did you have sponsorship throughout your running career?

I was very fortunate to have sponsorship from Gola. They even made me a pair of shoes to fit to the specification I gave them although they only arrived two days before the race, which wasn't ideal. They were built on a spike last, as were Ron Hill's World Tens at that time. However, whereas Ron Hill's had nothing on the soles, other than a tiny piece of polyurethane, mine had quite a lot of cushioning, and they had holes all over them. I guess that was strange in those days. We look back and laugh now, but they were very good for a couple of years. It was still very much the Oxbridge thing in athletics in 1970, and the great majority of the British athletes at the Commonwealth Games were university people. They weren't many people like Geoff

Capes and I, who were working manually. I don't think he was working for the police at that time. You couldn't get Adidas or Puma shoes, or anything like, that for neither love nor money because it was all stitched up. A little bit later, I got sponsorship from Dunlop. They were trying to get into the running shoe market and were very good to me for a couple of years. Nike were also very good. So, it was just bits here and there really.

Did you earn any money?

No, I never had any financial gain from athletics, neither from sponsors nor from races. I did a race in Rome once with Bernie Plain where there were cash bonuses at the end of each lap, but naively we didn't realise why they were all sprinting. No one had told us. There was probably nowhere else other than Italy doing that at the time though. What I did gain from running were some very good friends, and it got me all over the world, including the iron curtain counties. It got me to China just before it opened up to tourism and to Japan, South America and North America. Australasia was about the only place I didn't get to go. I also raced in just about every country in Europe. It was great!

Did you get enough rest and sleep?

I used to get seven or eight hours sleep every night although I am one of those people who probably go to bed too late. Before the 1972 Olympics, there was a lot of publicity about Ian Stewart going part-time, which was unheard of in England in those days. From what he tells me, I don't believe he was doing any more training. It just allowed him to eat and sleep after his first training run instead of being straight back at the workbench. He was a gunsmith or something. I can see logical advantages in doing that. However, I can also see a lot of boredom in being a full-time athlete unless there are other things you are doing. I never ever considered that. Nowadays, with things like job share, I might have.

Did you have regular massage or other treatments?

I think the athletes of the 1970s, certainly from a long-distance point of view, could have made all sorts of improvements, in terms of being able to train better and keep away from injuries, if we'd had more physiological support like physiotherapy and massage. I was very lucky in that the Great Britain team physiotherapist for many years, Ted Chapel, lived nearby in Worcester Park. He had a physiotherapy business, but he didn't charge athletes. I used to see him regularly. There was always an open door and a cup of tea, and you'd often meet other Surrey athletes and international runners there. He was around from after the Tokyo Olympics, and he was very good. When I was younger, I had stress fractures almost every year in either my toes or my shins. It was probably because I was a slight build and running a little bit too far for my age. Plus, in those

427

days, you didn't have the types of training shoes that you have now. If you were lucky, you had a pair of shoes called Tiger Cubs, which cost a pound-and-a-half. They had canvas uppers and no support whatsoever. There certainly weren't the heel counters and materials that are around now to try to protect your legs and back from the injuries caused by the jarring of running. Ted Chapel was very good though with the lower back, and he sorted out any problems I had in that area. It was always a fine line between being fit and getting ill. I often had throat infections and occasionally I'd get mouth ulcers. I had a cartilage out three years ago but that was more likely due to football and trying to do skills with 10 and 11 year olds! I think I did more damage through football than running although it might also have been wear and tear. Back in the early 1980s, in fact 1983, I had a car crash. I received seat belt damage across my whole pelvic area, which damaged the rectus sheath. Funnily enough, it is an injury that a lot of footballers get, and it is the injury that Dave Moorcroft had to have surgery for. It's like a double hernia operation. They did tell me that it wasn't altogether to do with the seat belt hit but also the wear and tear of running over the years. I went two years before I could have the operation, and I really couldn't get any knee lift at all, as it gave me terrific pains after a few miles. I also had a major scare in 1985. I was very it, and I remember I trained twice on that particular Thursday. I did a good session at lunchtime and another good track session in the evening. I was really buzzing and ready for something at the weekend. However, I woke up on the Friday morning feeling like I had been kicked around the bedroom by a horse. So, rather than my planned run to work, I got Sue [his wife] to give me a lift to work. Later, I collapsed and was rushed to hospital. I was put in the heart unit of intensive care for two days. Luckily, it turned out that it wasn't a heart attack or stroke. Instead, I had pleurisy and viral pneumonia, which had set in overnight. The virus was so bad that it had affected the lining of my heart although thankfully not my actual heart muscles, and the pains were to do with the fluid in the lungs. It took me a year trying to get back to the level of training I was doing before. However, my times were still way down. The International Athletics Club were very good, and they sent me for complete BUPA and stress testing. The results said that there was nothing wrong with my heart and no scars or anything, but from these tests they came to the conclusion that I was doing the wrong type of training. Apparently, I was doing too much slow running and not enough speedwork. Once I was released from the BUPA testing, I felt fine and sort of got back again, but I was two or three years older, and so I decided I wouldn't do any more serious marathon running and would just run more for fun with the lads and for the club.

What do you think were the key factors that made you and the others so good in this era?

I know what made me good at the time: it was because I was competitive. What made me competitive stemmed from when I was a boy, in terms of when I was a boy I was up against youths and then as a youth I was up against juniors and then as a junior I was up against seniors. My peers were Ian Stewart; Andy Holden; Tony Simmons; Norman Morrison, who actually did a four-minute mile; John Bednarski, who won the International Cross-Country and Dave Bedford. We competed against each other in the National, the Inter-Counties and so on. If I wanted to be successful and compete against these people in the major championships, then I had to get myself to a particular level of fitness. It was the background and apprenticeship that I did as a boy, youth and junior with that particular group of people that I think helped me and stood me in good stead for when I entered the senior ranks. It was very competitive because the people you came up against were just so good. If you wanted to at least keep on terms with them and compete at that level, then you knew what you needed to do and that was that. I don't think the standard is there today. If you look at the 10,000m, and you go back to the days of Bernie Ford, Tony Simmons

Dave Black and Brendan Foster in the mid/late 1970s, they all ran a lot quicker than people are today. When Brendan Foster had the world record of 27.30, the other guys all ran around 27.43 to 27.45. If you look at the rankings for 10,000m now, I don't think anyone has run as fast as 27.45. It is 20 years on and 10,000m runners are not as good. Ian Stewart won the Commonwealth Games, and Ian McCafferty beat Keino in 13.15. I know Dave Moorcroft broke the world record, and people are running faster than that now on the world stage, but there aren't many running those sorts of times in the UK. It's not logical. We also had a very gifted group of 1500m runners like Coe and Ovett, and Elliott and Cram, as well as many good 800m runners, but the standard really isn't there today. If they haven't got the incentive of the major games, because of the fear of being completely overawed by the Kenyans or by people from somewhere with an enhancement situation, then they've at least got a financial incentive now. If they are good enough, they can go all over the world. They can set themselves a schedule of races to do and make good money from it. The people are just not coming through. If you consider the Kenyans are supposedly good because they come from altitude and walk or run everywhere from when they are old enough to walk and run, you could maybe compare that to the hardships that people like Ron Hill, who was a little older than me, had to put up with. There was a lack of food around after the war, and they walked everywhere. They weren't taken to school by their parents. There was also far more sport in school back then than there is now. You can follow that on to my generation, which is 10 years on from Ron. We certainly didn't have a car, and I used to walk everywhere. I'd even save money on the bus fare by jogging to the cinema and back. Another 10 or 20 years on, and things are getting worse and worse with kids having very sedentary lifestyles. Now they sit and play computer games all day. Things were definitely harder when I was a boy. When I got married, I had a scooter, not a car. Nowadays, people want everything on a plate, and things are too easy. Parents buy their kids a car. My parents would never have been able to buy me a car. I think all the way down the line we are making it so much easier for our kids, and it is just another nail in the coffin. I think it really has had an effect on people.

About Gabrielle

I was born in London and attended Nonsuch High School for Girls in Cheam. Being a rather free-spirited person and finding the constraints and curriculum of an all girls' grammar school a bit too much, I left at 16 to start a job in structural engineering in London.

However, I later returned to academic life and obtained both a BA (Hons) in Sports Studies & History and an MSc in Sports Science. During this time, I also became a pretty good runner.

I had been a half-decent swimmer and netball player at school but only got into distance running after hanging out with my friends: Gary Staines, Stuart Paton and Kevin Sturman, who all ran for Belgrave Harriers. They humoured me when I showed some interest by taking me out for some short jogs, which I could barely complete.

It must have surprised them when I joined Belgrave, and I suspect they thought the novelty would soon wear off, but it didn't, and I eventually gained an Athletics National Championship (AAA) medal. I can be quite stubborn and persistent!

While the guys at Belgrave sparked my interest, it was Geoff Hill (Swansea Harriers) who was really inspirational, and it was through his careful guidance that I reached the level I did on the track, road and cross-country. There were a few tantrums along the way, but he managed to ignore most of those and gently nurture his charge. Without him, I don't think I would have achieved half as much. I must also pay tribute to my various training partners: Paul Collicutt, Tony Holborn, Kurt Hoyte, Andy Mitchelson and anyone else who had to suffer my moaning when training on cold winter nights.

After having surgery on a calcaneal bursitis and cyst, I retired from running and travelled about for a while, including spending long periods of time in Portugal. It was at this point that I started my career as an author and wrote two books about buying property there.

I am now back living in London and spend my time writing, working part-time and throwing large pieces of metal about in the gym. The rest of my spare time is taken up attending rock & metal gigs and drinking wine with good friends. You can read more about me on my website at www.gabriellecollison.com.

Appendices

The following lists show British men and women who were ranked in the world top 100 at some point during each decade. While they may have been ranked in more than one year, I have only shown their best performance during the decade. If the time is not their PB, this is shown in brackets. *Other performances, which didn't make the world top 100 in their year but were quicker than the last person listed (or sub 2.38 for women in the 1980s), are also shown underneath.

British Marathon Runners Ranked in World Top 100 (1980s) - Men

Steve Jones - Chicago 1985 - 2.07.13
Charlie Spedding - London 1985 - 2.08.33
Geoff Smith - New York 1983 - 2.09.08
Allister Hutton - London 1985 - 2.09.16
Hugh Jones - London 1982 - 2.09.24
John Graham - Rotterdam 1981 - 2.09.28
Mike Gratton - London 1983 - 2.09.43
Tony Milosorov - London 1989 - 2.09.54
Gerry Helme - London 1983 - 2.10.12
Kevin Forster - London 1988 - 2.10.52
Chris Bunyan - Boston 1983 - 2.10.55
Nick Brawn - New York 1981 - 2.11.09
Dave Murphy - Sydney 1983 - 2.11.18
Dave Cannon - Montreal 1980 - 2.11.22

Paul Davies-Hale - Chicago 1989 - 2.11.25
Dave Long II - London 1988 - 2.11.33 (PB: 2.10.30)
Malcolm East - Boston 1981 - 2.11.35
Kenny Stuart - Houston 1989 - 2.11.36
Steve Kenyon - Gateshead 1982 - 2.11.40
Jimmy Ashworth - Berlin 1985 - 2.11.43
Jim Dingwall - London 1983 - 2.11.44
Fraser Clyne - Sacramento 1984 - 2.11.50
Steve Brace - Chicago 1988 - 2.11.50 (PB: 2.10.35)
Martin McCarthy - London 1983 - 2.11.54
Mike O'Reilly - Columbus 1989 - 2.12.06 (PB: 2.10.39)
Dennis Fowles - London 1984 - 2.12.12
John Wheway - London 1988 - 2.12.13
Dave Long I - Miami 1982 - 2.12.17
Trevor Wright - London 1983 - 2.12.29
Derek Stevens - Duluth 1984 - 2.12.41
Ray Crabb - London 1983 - 2.13.15
Norman Wilson - Boston 1981 - 2.13.16
Mike Hurd - Chicago 1982 - 2.13.17
John Boyes - Maassluis 1985 - 2.13.20
Ieuan Ellis - Beijing 1986 - 2.13.21
Chris Garforth - Otwock 1980 - 2.13.27
Lindsay Robertson - Frankfurt 1987 - 2.13.30
Dave Clarke - Stockholm 1989 - 2.13.34
Michael Kearns - London 1981 - 2.13.37
Ian Thompson - Birmingham 1981 - 2.13.50 (PB: 2.09.12)
Graham Laing - London 1981 - 2.13.59
Brian Cole - London 1981 - 2.14.01
Stan Curran - Rotterdam 1981 - 2.14.08
Ian Ray - Gateshead 1982 - 2.14.08
Andy Robertson - Sandbach 1981 - 2.14.23

*Steve Binns – Chicago 1988 – 2.13.32
John Caine – London 1983 – 2.13.43
Mervyn Brameld – London 1983 – 2.13.48
Mike Bishop – Paris 1987 – 2.13.48
John Offord – Maassluis 1984 – 2.13.52
Mark Burnhope – London 1985 – 2.13.54
Adrian Leek – Pittsburgh 1987 – 2.14.03
Martin Brewer – San Francisco 1984 – 2.14.07
Carl Thackery – Liverpool 1989 – 2.14.19 (PB: 2.12.37)

British Marathon Runners Ranked in World Top 100 (1980s) - Women

Veronique Marot - London 1989 - 2.25.56
Priscilla Welch - London 1987 - 2.26.51
Sarah Rowell - London 1985 - 2.28.06
Sally-Ann Hales - London 1985 - 2.28.38
Joyce Smith - London 1982 - 2.29.43
Paula Fudge - Chicago 1988 - 2.29.47
Ann Ford - London 1988 - 2.30.38
Angie Pain (Hulley) - Seoul 1988 - 2.30.51
Susan Wightman (Tooby) - Seoul 1988 - 2.31.33
Lyn Harding - London 1989 - 2.31.45
Gillian Castka (Burley) - Florence 1984 - 2.32.53
Sheila Catford (Boyde) - London 1989 - 2.33.04
Carolyn Naisby - Florence 1987 - 2.33.22
Sally Ellis - London 1989 - 2.33.24
Lynda Bain - London 1985 - 2.33.38
Jill Harrison (Clarke) - London 1989 - 2.34.19
Heather MacDuff - Eindhoven 1988 - 2.34.26
Alison Blake - Bedford 1982 - 2.34.35
Sandra Branney - London 1989 - 2.35.03
Carol Gould - New York 1980 - 2.35.04
Susan Crehan - London 1988 - 2.35.10
Karen Holdsworth (Goldhawk) - Berlin 1985 - 2.35.18
Julie Coleby (Barleycorn) - London 1984 - 2.35.53
Margaret Lockley - London 1984 - 2.36.06
Kath Binns - Windsor 1982 - 2.36.12
Glynis Penny - London 1983 - 2.36.21
Julia Gates (Armstrong) - London 1986 - 2.36.31
Lorna Irving - Edinburgh 1986 - 2.36.34

Gillian Horowitz (Adams) - London 1984 - 2.37.10
(PB: 2.36.52)
Caroline Horne - London 1985 - 2.37.26
Iness McLean - Laredo 1985 - 2.38.17
Susan Morris (Hassan) - Essonne 1981 - 2.42.12
Rosemary Wright - Gloucester 1981 - 2.43.29
Leslie Watson - New York 1980 - 2.45.39 (PB: 2.44.18)

*Rosemary Ellis - London 1989 - 2.35.32
  Marina Stedman (Samy) - London 1989 - 2.36.32
  Moira O'Neill - Dublin 1988 - 2.37.06
  Debbie Noy - Birmingham 1989 - 2.37.24 (PB: 2.35.18)
  Sandra Mewett - Houston 1988 - 2.37.36
  Alison Gooderham - London 1988 - 2.37.49

British Marathon Runners Ranked in World Top 100 (1990s) - Men

Richard Nerurkar - London 1997 - 2.08.36
Paul Evans - Chicago 1996 - 2.08.52
Jon Brown - London 1999 - 2.09.44 (PB: 2.09.31)
Steve Jones - Toronto 1992 - 2.10.06 (PB: 2.07.13)
Allister Hutton - London 1990 - 2.10.10 (PB: 2.09.16)
Dave Long II - London 1991 - 2.10.30
Steve Brace - Houston 1996 - 2.10.35
Mike O'Reilly - Fukuoka 1993 - 2.10.39
Eamonn Martin - London 1993 - 2.10.50
Dave Buzza - San Sebastian 1993 - 2.11.06
Gary Staines - Chicago 1996 - 2.11.25
Paul Davies-Hale - Carpi 1991 - 2.11.57 (PB: 2.11.25)
Mark Hudspith - London 1995 - 2.11.58
Kevin Forster - Tokyo 1991 - 2.11.59 (PB: 2.10.52)
Jon Solly - Twin Cities 1990 - 2.12.07
Mark Flint - London 1994 - 2.12.07
Andy Green - Paris 1993 - 2.12.12
Carl Thackery - Carpi 1992 - 2.12.37

*Peter Whitehead - London 1995 - 2.12.23

British Marathon Runners Ranked in World Top 100 (1990s) - Women

Liz McColgan - London 1997 - 2.26.52
Marian Sutton - Chicago 1999 - 2.28.42
Sally Eastall - Sacramento 1991 - 2.29.29
Yvonne Danson - Boston 1995 - 2.30.53
Veronique Marot - Houston 1991 - 2.30.55 (PB: 2.25.56)
Andrea Wallace - London 1992 - 2.31.33
Nicky McCracken (Morris) - London 1990 - 2.33.07
Karen McCleod - Victoria 1994 - 2.33.16
Suzanne Rigg - Berlin 1995 - 2.34.21
Sally Ellis - London 1991 - 2.34.42 (PB: 2.33.24)
Debbie Noy - Beijing 1991 - 2.35.18
Sheila Catford (Boyde) - Firenze 1991 - 2.35.37
(PB: 2.33.04)
Angela Pain (Hulley) - Auckland 1990 - 2.36.35
(PB: 2.30.51)

Sally Goldsmith - Vigarano Mainarda 1996 - 2.34.11
Lynn Harding - San Sebastian 1993 - 2.35.04
(PB: 2.31.45)
Hayley Nash - Victoria 1994 - 2.35.39
Danielle Sanderson - Helsinki 1994 - 2.36.29

British Marathon Runners Ranked in World Top 100 (<2009) - Men

Mark Steinle - London 2002 - 2.09.17
Jon Brown - London 2005 - 2.09.31
Tomas Abyu - Dublin 2007 - 2.10.37

British Marathon Runners Ranked in World Top 100 (<2009) - Women

Paula Radcliffe - London 2003 - 2.15.25

Mara Yamauchi - London 2009 - 2.23.12

Elizabeth Yelling - London 2008 - 2.28.33

Kathy Butler - Chicago 2006 - 2.28.39

Hayley Haining - London 2008 - 2.29.18

APPENDICES

Lightning Source UK Ltd.
Milton Keynes UK
UKOW04f1944170415

249871UK00001B/1/P